BEYOND
HORIZONS

Major Ashok Kumar Singh is the first physically handicapped yachtsman to sail around the world in a yacht. Schooled at the Rashtriya Indian Military College, Dehradun, Major Singh is also an alumnus of the National Defence Academy (NDA) and the Indian Military Academy (IMA). He was awarded the President's Gold Medal at the NDA, and the Sword of Honour as well as the President's Gold Medal at the IMA. He was commissioned into the Corps of Engineers of the Indian Army. He has been decorated with the Kirti Chakra and the Sena Medal for gallantry by the army, and the President of India's Tenzing Norgay National Award for adventure.

Major A.K. Singh can be contacted at trishnayacht@yahoo.com.

BEYOND HORIZONS

AROUND THE WORLD IN A SAILING BOAT

MAJOR A. K. SINGH

With a foreword by
Rakesh Sharma

RUPA

First published by
Rupa Publications India Pvt. Ltd 2014
7/16, Ansari Road, Daryaganj
New Delhi 110002

Sales Centres:

Allahabad Bengaluru Chennai
Hyderabad Jaipur Kathmandu
Kolkata Mumbai

Copyright © Major A.K. Singh 2014
Foreword copyright © Rakesh Sharma 2014

The views and opinions expressed in this book are the author's
own and the facts are as reported by him/her which have been
verified to the extent possible, and the publishers are not in any
way liable for the same.

All rights reserved.
No part of this publication may be reproduced, transmitted,
or stored in a retrieval system, in any form or by any means,
electronic, mechanical, photocopying, recording or otherwise,
without the prior permission of the publisher.

ISBN: 978-81-291-3006-8

First impression 2014

10 9 8 7 6 5 4 3 2 1

The moral right of the author has been asserted.

Printed by Parksons Graphics Pvt. Ltd, Mumbai

This book is sold subject to the condition that it shall not,
by way of trade or otherwise, be lent, resold, hired out, or otherwise
circulated, without the publisher's prior consent, in any form of
binding or cover other than that in which it is published.

I dedicate this book to my wife, Asha, and to my daughters, Akshi and Aditi, who gave up so much to see my dream fulfilled—my grateful thanks.

CONTENTS

Foreword — xi
Prologue — xv

1. The Idea (1978) — 1
2. The Nagging Delay and the Emerging Plan (1979–1984) — 10
   Red Tape — 10
   Life Goes On... — 15
   Things Start to Move (1984) — 16
3. The Crew and Sail Training (August–October 1984) — 25
   The Boat — 25
   January 1966–December 1969
   The Memory Lane to School: Rashtriya Indian Military College — 35
   Fifteen Going on Sixteen — 39
   NDA 1969–72 — 40
   Peacock Bay: 'Shamming' — 40
   The National Championships, Royal Connaught Boat Club, Pune, 1971 — 42
   Sailing Trials for the Youth Olympics (1972) — 43
4. Sailing Begins: Back to October 1984 — 46
   Trishna of India — 47
   Trishna Sets Sail (12 October 1984) — 51

Southampton to Gibraltar	53
In Alderney Harbour	54
Mooring at la Coruna Sailing Club	58
The Rio Tejo-Lisbon	60
Sailing to Gibraltar	63
Gibraltar to Port Said	67

5. Onwards to Malta, Closer Home (November–December 1984) — 72

6. Port Said to Bombay (December 1984–February 1985) — 89

The National Defence Academy — *111*

Ronnie	111
Kanshi Ram	114
Man-handling	118
NDA! Oh NDA!	119
What's in a name?	120
The 'Undies'	122
Moral Lectures	123
Time	125
Sneak-peeks	126
The Freedom Train	128
Smelly punishment	129

7. For the Un-Initiated — 134

The *Trishna*	134
Boat Handling and Routine Aboard *Trishna*	142

Asha Speaks — *147*

Loss of Limb — *153*

8. *Trishna* in Mumbai: The Story Continues — 162

Asha Speaks—The Sailing — *172*

Regiment — 179

	Part II: Sailing around the World	183
9.	Mumbai to Mauritius	185
10.	Mauritius to St. Helena Island (30 October 1985–10 December 1985)	195
	NDA II	*216*
11.	Big Ocean, Tiny Boat: St. Helena to Balboa and Sailing Into the Pacific Ocean (10 December 1985–5 April 1986)	218
	Ascension Island	219
	Brazil	224
	Belem	228
	Leaving Belem	229
	Suriname	231
	Guyana	233
	Trinidad	236
	Barbados	237
	Jamaica	238
	The Panama Canal	239
12.	The Mightiest Ocean on Earth—the Pacific	246
	The Sail to Auckland	246
	Puerto Ayora	249
	Taiohae Bay	255
	Papeete	258
	Bora Bora	261
	Rarotonga	264
	Suva, Fiji	269
	New Zealand	273
13.	The Tasman Sea and the Sail from Auckland to Darwin	277
	Sydney	281
	Green Island	289

	The Great Barrier Reef	291
	Thursday Island	294
	Darwin	297
14.	**Return to Oriental Waters: The Sail from Darwin to Singapore (13 October1986–19 November 1986)**	**301**
	Benoa, Bali	305
	Singapore	308
15.	**The Sail Home: Singapore to Mumbai (27 November 1986–10 January 1987)**	**310**
	Georgetown	311
	Campbell Bay	313
	Sighting Sri Lanka	316
	Second New Year Celebration	317
16.	**Mumbai**	**320**
	Asha Speaks—'They are Back!'	*322*
	AK Speaks—The Morning After	*324*
17.	**Quiet Thoughts**	**326**
	Epilogue in Retrospect—A Disclaimer	*332*
	Annexe 1: Perspective on Sailing in India	*336*
	Annexe 2: 'Abandon Ship' Survival at Sea	*341*
	Annexe 3: A Note on the Beaufort Wind and Sea Scale	*345*
	Annexe 4: Getting to Know Nobby	*349*
	Annexe 5: Good Will, The Real Mantra	*355*

FOREWORD

Beyond Horizons begins with the author's statement that 'all ideas begin small'. How true and insightful!

Frankly, I was unaware of Major A.K. Singh's remarkable journey, both personal and the one he undertook in *Trishna*. Having been previously acquainted with Col 'Tipsy' Chowdhry, AVSM, and being aware of his contribution in the *Trishna* saga, I was both curious and intrigued when A.K. called me up and invited me to write a foreword to his book. That short conversation made me wonder about his role in that record-setting event.

As I put down the book now, I am humbled and deeply impressed by this man's single-minded dedication and never-say-die spirit. Humbled because, many a time I have had to put peoples' perception of my own journey into perspective and I usually do that by quoting the example of Mr Amitabh Bachchan and Bharat Ratna Sachin Tendulkar. I try to explain that their feats are more praiseworthy as they have delivered excellence over a long period of time. To illustrate the difference graphically, I usually draw their attention to the difference that exists between a star and a meteorite. The former burns bright, always, while the latter creates a compelling celestial firework once and then vanishes from sight forever! A.K.'s achievement falls in the star category—not because what he achieved was never done before or that he has done so many times over, but that he achieved it while battling seemingly insurmountable odds.

The sceptic in me asked at first: what is an army guy doing, messing around with the sea? I mean army blokes were supposed to live off the land, not the sea! So, here was a person who was quintessentially army, had damaged and lost the use of a limb in a *flying* accident, no less, and then, chose to continue his love affair with the sea!

Being an alumnus of the National Defence Academy, A.K. always had the pedigree to over-perform and succeed when faced with unexpected odds, but to remain steadfast, rediscover the drive to remain focused and motivated, despite having faced a life-threatening episode and, subsequently, a life-altering medical procedure, demonstrates a rare, awe-inspiring personality.

More than a travelogue, here is a heart-warming saga of how an apparently uninterested boy, seeking to malinger while under training at the NDA, chanced upon his passion accidentally—sailing. A passion that later happened to be the 'pivot' he used to leverage his willpower and overcome the lowest phase in his life. He ends up achieving what he probably would never have attempted had he not had the opportunity to face and overcome adversity. This is the story of a remarkable individual who defines the stuff heroes are made of, one who has never let circumstance dictate the ebb and flow of his life. Like a true soldier, he charted his own path, unfazed by the prospect of a difficult terrain and a daunting landscape strewn with obstacles.

Asha, his wife, describes in poignant detail how the family rallied together to support this man through his darkest hours. Anyone who has had to face such reverses in life knows that a patient's mental and physical recovery requires clarity of thought, undying faith, a sunny disposition and loads of compassion shown by all family members involved in the rehabilitation process of the patient. And, all this takes nothing away from the patient's own resolve and will to heal.

This is a stirring account of personal courage, the fight and subsequent triumph against depression, facing the fury of nature while negotiating storms at sea and, the blessed relief on sighting land after reaching the limits of physical and mental exhaustion; an account of a hurried change of a damaged prosthetic limb, taken on without adequate trial and re-fit so as not to jeopardize the team's mission; and of the decision to bash on regardless, as there was a job that needed to be completed. All of this is the stuff heroes are made of.

By the time I came to the end of A.K.'s remarkable journey, I felt well and truly guilty for having flown around the globe, once every ninety minutes, in relative comfort and luxury, at a height of 500 kilometres—well above the fury of nature—while A.K., doing the same, battled the elements under extreme conditions and that too carrying a physical impairment! All he had with him for fifteen long months was an iron will that never failed him.

I must also thank the author for sharing his story, even though revisiting those painful events must have been very emotionally draining. The bonus is Asha's story within this story. It just tells us that heroes happen only *with* the unstinting support of heroines!

By the time you are done reading this book, you will feel privileged to have come to know a special kind of person. They are few and very far between. I doff my hat to him and to the other intrepid sailors of the *Trishna* who have done both themselves and our country proud by circumnavigating our beautiful planet while braving the fury of nature and coming out triumphant.

I salute you all!

Wg Cdr (Retd) Rakesh Sharma
Ashoka Chakra
Research Cosmonaut

PROLOGUE

There was a muffled crack as my limb snapped. I clutched the railing as the *Trishna* was flung about in the heaving seas. Suddenly, the boat rolled violently to one side. Her beam went so deep under that I thought she would go over completely, but, miraculously, she came up on top of the giant wave again.

The end, I thought, could not be far now, as I huddled in the corner of the cold and wet cockpit after we settled the boat to hove-to in the insurmountable sub-zero storm. We would all go down in this cold gray sea, thousands of miles from home. Perhaps the best thing to do would be to lie down, and let sweet sleep take over, and with it hypothermia and death would soon follow. After all, how could I have imagined that, with just one leg, I could sail the mighty oceans all the way around the world?

CHAPTER 1

THE IDEA
1978

All ideas begin small; but once they take root and begin to grow, they become obsessions. That's when ideas become troublesome for they will just not be wished away. They refuse to disappear or be forgotten, forcing one to act. Why does one do anything at all? How can one merely breathe to live, eat and die?!

It all started like any other idea: in a small way. It was one of those things you didn't want to tell anyone about so they didn't laugh at you. It might sound ludicrous, so unimaginably, unrealistically unachievable. It was actually a simple wish, a longing, a desire—to sail around the world. And it waited, demanding fulfilment.

As with all such ideas, the more one keeps it secret, the more it nags—and grows. And it raises questions. Could it really be done? Why not? Several people had done it—so obviously it could be done. But how was one to do it? Where would I begin? Whom could I ask? No one I knew had done anything like this. But I had read nice stories about adventurers sailing the oceans. Stories that enthused, urged and challenged one to do something worthy in life. One could feel, 'This could be done here too...not only in far off lands, by unknown, strange and distant people'. Hadn't Joshua Slocum sailed a wooden hand-built boat with wooden spars, cotton sails, and natural fibre cordage and ropes, all the way to Cape Horn and around the world from 1895 to 1898? He had built the *Spray* from the carcass of a boat bequeathed to him. These days, people in the developed world build boats from kits, and sail large distances. Why couldn't I build one? But I didn't dare voice any of this. I could already hear what people would say: no one from Asia, except the Japanese, had sailed around the world. And that was in 1978. In fact, barely 40 to 50 teams had sailed around the world in anything smaller than 38-footer. Anyone who heard me would call me mad—would say that I was being an adolescent, attention-culling fool!

But I told myself, people *do* think of doing things. And people *do* make unusual things happen. They don't *always* worry about what other people may say or think.

This distant dream, this secret obsession, this ultimate goal continued to haunt me. And soon, it spurred me on to find out about how it could be achieved. Several years before re-building the *Spray* and sailing alone around the world, Joshua Slocum had built the 35-footer *Liberdade* with wood from the forest hewn with his own hands, after being shipwrecked in southern Brazil, and sailed the 'junk rigged' boat[1] with his family, back home, and all the way to Boston. With the much advanced boat-building techniques now available, surely I could do the same, and build a boat here in Pune! I began reading up and got down to studying the aesthetic flow of the 'lines' of the hull of a sailing craft. Lines were important to the glance of a trained eye since they determined how a boat would behave in the different moods of the mighty oceans, particularly in stormy weather.

So I proposed to build my boat myself, right there in Pune. But then, along came Harry Kapoor, with his own views.[2] 'Oh! So you want to build a boat and sail around the world? I say, this boat building will consume your life! If you want to make your trip in real-time, get a good boat from the sailing spots of the world, and set sail—and yes, not east-about as you are planning, but west-about, with the trade winds. Don't worry about Asian maritime culture—all those Arabian *dhows*, or sailing to Indonesia and eastwards to revive maritime history. Let us just plan hard for the round-the-world sail.'

Of course we had been sailing dinghies in coastal waters

---

[1] A 'junk rig' is a type of boat rig.
[2] Brigadier HK Kapoor, founding president of the 'Optimist Sailing Association of India' for children under 14 years' age, with a lifelong involvement in national and international sailing. He held several appointments of the Yachting Association of India over many years, under the banner of the Corps of Engineering Sailing Club.

*The sailboat Albatross sailed from Mumbai to
Bandar Abbas (Iran) and back.*

and in-land lakes for years—so we were not totally new. We had even sailed the 18-footer, open day-sailor boat *Albatross* from Bombay to the Persian Gulf port of Bandar Abbas and back in 1977, under the innovative Major Paramjit Singh Pammi, who had conceived the daring voyage across the Arabian Sea in a drop-keel, shallow-water sailing dinghy, scarcely suited for the voyage he accomplished. We navigated using astronavigation and elementary seamanship on the way. This gave me the much needed beginner's confidence. But crossing the Arabian Sea is not the same as crossing the Pacific Ocean, and the mighty oceans had not yet revealed to us how little we knew! They say little confidence is a dangerous thing. Dangerous enough for ill-prepared people like us to go ahead with a plan to sail around the world. How right they were! It now seems providential that we did not know so then. Just as well, for had we known, the unattainability of my dream may have dawned upon me. The idea may have appeared more foolhardy than it seemed at that time, and who knows, rationality may have prevented us from assuming that such a voyage was within our abilities, while actually it turned out to be closer to the outer boundaries of the sailing background, experience, facilities and abilities we possessed at that time.

Plan hard we did. We got down to the job with a will.

It took a few months of detailed research. There was virtually no material to start our search with. No one had the remotest idea what we were looking for. No blue-water yachtsman to mentor us, no literature except for adventure books in bookstores. And definitely no technical ocean sailing books anywhere—neither at the British Council Libraries, nor in the United States Information Service (USIS) Centres, both of which I scouted for any material that may be useful.

I was posted at the College of Military Engineering (CME), Pune at the time, and on scouting its library, I hit it rich. Decades ago, some officers of the Royal Engineers had instituted sailing as a sport in the narrow restrictive waters of the river Mula, which runs through the CME. Two of them had actually designed a plywood dinghy, and built it there. It was called the *CBK* (after their initials), and we regularly sailed it in local regattas held by the CME, the National Defence Academy (NDA), Pune, as well as in Mumbai. Their love for the wide blue yonder was backed by a healthy collection of books in the CME library on almost all aspects of sailing: yacht design, boat-building, sailing in the high seas, etc. The collection though, was far from exhaustive, with just about a book or two on the technical subjects, and a few more by yachtsmen recounting their trans-ocean voyages.

But I had found my starting point—I began sponging these books up! I took two suitcases full of books on boat design, yacht construction materials, cruising, and anything else to do with ocean sailing, and went off on a twenty-day holiday to Lucknow. Reading and reviewing two dozen books in twenty days was quite a job. The basic fabric of our plan was woven that October and November, during the many days and nights of brainstorming between Harry and me. First we would buy a suitable boat in England, and sail it down to India. The circumnavigation proper would start then. We would sail westwards from Bombay, through the Panama Canal—instead of the rougher South America and Cape Horn. This was a considered decision: it seemed foolish to take on Cape Horn in our maiden trans-ocean venture, since we had no idea of ocean sailing whatsoever. We reckoned we'd do that another day.

It was time now to chalk out the plans with the team[3]. AP took on route planning, meteorology and navigation; Soma Pillai concentrated on finding out what kind of training we needed; and I took on the responsibility of selecting a boat, acquiring all the equipment needed, making the criteria for crew selection.

Early in 1979, once the plan was finalized, Harry put it through the military channels of command: after all he was the General! And then, a long period of waiting began. It took about six years for the bureaucracy to finally approve the idea—roughly five times what it took for us to sail around the world! No wonder we still feel that our main battle was on land—with paper and pen—and not with storms at sea! Talking any more about what all it took to get going will open a Pandora's Box that may need another book!

But yes, the mention of a few oddities may be pertinent here: I was confronted with government officers asking why we wanted to be accompanied on our journey by a helicopter.

---

[3]The team was to ultimately consist of ten members, with six on the boat at any one time. The four permanent crew members who sailed all the way both from Gosport to Mumbai as well as all the way round the world were to be: Maj K.S. Rao, the skipper; Capt. Sanjeev Shekhar; Capt. Chandrahas Bharti; and myself. The other crew members were Col TPS Chowdhary, the team manager (Tipsy, who sailed from Gosport to Port Said, and from Panama to Sydney); Maj Amreshwar Pratap Singh (often referred to as AP in the book, sailed from Gosport to Mumbai, and from Mumbai to Panama); Capt. Rakesh Bassi (sailed from Mumbai to Trinidad); Lt. Navin Ahuja (sailed from Trinidad to Auckland); Maj A Bhattacharya (sailed from Auckland back to Mumbai) and Maj S.N. Mathur (sailed from Sydney back to Mumbai). In addition to these ten, Capt. M.S. Pillai, a.k.a. 'Soma' Pillai, sailed from Port Said to Mumbai.

I was nonplussed. Of all things! Where did this helicopter come from? Then I remembered that, on hearing of our plan to sail around the world, some helicopter pilots had been heard talking—over drinks one evening at the bar—that it was probably a good idea to accompany the boat by chopper! I had thought nothing of it then, but I did not in my wildest imagination believe that such an absurd idea could become a stumbling block for our simple plan to cross the oceans in a small boat. The government officer concerned must obviously have not checked the source of his information, and I was relieved when this absurd matter did not surface again.

Then again, someone else from one of the ministries remarked that allowing a team of serving army officers to go sailing around the world was tantamount to sending them on a sun-and-sand holiday! I guess they were thinking of Mediterranean beach travel brochures showing sailing boats with beaches, sun-umbrellas, and the like! So we got down to explaining the facts of our voyage: that we were planning to cross the mighty oceans which, in their fury, could throw occasional vicious storms that could—and did—sink big ships and small yachts alike. We quoted some famous ocean voyagers and cited their descriptions of both the raw fury of the oceans as well as their grandeur and lure they hold for adventurers.

All this was to bring home the point that these were the words of the survivors—the other kind didn't live to tell their story! Promptly, the concerned ministry wrote that if it was going to be that dangerous, and if anything was to happen to the crew, their families would sue the government for damages. So why send the team at all? As it turned out, we all gave an undertaking that we would not hold anyone but ourselves responsible in case of death or damage, and also agreed not to sue the system for damages. Finally, we agreed to sail round the world on specially sanctioned leave so we could not claim any duty privileges.

A lot had happened during those six years. The provisional crew of seven we had selected in 1979–80 had broken up—not a few of them thinking it not a 'career oriented' project for upwardly mobile Army officers that we were, even if we did succeed.

> A large peace-time standing army needs to keep its young men constructively occupied to expend their energies. While the paperwork with various ministries was getting along at a slow pace, we kept busy with regular yachting regattas at various competitions. Some of my energies also went into the novel idea of re-engineering my old Royal Enfield motorcycle. I replaced its robust petrol 350 cc engine with a small new engine that ran on diesel, which was very economical: at 85 kilometres to a litre of diesel at a time when it cost a mere Rs 1.10 to a litre! There were several wagers lost and won at the College of Military Engineering concerning the innovation. Many said it would never run. Others said it would run either too slow or not at all satisfactorily, since I was not, after all, an automobile engineer, and there were gear ratios, rpm, calorific value of fuel and other such technical factors to consider.
>
> The motorcycle ran well enough to drive me and my golden spaniel puppy, Golda, all the way from Pune to Ludhiana in Punjab and back, during the ensuing term break.

CHAPTER 2

THE NAGGING DELAY AND THE EMERGING PLAN 1979–1984

Red tape

Time was dragging on and we were nowhere near our starting point. Bureaucracy, systems and too many people in too many sections of various ministries delayed things, questioning each aspect—the hows and whys of a plan that had never been attempted before. There were at least two false starts. The first was in 1980 after which we were asked to stand down for a while. 'A few more days, boys,' we were told.

All the while, I struggled to fill-in-the-blanks of our project and these were un-ending. There were many unknown areas, since I had not yet met a person with firsthand experience of sailing round the world or having crossed oceans in a small boat, to quiz and learn from. Firming up on all details is a continuous seeking and learning process. And I was, all along, seeking and learning. After all, this was the time to do it while things were still taking shape. The middle of the ocean was hardly the right place for rethinking plans and questioning the founding blocks of the project. I left no stone unturned. I scouted all possible libraries and met all the relevant people—including the many I had thought relevant but who clearly told me 'I haven't the foggiest!'

Among the many questions were those relating to the size, type, construction, design and material of the boat. Others included its inside layout, fittings, equipment, sail plans and rig, crew numbers and composition, criteria for crew selection—age, qualifications, sailing experience, etc., the route to be taken and passage planning—which ocean during which month of the year, what sort of crew training and boat handling, safety gear, personal gear, navigation equipment—maritime charts and sextant, etc. (there was no sat-nav or GPS those days, there wasn't even the cell phone!), electronics, communication gear (there were no satellite phones in those days), life-saving drills and gear... the list was really quite endless. There never is such a thing as too much planning for a small boat wanting to cross the oceans. Critical situations pop up during every voyage in the middle of nowhere—stark revelations of where one faltered in planning.

I would ask shippies about navigation. Anyone remotely connected with the remotest aspect of sailing would be quizzed to the point of discomfort. In my quest, I met a lot of helpful people, but also some not so forthcoming. In many ways, the six years' wait between the writing of the basic plan to the time we got the go-ahead, helped fill in critical gaps and details, unveiling slowly the true size of the mammoth task we had such little understanding about when we started. It certainly appeared now that we had bitten far more than we could chew then. Thankfully, the revelations added more spur than brakes to my resolve.

'To check out my facts', the Sapper Adventure Foundation agreed to fund me for a fortnight's visit to the UK provided I share the expenses. The trip really helped me get all my answers. I went from boat yards to sail training establishments, and met several people involved intimately with the business of sailing. I am grateful to the then Engineer-in-Chief, Lieutenant General SN Sharma, as also to the Commandant of the College of Military Engineering, Lieutenant General Parikshit Puri, Major General Harry Kapoor, and Major General VP Yadav, who reposed their faith in the project and in me, gave wisdom and direction, and pushed the project as one combined Corps of Engineers' aim, despite the omnipresent pressures of their high professional army responsibilities. It took colossal effort for the plan to crystallize and later materialize. Without the combined and very high powered commitment of all these gentlemen, our plan might never have seen the light of day—such were the odds stacked against it, and the planning effort required.

The final crystallized plan was something like this:

The boat would be made of glass reinforced plastic (popularly called fibre glass or GRP). It would be about 35 or 36 feet long overall, with an aluminium mast and boom (popularly called spars), and a Bermudian sloop rig—although a cutter or ketch rig would also do. The rig is the layout plan of the sails and spars combined, and as many as a dozen or more rigs for sail boats are in existence, including the dhow, the Chinese junk rig, the gaff rig, the lateen rig, the square rig, the sloop, the cutter, the yawl, the ketch, etc. Each has evolved in response to the purpose and the seas it is popular in. Similarly, boats are built in a variety of materials like GRP, wood, plywood, ferro-cement, steel, aluminium, and a variety of construction techniques in wood and plywood like foam sandwich, clinker, carvel, and others. Hull construction and design too could be of several types—the classic long-keel, the fin and skeg, the underslung or spade rudder, the delta keel, the bilge keel, the broad beamy spacious comfy-boat, or the uncomfortable but infinitely safer less beamy designs, and so on. Describing the design or the lines of a boat to the uninitiated sailor is difficult. Suffice it to say that hulls are designed with a view to creating the most desirable hydrodynamic response during all points of sailing, particularly during extreme weather. At the same time, it should afford reasonable comfort and speed desirable during fair weather.

The result, as can be guessed, is always a compromise, and one has to decide where one's requirement lies between the scales of safety on the one hand and comfort on the other. So, there are designs and designs, just as there are choices of every other type in rig, material, construction, etc. The task of selection can be likened to that of a connoisseur of any delicately artful things in life—where knowledge complements experience to finally give you what you need. The process is also never ending. In the end, it is desirable that your boat sees you through the vagaries of a tropical force ten storm (on the Beaufort scale of storms and sea-state) as well as affords you the minimum wherewithal essential to long ocean passages.

The design should be a self-righting one. This means that if the weatherboards and companionway hatch[1] are shored up, and if the sails are dropped and stowed or lashed before a wave, or the weather capsizes the boat, the ballast or lead in the keel, helped on by the encapsulated air in the upturned cabin below, pushing to come up, and the wave action in the storm swinging the keel, creating a 'couple' of forces, will help the boat upright itself and the crew, lashed on to the boat using steel life-lines, will have a chance with the thus up-righted boat to save themselves and , with luck, sail her. For this, the ballast ratio—the weighted lead in the keel compared with the overall weight of the boat—should be over 40 per cent. Of course, this value is complemented by the design, as the up-righting forces depend on both ballast ratio and the design in the end. A 32-footer was all that we could afford, and it was possible to sail around in one too; but a 35 or 36-footer would definitely have been more useful.

---

[1] The companionway refers to the steps leading down from cockpit into the cabin below decks. Weatherboards are used to close this passage so as to prevent waves from flooding, swamping and thereby sinking the boat.

Life goes on...

With the green signal for our project being nowhere in sight, and after considerable delay, I decided to let the normal course of life flow: in 1980, I married Asha, whom I had never met before, in the traditional Rajput style of arranged marriages. I figured that I might as well get married—after all, who knew how long it would take for our plan to get going? Moreover, at that time, I had no money in my pocket to buy the boat, and get on with it.

And then, three years later, my life underwent a rude change: I lost a leg above the knee in March 1983 during treatment at the Army Hospital in Pune, consequent to a hang-gliding crash over a fortnight before the emergency operation for gas gangrene. Everyone, including several medical experts said that it was a clear case of gross medical negligence. But, weighing all things, it appeared better to move on rather than allow events, particularly those that may be explained away as statistical unintended blunders, to bog me down, sapping away the richness of living, and weighing me down with the disgust and lack of relevance of recompense or retribution instead. I now feel vindicated by my decision at that time.

There were other injuries too, to the hands and legs, seven fractures in the jaw, and the loss of several teeth. My jaw was held together by stainless steel wires, and my teeth were never thirty-two again.

Still, when the project was finally given the green signal in June 1984, things picked up very quickly.

My diary entry at the time:

> 15 April 1984, 1410 hours
>
> Left hospital in August 1983, posted to Gwalior to convalesce and recover—both physically and mentally—with Asha's job in Gwalior. Had written from the hospital itself to General (Kapoor) that I would be functional by October (1983), and was still to be considered very much in as far as the sail round the world was concerned.
>
> Took part in the quadrangular Thimayya Trophy sailing championship at the National Defence Academy in August (from the hospital on an out-pass) and in the National Team (sailing) Championship in December. Seabird class nationals in February/March 1984. Windsurfed again!— Oh! What a feeling—in December. No matter only for a hundred metres, though.

Things start to move (1984)

There now appeared on the scene a man with a phenomenal drive and stamina for work. If this were not enough, he was charming and possessed of an infectious sense of humour too. Colonel TPS Chowdhury—called Tipsy because of his initials and not for any 'spiritual' tendencies—had helped to push through our project in New Delhi, and was nominated as manager of the team which now consisted of Major KS Rao as Skipper, AP, myself, Soma Pillai, and four others: Captains Bharti and Shekhar, and Majors Bhattacharya and Mathur. While all four had varied dinghy sailing experience in local regattas, Bharti and Shekhar, both barely twenty, were selected to add a touch of youth to the team. This was done on the advice of Lieutenant General Parikshit Puri, then Engineer in Chief of the Army, and Chief Patron of the project, and General SN Sharma, since having retired from the post, but not before a whole-hearted push which put the project well and truly on track. Mathur and Bhatta were to control affairs at Delhi and Pune, our two administrative bases, in addition to each being earmarked to sail a part of the voyage later.

Diary entry:

15 July 1984

Took leave, went to Delhi and did some work on the round-the-world project, or it would have been put off by a year, if not shelved yet again. General VP Yadav and Mr KP Singh Deo made a wonderful combination in parrying the project with the various ministries; General PR Puri gave whole hearted support and overall guidance; the Vice Chief, General K Sundarji too, was highly enthused by our cause. The never-ending task of getting various sanctions through the North and South Blocks, Udyog Bhavan, Sena Bhavan, Shastri Bhavan, Reserve Bank of India (for the foreign exchange needed to buy the boat), State Bank of India, Air India (for complimentary air passage for the crew). Tipsy's optimism and dynamism were priceless.

One by one—slowly at first, then rapidly—things began moving. Mr Baljit Gill of the Department of

Sports, General Narindar Singh of the Sports Authority of India, Commanders Joshi and Shahane of the Yachting Association of India, and the Chief of the Naval Staff, Admiral OS Dawson, all gave their blessings and unconditional support. Colonel Tankha of the Army Adventure Foundation, Mr Sen of the Director General Technical Development, the CCIE and the Joint CCIE at Udyog Bhavan also gave their blessings. Then there were the clearances and approvals that were received from the Minister of Civil Aviation, Ministry of Finance (Defence Finance), Miss Deepali Pant, Miss Abha Joshi, various clerks, typists, Mr Nair from the Land Customs, Mr Rajinder Prakash Sondhi, Captain Kohli of Air India—who, during his days in the navy, had put nine atop the Everest in 1963. Tipsy was everywhere at once seven days a week. Mr Khizer Ahmed, Joint Controller of RBI was also very supportive.

Mr KP Singh Deo was the Minister for Youth Affairs and Sports, an avid water-sports enthusiast and mentor to several sportsmen. General PR Puri was then the Engineer in Chief (E-in-C) of the Army, and held the project close to his heart, having seen it through from its inception stages. It was directly under his wings earlier, when he was Commandant of the CME, that the project was born, and now he was its chief mentor.

There were many more helpful people in key positions who furthered the seemingly endless process of granting us sanctions, which they did with enthusiasm and a word of encouragement and exhortation for the project, whom I am sure to have missed out. The time elapsed has dulled the memory. There were also multiple people dealing with different stages of the sanctions and approvals so each of us was not intimately in touch with the process as a whole. To each and every one who helped, I wish to say, I hope we fulfilled the hopes you reposed in us when you gave your enthusiastic support and the much needed official sanctions. My grateful thanks to all who helped.

The Army had granted us special leave. Money to buy the boat had been raised through sponsors by the Sapper Adventure Foundation, under the E-in-C. We already had a name for the boat: *Trishna*. It was chosen by Harry; it meant a deep-rooted desire to achieve or attain something elusive or unattainable, and it rhymed with 'Krishna' as well.

'AK, do you think you can still sail? I mean...after your amputation?' asked General Puri.

Sitting upright and at attention, before the seniormost General in my Corps of Sappers and Miners and one of the chief mentors of our project, all I could say was, 'Sir, I'll never know unless I try.'

I thought to myself, 'I'll be damned if I give up without trying to find out! After all those years of work...'

At the beginning of our project, we had no ocean sailor to guide us. Now we finally had a go-ahead from the government, but, well, I certainly had not heard of any amputee who had sailed round the world. Only much later (after I finished my voyage successfully, in fact) did I get to know about and correspond with the legendary Tristan Jones. So, who was I to ask?

Only I could find the answer to whether or not I could do it.

'In any case,' General Puri continued, 'we need you to go to the UK and select a suitable boat for the job. After all, you have done so much work studying boats and the voyage.'

I asked for, and was permitted one companion, mainly due to my recent above-knee amputation and related ambulation problems. I requested for Tipsy to accompany me since his brother who had a foot-hold in London could be of some help. We were to go to England ahead of the rest of the crew. While Tipsy was to organize all administrative matters there—accommodation for the crew, refresher sail training facilities, opening bank accounts, etc. I was to select the boat. So, on 15 July 1984, Tipsy and I found ourselves on board an Air India Jumbo bound for London. The excitement of finally being on our way and the good in-flight beer kept our spirits up all through the ten-hour flight.

Diary entry (undated):

> I am finally on my way to the UK to select and get the boat, to fix up training, and prepare the ground for detailed pre-voyage planning and the sail back to Bombay.
>
> Asha and Akshi, will, as always, be at Gwalior—away from me, and we will shorten our lives by a few years worrying about each other. There never has been a 'home' for us—unless living in a house for up to six months at a time can be called a home. God is with us, and the future will decide the correctness and wisdom of our actions.

In England, I first made a list of boat marinas, yacht brokers, and private advertisers and then began visiting them one by one. Over four hundred boats were considered, and dozens of marinas were visited between Salcombe and Ipswich along the southern coast. I made inquiries about yachts as far away as Glasgow, the Channel Islands, and even Spain. The list of probable boats was narrowed down to fifty, then to fourteen or thereabout. This was done after close inspection of each craft and its design and construction, the credentials of the designer and builder, the history of the boat, its suitability for our purpose, and so on. Since like most contemporary Indian adventurers, we didn't have much money, we had to settle for a used boat—at a third of the price of a new one.

Neil Carlier, a Brigadier of the Royal Engineers and an accomplished blue water yachtsman, had kindly agreed to render all advice, guidance and help, which came generously. This was the result of informal 'old boys' networking between Indian and British Sappers as well as the sailing communities of the two countries.

Fourteen boats were shortlisted and closely scrutinized, and then the final list of five was before us, of which one in particular was fully fitted out by its current owner for an ocean passage. However, perhaps motivated by our efforts, he backed out saying that he himself had begun considering a long passage instead of selling his boat!

On 9 August 1984, Neil and I took a look at the 36-feet-long Swan class sloop called *Guinevere of Sussex* as she lay at her moorings at Brighton. I had seen her two days earlier, along with David of David East Yachting—a handsome and affable broker later to become a lifelong friend—and had liked her immensely. She had those fine little points, both in design and construction, that spell quality. She had been designed as a fast cruiser by Sparkman and Stephens of U.S.A., and built by Nautor of Finland. Although more than 14 years old, she had been maintained well, and was easily on the top of our list.

Meanwhile, Harry had joined us and had taken charge of all the goings-on. Better this than biting his nails sitting far away in India, worrying whether I was on the right track. Finally, unable to stay away from the action, he had reached the UK along with Maya, his wife, on 5 August 1984. All through Harry's sailing life, Maya had mothered the hordes of young sailors spawned by the 'International Optimist Class Association' regattas—a class of which he was the founding father.

It was just as well that Harry was with us, since so much co-ordination was needed at the macro level.

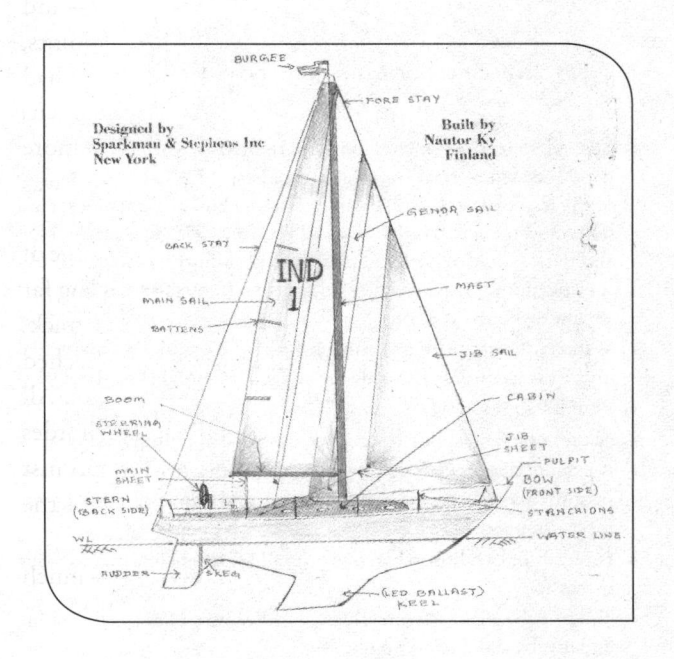

Sketch of *Trishna* Showing the Basic Parts of the Boat

TRISHNA of INDIA

SWAN-37 SLOOP

Specifications and other boat details

- Overall 36 feet, 5 ¼ inches long (11.18 metres), with a draft (water depth needed to float) of 6 feet, 1½ inches (1.88 metres). Weight of the lead ballast: 7,300 lbs, bolted to the hull using stainless steel bolts, and measured sail area of 598 sq feet (55.5 sq metres). Hull and deck moulded with high strength glass fibre to Lloyds 100A1 specifications. Gross weight reckoned at 10.5 tons; and lead keel weight reckoned at 6 tons.
- Water tanks comprising two nylon tanks of 25 gallons each, situated under the berths on each side in the cabin/saloon below the decks.
- Bermudian sloop rig.
- Mast, boom and spinnaker pole of anodized aluminium alloy.
- Accommodation included two quarter berths, two berths in main saloon, two pilot berths in main saloon, and two fore-cabin berths for use in ports.
- Fore-cabin: two lift-up berths, with sail lockers below and stowage spaces above.
- Toilet: Baby Blake Marine Toilet, with sea water inlet and flushing outlet valves, and hand pump.
- Main cabin (saloon): two settee berths, one each on port and starboard side, a pilot berth on each outboard and above the settee berths. Cave lockers below pilot berths.
- Full sized chart table: with a forward facing navigator's seat.
- Aft cabin: two quarter berths, one on each side under the cockpit area.

CHAPTER 3

THE CREW AND SAIL TRAINING
August–October 1984

The Boat

As I saw her again, my heart lifted. She was a graceful little craft, carrying aloft a proud and stately mast nearly 50 feet high. Built in fibre glass, she weighed nearly 10 tons, of which 6 tons were in the lead ballasted fin keel. To a seaman's eye, she was pure joy. Her graceful lines hid a strong and resilient body, capable, as we were to soon find out, of riding through horrendous storms and taking a tremendous beating at sea. She was a soothing sky blue, with a white cabin roof and teak inlaid decks. One of her previous owners had replaced the tiller with a steering wheel, which suited us since a wheel is far better for long voyages.

Like all things feminine, boats are both simple and very complicated. They may appear simple to the undiscerning eye. But to a yachtsman, a boat is not just a boat. The various shapes and curves of the hull greatly affect the behaviour of the boat in various moods of the sea. Basically, boat selection is a balancing of compromises. In a rough sea, fast, narrow hulls are very uncomfortable when compared with slower beamier (wider) ones. Thus, more roomy and comfortable designs might seem preferable, but they tend to compromise on seaworthiness. Also, room is at a premium in small boats. However, while a wide and roomy boat may heel less, it will not upright itself in case it capsizes. So one needs to get the right blend of safety, comfort and speed for the job.

Our survey had indicated that the *Guinevere of Sussex* was a little behind on preventive maintenance, so I got the owner to cut down the price by £2,000, to £28,000. I don't think I lost too much goodwill in our bargaining, though the owner did not exactly become my best friend for life in the process!

Diary entry:

23 August 1984

Boat selection has been a heck of a rewarding job! I feel nearer to realizing the desire... Endless toil and dedication ahead—out of that is going to grow the sweet taste of riding the waves high in a fine wind on a sound hull. Closeness to Nature can be such an addiction! Confirmed a final go-ahead for buying the boat. Promised to have the money transferred today. Big thing in my life today—culmination of a dragging six long years of turbulent and troubled family, personal and professional life.

KS, AP, Bharti, and Shekhar flew in from India and joined us in Gosport, Southampton on 9 August, and after a quick refresher course on astro-navigation, we were ready for *Trishna*. Tony Atkin, the erstwhile owner of the boat, his wife June, and their eight-year-old daughter Elizabeth drank a change-of-owner toast with us on 28 August 1984 on her moorings at the Brighton Marina, and the proud boat had new masters.

Diary entry:

29 August 1984, 0133 hours
On board the *Guinevere of Sussex*

Met Tony Atkin at 2000 hrs on the 28th—checked out the boat with him for an hour, finally drank a 'change of owner' toast at about 2100 hrs, along with his gracious wife June and their daughter Elizabeth. He mellowed down a bit and even became friendly! He had been mad so far, as I had managed to get the price down to £28,000 from his asking price of £30,000 because of the survey report.

Our first sail on the *Guinevere* (permission to change her name had not yet been granted) turned out to be rather uncomfortable and distressing. We were to sail her down to her new berth at the Joint Services Sailing Centre (JSSC) at Gosport 40 miles away. This had graciously been made available to us free of charge by JSSC.

Ron Gravells, our sailing guru, arranged through the good offices of Brigadier Neil Carlier, had kindly agreed to tutor us in the finer aspects of big boat handling in blue waters for a small fee, and was there to meet us. We had not yet got our rough weather sailing gear, and though we were grossly inadequately clad—without sailing boots or storm suits, he reluctantly decided to go ahead with the first sail on our boat.

The Gods had probably decided to break us in straight away: the head winds soon increased to 40 knots (about 75 kmph). We were seriously ill-clad for the biting cold at 4°C with a high wind chill factor as we sailed on the highly tidal, reef ridden waters for fifteen hours, through the dark, moonless night, negotiating a busy shipping channel, feeling cold, soggy and terribly seasick. It was a miserable beginning. But it was probably just right for me to start finding the answer to the big question: could I sail a big boat across the oceans? Could I sail her at all?

In the cold squalls, with all of us terribly wet and seasick, the delivery-crew skipper brought by Ron to skipper us on this sail, uncertain about our abilities, said, 'Will someone go up and reef the main sail?' As the uncertain, seasick crew did some soul searching on this, I just had to find out: would I be able to sail her in a squall? As if answering a call, I advanced on the mast negotiating the wildly jumping wet deck on all fours even as someone said, 'AK not you...'

'Why not?' I shot back in the cold storm, and winch handle and chuck in hand, bracing against the life line holding me to the mast, applied myself to the job at hand. And, the Gods be praised, I did it! I had the main reefed!

Working slowly and unsurely at first, I was soon filled with a renewed glow of confidence deep inside as I found the answer—I could sail the boat! Though seemingly insignificant for others, for me it was a decisive event. I had my answer, and that is all that mattered. If I could reef the main sail in a storm, I could sail the boat!

We reached our mooring at Gosport cold, tired, and wet in our borrowed storm suits in the middle of the dark and stormy night, and promptly dropped off to sleep in the boat's bunks—wet suits and all.

Since she was a used boat, lots of repair and maintenance was needed to get *Guinevere* ready for the passage to Bombay. So, after hoisting her out of the water at Gosport, we set about our work in right earnest.

Boat work was more than just boat work. The stem-head fitting was causing some anxiety. There was some water leaking through. The fore and aft stays needed a change. Winches needed to be serviced; so did the sea cocks (for letting in sea water through valves, into the galley sink for washing dishes, and for flushing out the sea toilet, thus conserving fresh water).

Diary entry:

2 September 1984

> Never-ending work for preparing the boat takes most of the day. Rest goes into planning and thinking about it and in pre-empting the various problems that might come up.

It was more than just hard work. There was so much to do and such little time to accomplish it all, for we did not want to miss the sailing-out season. The last boats sail out of South England by mid- to end-September, since after that the Atlantic weather moves in.

Diary entries (undated):

> Tired and sleepy—dropping off as I write; have been like this most of these past few months. Have had only five and half hours of sleep (each night) for almost as long as I can remember. Good practice for the watch-keeping on the boat coming up! Feeling-less—probably moving too fast...
>
> Worked on the boat till 0215 hours... There just aren't enough hours in the day. I think I must sleep now...lots to do tomorrow.

Preparation to sail the oceans involves being wholly dependent on oneself in terms of boat handling and survival at sea, as well as boat maintenance and repairs, including emergency repairs. No help is normally capable of reaching you in time during an emergency at sea, even if the VHF radio's SOS signal gets picked up by a passing ship. The range of the VHF is, in any case, only about 15 or 20 nautical miles (about 22 to 35 km under ideal conditions). A good yachtsman knows everything about everything on his boat, and has the ability to anticipate what can go wrong so far as the equipment is concerned. He should have a nose for smelling out trouble before the trouble smells him out in the middle of the ocean.

With a fourteen year old boat like *Trishna*, this meant removing, servicing and re-installing almost every piece of sailing and safety related equipment. This is the only way one can be sure of when it was last done and how long it can be relied upon before a review becomes necessary. There is no short cut—and doing it yourself is the only way of ensuring safety of the boat's life and yours in the middle of a dark stormy night, thousands of miles from anywhere. All standing and running rigging was looked into minutely. Since it is impossible to tell with old stainless steel how much stress it has already taken and when it may give way, most of it was replaced with new rigging, and load-bearing deck and hull fittings. All sails were closely inspected, repaired, washed and stowed to make sure they were ready for quick sail-changes at sea in rapidly deteriorating weather—after all they were the motor of the boat.

All winches, sea cocks, fresh water tanks and cocks, the loo and its plumbing were taken apart, serviced and re-installed—all by the very persons who would have to rely on them for their safety and comfort at sea—meaning ourselves. A sea cock leaking at sea may take in sea-water more rapidly than one can bail it out, particularly if it jams and can't be shut! The cooking gas mini-cylinders, the gas pipeline with its rubber hose, and burners were specially looked into for perished parts overdue for change. Boats have been known to sink due to a fire on board in the middle of an ocean! The steering column and the rudder post with complete rudder movement were checked for perished links and split pins, to make sure they did not give way during heavy weather, for a rudder can be subjected to tremendous forces during a heavy sea.

The Volvo Penta inboard engine used for charging batteries every day and for minimum emergency propulsion was serviced. The electrics, electronics, charts, navigation equipment, all were handled, checked, listed and stowed such that they may be of use under the most un-imaginable conditions at sea. The emergency self-inflating life raft, the life buoys, dan-buoy, the EPIRB (the emergency position indicator radio beacon, that, once activated, automatically sends out an SOS signal when launched), and a host of more such stuff was looked into under the proverbial microscope. In other words, *everything* was serviced, repaired and stowed for immediate and effective use in an emergency.

A hand-held compass, binnacle compass, fog horn, hand-held search light (to focus on man-overboard or shine at an onward coming ship threatening to run us down at night), storm suits, life-lines and life-jackets were all refurbished. All systems were checked and overhauled. A new coat of anti-fouling paint was splashed on. We also added on one of the latest gadget of the day: a satellite navigation system, the size of a radio receiver.

Truly, the list is endless when preparing a yacht for voyage at sea. Endless also are the days of hard work merging into nights of continued hard work under jury-rigged lights—and then collapsing into a dead tired stupor of a sleep for a few hours before beginning all over again the next day. At one point in our preparations, it seemed there just wouldn't be time enough for it all. But everything did get done and, finally, she was lowered again into her element.

Diary entry:

> 23 September 1984
>
> We are sailing out daily and getting to know the boat well. There are so many small things to be done on board; it is almost a never ending job.

We sailed hard. The next month was consumed in boat repairs, re-fitting, sail training, along with tackling the endless list of tasks, big and small, that go into planning and preparation of this kind. There was paper work, including half a dozen registrations, insurances, permissions, intimations, and what have you. There was a long list of stores and supplies, and an even longer list of things to be checked out in an old boat: repairing and/or changing, as also fitting in equipment specifically needed for long voyages. We worked on the assumption that Murphy's Law, invariably holds good at sea: 'if anything can ever go wrong, it will', and when one least wants it to!

Sail training in the temperamental weather of the English Channel—with its unpredictable and nasty squalls, extremely strong currents, reefs and rocks all over—was the best training for the circumnavigation we had in mind. We sailed to Cherbourg across the Channel to France; and then, on our way back, we set sail for the Channel island of Guernsey.

Diary entry (undated):

> Guernsey is one of the five British Channel Islands—the others being Sark, Jersey, Alderney and Herms. We got late sailing out, missing the tide by one hour. It was enough to

force us to alter course midway, for Alderney. Tides and rocks in the Channel are treacherous. Shipping is heavy. Tides at times run at 8 to 10 knots! With a boat speed of 6 to 8 knots in a good breeze, we were moving backwards when sailing against the tide, or covering an awesome 16 to 18 knots when running with the tide. With or against, tides could not be ignored. Reached Alderney at 11 p.m. Entering a harbour under the conditions was very tricky, sharp rocks—many under water—all around. Perfect coastal navigation and boat handling are demanded. Sailed off for Guernsey next day, after rest and taking on water, at about 1500 hours, bang on the tide! Reached there in about 4 to 5 hours, and entered the harbour of St. Peter's Port. Rested and lounged there next day, before setting sail back for Gosport at mid-day, on 18 September, reaching after a fifteen hour sail.

2 October 1984

We are now getting the boat ready to sail to India. We will sail out on 12 October. Quite excited. Everyone is working hard. Boat is more or less ready, with food, water on board, and all repair work done. Small last minute things remain. Our route is to be La Coruna (Spain), Lisbon, Gibraltar, Ibiza, Malta, Port Suez, either Port Sudan or Jeddah, on to Aden and Bombay. Total distance is about 6,500 NM (1 NM = 1.8 km). We are capable of covering over 100 NM in 24 hours. Should take about 3½ months after catering for the vagaries of winds. In the Red Sea, winds may be either strong head winds, or very light; and after Aden, expecting light to very light winds.

January 1966–December 1969

The Memory Lane to School:
Rashtriya Indian Military College

The Prince of Wales' Royal Indian Military College is situated in the lush green foothills of the great Himalayas, in the beautiful and tranquil Doon Valley in North India. It was re-named The Rashtriya Indian Military College (RIMC) after the British left India in 1947.

We may have been underage to take decisions on our future when we joined the College at the tender age of eleven, but at RIMC we were not 'boys' or 'students'; we were 'cadets'. We dressed in the Indian army's olive green uniform, marching, saluting, 'Yes Sir'-ing even boys who were ahead of us by a mere six months. We soaked in more than just the clean Dehradun air. We learnt all the true schoolboy values—standing by one's friends and not sneaking on them (or foes alike) before the powers that be (our seniors), who kept a close watch on our wrong-doings. We also nursed weird teenage notions, hero-worshipping senior cadets, nurturing lopsided ideas about girls, tackling our skewed emotional responses and the general sense of dislocation characteristic of this formative stage in life.

If one 'challenged' a fellow cadet, the gauntlet just had to be picked up—no matter what the consequences. So it was with challenges of all variety—going alone on a dark night into the hauntingly aloof Cricket Pavilion, or trying to catch a glimpse of the 'one-legged ghost' shovelling coal into the hot water boilers in the dead of night. So, if Harmeet, my best friend and buddy, said 'See if you can hold your breath for three minutes—particularly if you want to swim under water right across the swimming pool. I read somewhere that it can be done', and it just had to be done! It did not matter that I woke up from that session of breath-holding, dazed and light headed, with Harmeet holding the watch and shaking me vigorously saying, 'Thank God, you have come around! You passed out after two and a half minutes!'

> 'German Shoes-German Shoes,' they'd call after him.
>
> Anybody would. While all the boys sweated it out in strenuous physical training (PT), he strutted up and down the PT ground—'on doctor's orders,' he said—wearing peculiar, crudely-made black boots, tilted sharply outwards on both feet, and with heavily arched inner soles, supposedly to improve his severe case of knock-knees and flat feet. This cadet with an ostrich swagger seemed to be able to pull off the foremost audacious aspiration of any fertile, vicious and morbidly-free boarding schoolboy mind—shamming! That fine art of getting away without having put in honest work!

> He was a funny chap, this A.K. Singh II of the Chandragupta Section (there were two other A.K. Singhs senior to him in school: they were unimaginatively called A.K. Singh and A.K. Singh I—and this went on till A.K. Singh V!). He was lanky, and once asked the school RMO (Resident Medical Officer, the doctor at the College Hospital) how he could increase his weight so as to look more acceptable. Shockingly knock-kneed, with feet as flat as pans, and a head too small for his thin frame, he had an argumentative disposition which spurred most bullies into action. He was always fair game—seldom able to match up physically but never the one to give up. What riled the bullies the most was that he always seemed to get the highest marks in class! So, even while he did not have many friends, sometime or other, everyone did need his help—if not in Mathematics, it was in Physics or Chemistry. And this help was grudgingly solicited, and equally grudgingly given.
>
> Who *was* German Shoes? German Shoes was none other than yours truly!

Four to five years of life at RIMC—marching, saluting, 'Sirring' (mostly 'Yes Sirring'!)—taught us about life within a senior–junior hierarchy and also the hierarchy of the bully and the bullied; these are not small lessons to learn when it comes to grappling with the adult world—military or civilian. It sent home the message that in the world there was a place for you only if you had the courage to step out and carve that place for yourself. You learnt not to cry when you got hurt, since crying was not for 'men'. The long summer holidays, and the not-so-long winter holidays were special, since one got to return to the reassurance of one's family and eat home-cooked food!

At RIMC, we were gradually weaned away from home into the exhilarating freedom that carefree youth always yearn for. We learnt to use that freedom responsibly, ready to deal with the outside world, no longer seeking the protection and the safety of our homes. It was there that we imbibed basics of leading the life of a soldier—the vagabond! And all this, from the early age of eleven!

Looking back, I have come to believe that the college did its job well. Our calendar was crammed with school activities: studies, sports, cultural, and co-curricular, all designed to groom us from gawky eleven year olds into confident and capable sixteens. Notwithstanding the fact that at that time we'd try our best to avoid and circumvent all that we could get away with, we had a chance to grow up, and become more balanced young boys whose emotional energies were less burnt out and more used! Not everyone succeeded with flying colours but each one of us emerged wiser and surer.

Soldierly values and patriotic ideals seeped deep and wide into our dormant young minds and left their imprint for ever. As noveau-adults we learnt to seek responsibility and be responsible, instead of seeking the convenience of protection. One could ask: Did the life at RIMC push us to continue creating solutions to each prickly challenge that came our way? The answer would be a definite 'yes'. Collectivism and a strong sense of camaraderie were now embedded so deeply in our psyche that buddies received primacy over all other relationships. The realizations came in retrospect though; those were not the years to dwell on such profundities.

Fifteen going on Sixteen

After five years at RIMC we felt super-ready to join the National Defence Academy! After all, had we not joined the RIMC seeking future careers as commissioned officers in the country's Armed Forces? So, off we went from Dehradun to Pune, relinquishing one cadet-ship to take on the grown up, 'big boys' version at NDA. It was interesting to see that many of the first-year bullies at RIMC did not make it—perhaps they had concentrated too much on the bullying! And, in contrast, many of the quiet, 'decent' guys succeeded. Life was beginning to teach us some valuable, ever-lasting practical lessons that would help us to be more discerning, and choose the right path for ourselves as we grew older.

NDA 1969–72

Peacock Bay: 'Shamming'

There was aimlessness in the madness. The routine at the Academy left little time for any pursuit beyond the training programme. The fact of having been through almost the same routine at RIMC for over four years, took away some of the excitement from the NDA programme. 'Shamming', malingering, ducking, and conjuring up creative if vague excuses to skip activities became day-to-day challenges. Exchanging notes on how to get it right and refine successful strategies was an added occupation. Not everyone who tried got it right. Some got it right *back* on being found out! Of course, there was the unavoidable minimum standard required to be achieved, and so 'shamming' was best done *after* meeting the minimum standard set for academic and physical performances. Only in this way could one avoid the spotlight of the Directing Staff and Training Officers.

So, when there was a general call for the first year cadets to report at Peacock Bay to be screened for the formation of a core team of beginners to be introduced to sailing as a hobby, it seemed a good opportunity to create a 'shamming window'. Since Peacock Bay was at an extreme end of the campus, diametrically opposite our Squadron Lines and far enough away from the academic block, physical training and games grounds, it was a natural choice for the likes of me who wanted to escape the watchful eyes of the instructors and seniors. Of course, it was an effort to cycle all the way to the Bay, over a steep hill road; but the mental freedom of being away from it all was worth it.

Sushil Kumar Isaacs, the young Navy Lieutenant Commander (later to head the Indian Navy as its Chief of Naval Staff) got us all together. After a pep talk on how this was an opportunity for us to learn the very unique sport of sailing (not available anywhere else in the country), he divided us in pairs, and got us into the small Cadet Class dinghies to start off on our first sail ever. It wasn't bad at all! The boat went where it wished, since we were not yet masters of the sport, but we soon got the hang of it, and it was rather fun!

> We learnt the ropes of sailing, riding and swimming, in the most basic ways—monkey see, monkey do. Basic sailing skills were gleaned from the boat tending staff called 'tindalls'—the Namdevs and the Kamals Kanus, and Nagus—all from a particular remote fishing village in Ratnagiri, on the Karwar coast. They would yell, '*Kya karta hai?! Luppin luppin jao na!*' (How are you sailing? Go luffing into the wind close hauled!) We learnt basics of horse riding from the syces, or horse grooms, and also from the risaldars of the army's mounted units, posted to NDA for the job. '*Canto o o o r*', an intimidating holler... '*Arey cantor karo na, kya karta hai!*' (Cantor your horse! What are you doing?!).

> When unceremoniously dethroned by a wildly bucking animal, a loud command to 'mount!' left little time for one to recover from one's embarrassment. All one could hastily do was simply to mount the beast, probably for a repeat of the ignominy!

The National Championships, Royal Connaught Boat Club, Pune, 1971

'You could take part in the National Cadet Class Championship if you try,' said Sushil.

There weren't too many serious contenders; all in all, the best shammers among us seemed to have made the grade, because I found myself selected for the National Championships to be held on the Mulla–Mutha Reach at the Royal Connaught Boat Club in Pune. This seemed like a good mix of 'sham-and-achieve'!

By now, I had begun to rather enjoy the feeling of being free on the waves in the breeze, trying to move a boat well on its intriguing path around a regatta course. It was fun! It was not forced basic minimum training. It was not mandatory. I could achieve by choice. Some part of the aimlessness in the madness had disappeared, making way for a purposeful drive towards a vague distant goal which I could not yet see clearly, but had found worth gravitating towards. As the days of sailing turned into weeks and months, the tiring uphill bike-ride became a symbol of how much I wanted to reach the Bay a little before time to get a good boat rigged, and be off before the rest of the pack—that is, to be longer on the waters, to take more out of that day's sail! To learn more, give more, take more—all this became an obsession. And Sushil was always there to teach, to coach, to clarify and to search for answers in sailing books with us when problems turned technical.

We quickly outgrew the small Cadet Class boat and Peacock Bay, and off we were sailing in Mumbai, off the Colaba coast. Now we were sailing bigger boats like the International Enterprise Class and the CBK—indigenously designed decades ago, by three officers of the Indian Royal Corps of Engineers in the College of Military Engineering, Pune. The winds and waves created a heady combination and I found myself trying to better my skills at boat handling, honing racing rules and tactics in every spare moment. Soon, I actually became quite good at it!

Sailing Trials for the Youth Olympics (1972)

We heard that selection trials to sail for the country at the Youth Olympics at Kiel in Germany—the sailing venue for the Munich Olympics—were going to be held in Bombay. Could we do it? Why not? No doubt the Mumbai boys would be good—they had been sailing for years, and were on home waters. Would we be able to better them?

We did nothing but obsessively sail while we talked, thought, ate, slept and dreamt! Youth and enthusiasm can be a potent combination. During selection trials, the winds were expected to be strong. And tides were a new phenomenon to be mastered. We went into the trials with all we had. Though we did not realize it then, with two years at the Academy, 'all we had' had gained a lot more heft than the average seventeen year old anywhere in the world. When we found that our lean bodies did not weigh enough to battle the high sea winds, we wore three woollen jerseys under our heavy cotton-filled naval life-jackets, and took a dip in the sea to soak all the sea water possible, just to add on some kilos. This helped us to balance the boat and keep it on an even keel for maximum speed on the windward legs, as we hiked out over on the wind-ward side of the deck, precariously anchored by our toe-tips to our hiking straps, all muscles aching and groaning because they were pushed beyond their limits with the added 'ballast' weight leveraged well out-board. We were quite a spectacle for the rest of the fleet who did not dare laugh us off yet—not till they could see the results of these 'crazy' antics. To top it all, we had to work on the sails, the boat, and the equipment so that they were in the best possible condition for the races. Sleep was deep, and never enough after a day's hard sailing.

After all, the races could be won only if one's body, mind, and equipment worked in unison! As the trials progressed from one excruciating race to another, we gave it all that we could muster, given our capabilities and preparedness. Soon, our racing scores began inching ahead of the rest. And by the last race, we had clearly won!

Yes, sailing was now under my skin and I was fully soaked in my passion for taking my boat through rougher winds and higher waves. 'Shamming', once mastered, was giving way to greed—a hunger to better myself. As I sailed on, my self-image, confidence and self-esteem were enhanced and I began to feel the need to better myself in every sphere. A peculiar urge to continuously endeavour beyond excellence in everything I did was taking hold.

I think it had something to do with too many people taking for granted for too long that I would forever remain old German Shoes.

CHAPTER 4

SAILING BEGINS
Back to October 1984

Most of our three-month voyage to India was rather stormy and full of squalls. Our route took us south from the Solent, across the English Channel and the stormy Bay of Biscay, which is about 400 miles wide, past the coast of Brittany, past Spain and Portugal, with halts at La Coruna and Lisbon, and then through the Strait of Gibraltar. We sailed onwards across a winter storm-filled Mediterranean, on to the Suez Canal, and the mix of contradictions past and present that is Egypt today. We then traversed the Canal and the Red Sea, past the straits of Bab-el-Mandeb, across the peaceful Arabian Sea, and home to Bombay.
At Port Said, Tipsy was to leave to fly home, and Soma Pillai was to replace him. 'Champ' to some of us, he

had ruled the Indian single-handed dinghy sailing championship for over a decade. Soma later decided (on reaching Bombay) to pursue his dinghy sailing career, and so did not eventually sail with us around the world.

Handling a blue water boat is different from handling spirited dinghies. One cannot, so to say, sail a blue water yacht by the seat of one's pants. A yacht calls for coordinated action by the crew. Every situation at sea has its own drill, for seldom can help reach a yacht in time. Good seamanship is the ability to always do exactly what is best for the safety and comfort of the boat and her crew. As they say, at sea, if the boat lives, you live. It calls for repeated practice, and we got down to it day after day.

Ron Gravells, an ageless sea-dog agreed, for a fee, to train us on the finer points of big boat handling. He announced that he would henceforth be called 'Guru', and like a true guru he shared with us his wisdom acquired over decades of sailing the oceans in yachts.

Trishna of India

As the boat and her crew grew on each other, it was time for the *Guinevere* to become *Trishna*. Changing a boat's name is considered inauspicious because, normally, this is only done after a mishap or untoward incident involving a boat, like loss of crew at sea. Also, to a yachtsman, his boat is not inanimate; it is alive and spirited, with its own moods and eccentricities. So it was sad to 'terminate' *Guinevere*, even though she was immediately reborn as *Trishna*.

Guinevere of Sussex becomes the Trishna of India.

Diary entry:

10 September 1984

Bye bye, *Guinevere*. Hello *Trishna*! Permission to change the name (of the boat) came from the Registrar of Shipping, today. She is now *Trishna of India*! Today's work: on her stem-head fitting, fore-hatch, and change of name. She will uphold my name—for I have put my life into her. She is the result of years of hard work. She is a good boat.

Diary entry:

Night of 8 October 1984

AP and I worked on the boat till well past midnight. With AP inside the cabin and out of sight, I chose a moment of solitude to make a paper boat, with 'Guinevere' written on it, and floated her away in the dark. 'Guinevere' soon sailed into the beyond. Felt a strange emptiness. I was alone, so no one noticed my emotions. We loved *Guinevere*—she was our first boat. *Trishna* was the second. Thank you, good boat.

Trishna of India was painted in bold letters on her dark blue stern in the morning.

The first week of October 1984, the final week before sailing, sped by in a flurry of activity. Many a late night was spent stocking *Trishna* with water and food, repairing equipment, and checking out dozens of small but important items. Space and weight restrictions dictated that, as a rule, out of every ten useful tools and repair material we needed to carry, we select only one. Even so, I could not help marvelling at how we found space for so much. The layout of the boat below decks was not unlike a space capsule in terms of space management, with every inch of space utilized. At last all was ready.

Or was it?

Neil Carlier and Harry Kapoor decided to check us out.

Trishna sailed out to show her paces with both Harry and Neil on board. This involved a sail-out and sail-home exercise so that our boat handling drills could be assessed. It was a kind of a preparatory sail—a readiness check. We went out for a short sail in the Solent; all went well, until upon our return we attempted to bring *Trishna* alongside the jetty. The urgency of the moment, along with some over-enthusiasm, and definitely a certain lack of sailing expertise showed up then. The breast-line man, Chandrahas, stepped ashore with the mooring line and, restless to get *Trishna* to close the gap between the jetty and herself quickly, put all his weight on the mooring line to pull her in faster. But he did not factor in her weight of 10 tons! No doubt *Trishna* gained some momentum, and began to close in rapidly. But then, when it became clear she would arrive with a hard thump on the wooden jetty, she had to be fended off with equal energy!

Neil decided to demonstrate to us how to bring the boat alongside 'correctly'. But *Trishna* came alongside the wooden jetty yet again with a less-than-gentle thump! Given that Neil had been part of two around-the-world voyages, it was a somewhat awkward moment. I suspect the urgency of his desire to transfer all his seamanship and boat handling skills to us newbies all at once had something to do with it. However, it brought home to us that anyone can make mistakes at sea, even when least expected. In the end, he and Ron gave a green signal to boat and crew, and we were off!

Trishna Sets Sail (12 October 1984)

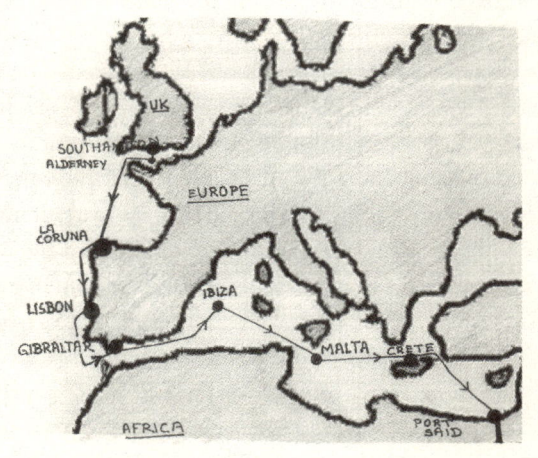

Route Map: Southampton to Port Said

The Gurkha bagpiper of the Queen's Gurkha Regiment played a favourite martial tune on that bright sunny October afternoon. A small crowd had gathered on the jetty to see us off. We also had a pundit on board. He had journeyed from London for the occasion, and was at his hymn-chanting best.

In heavily accented English, he began: 'Krishna means a good name...'

At that moment, Tipsy, standing next to him, whispered,

'Punditji, it is *Trishna*, not *Krishna*!'

Whereupon, the man of God continued smoothly: 'Yes, as I was saying, *Trishna* is a name which means something good to go on water.'

Of course this was not the meaning at all; but then, the Gods are forgiving and merciful. Someone popped a bottle of champagne, and amidst cheers and good wishes, *Trishna* slipped her lines and eased away from her jetty.

As I watched Neil waving us off, I wondered if he really believed we would succeed. In his farewell speech just before we had sailed, he had recounted his mixed feelings at the sight of the odd combination of a small Sikh in his forties, and a tall one-legged man, walking into his office two and a half months earlier and saying that they wanted to sail around the world. He had, nevertheless, rendered invaluable help, and one could see that, by now, he too had taken our venture to heart. If at all he had any reservations, he'd kept them to himself—in typical English fashion. Harry too, hid his feelings behind a straight smile as Maya and he waved us off.

> The excitement of the send-off over, Tipsy began looking for his left sailing boot, only to find that I had slipped his size 7 shoe on to my wooden leg, and had left my size 10 for him instead!

We quickly settled down to our routine at sea. Two 'watches' of two men each were formed—named in accordance with boating tradition as the 'Starboard' watch and the 'Port' watch . A 'watch' would man the boat, taking turns at sailing her for four hours before handing her over to the other watch. A fifth man would clean the ship, do all the cooking, and be on standby. He was the 'mother watch'. The mother watch changed by a system of rotation among the watches every day, but since Shekhar had been given the additional charge of rations and water—termed victualling in the seafarer's language—he soon earned the nickname of Mother Superior. The skipper's job was to see that all of us did our jobs.

The sail to Bombay was a personal challenge for each of us and especially so for me. A lifetime of planning and sacrifices were invested in our endeavour. Asha's personal sacrifices were undoubtedly greater than mine as also my young daughter Akshi's privations and anxieties that stemmed from long separations from her father. The highs and lows of their lives too were now inseparably intertwined with my obsession to sail around the world. Each day I faced the innumerable problems of sailing with a wooden leg. Could I last out—not just for a few hours, but for weeks on end? If not, I would have to withdraw from the team. There absolutely could not be any 'pile-on passengers' on such a venture.

Southampton to Gibraltar

Sailing off Cowes as we began our passage to India, the enormity of what we had set out to achieve struck me in large measure. It was too good to be true and incredibly overwhelming! We were on the verge of pulling off what had seemed at one point to be impossible! It was up to us and God Almighty to make it happen. The sheer bliss of knowing that no one could manipulate us into giving up the idea anymore—and this was indeed the beginning of our adventure—sank in as we sailed onwards, and the receding skyline faded into the horizon.

Fair winds, 10 to 15 knots, coming from the direction we wished to go, south by south-west, were not the best for boat speed, but were okay to start the long journey home. We were tacking into the wind all day in flat seas, till even these winds died off completely. We put into Alderney anchorage at 1830 hours on 13 October 1984.

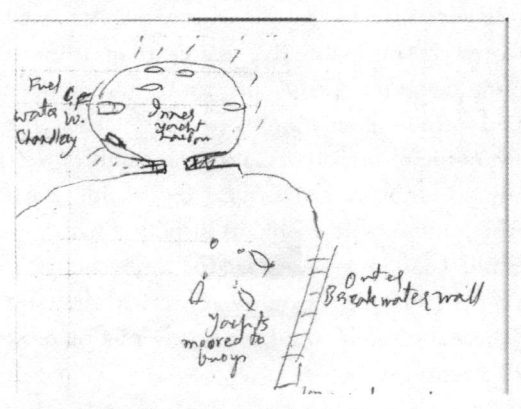

The Anchorage at Alderney Harbour

In Alderney Harbour

For the first few days at sea, I experimented with various ways to remove and store my limb and my storm suit trousers so that I could put them back on in the shortest possible time. I tried removing the limb and the trousers separately, then the limb with the trousers still on it, and also removing both only during the day off-watch time, keeping them on throughout the dark hours when an emergency can develop rapidly. It was also important to give some rest to my stump, and air it regularly.

I had mentally begun to work on a rough plan to remove, dry out and clean my artificial limb as well as my stump which would fit into the rotation of watch changes. I started keeping it on all night, on or off watch, removing it only during off-watch hours in the daytime.

Diary entry:

13 October 1984

> Stump is OK so far, but there is a lot to be learnt yet about going to sea with a wooden leg. We are 80 miles closer to home!

Anchoring out for the night in Alderney, the next day at 1100 hours, we went into Braye inner yacht harbour for water and fuel—all provided by Richard of Mainbrayce Marine, probably the sole operators in this small place. He was also kind enough to gift *Trishna* a log book. We left the harbour with no winds, going through a 5 nautical mile (7 to 9.5 km) wide patch of dense fog, where visibility was down to 50 metres at times.

We were under the influence of the high pressure lying at north and north-east of France and south and south-east of the UK—so there were flat, calm seas, accompanied by a gentle swell—the breathing of the Atlantic Ocean. It got very foggy now and then. We got a scare as we passed the Ushant—or the Ile Dussant—into the Bay of Biscay, through the Channel du Fromveur. We came too close to the left side, where tides set in 75 minutes before they do in the rest of the channel and, at one stage, we thought we would surely be pushed back to the north, and probably onto the rocks.

> Five days into the sail, I was keeping the limb on most of the time, wearing it along with the full storm suit even while I slept. I planned to remove it once a day for about four hours to air out the condensation that takes place inside the limb as also inside the weather suit, making it uncomfortable and clammy.

There were plenty of dolphins in these flat seas. Three birds flew with us for over four hours, perching on the boat, plucking out flying insects. They even perched on us at will—on our heads, shoulders and thighs as we sat motionless on lookout watch in the cockpit—never suspecting we could harm them. Their innocence was both touching and refreshing! There were calm, windless days, which were quite frustrating—but that is part of sailing.

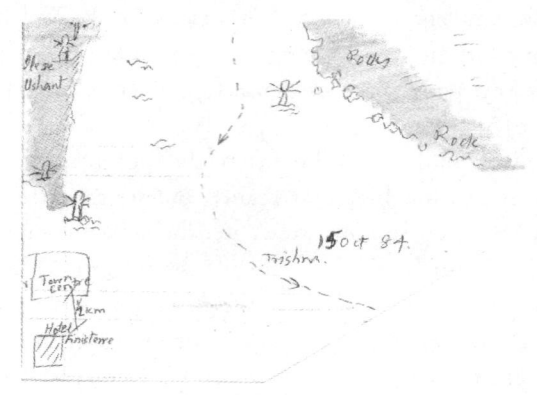

The Ushant Passage

Diary entry:

17 October 1984

The evening brought a radio forecast of gales and storms off Finisterre, and the night brought the storm itself. And how it hit! Down canvass to storm jib, and 12 reefs in the mainsail, and even then it was difficult to keep the boat under control and speed down—just off the wind—any closer and we would involuntarily tack. Peak winds were recorded at 50 knots or over 90 kmph (1 knot=1.8 kmph).

Boat stood up very well. Well done, *Trishna*, *Guinevere* would have been proud of you! Crew were good too; it is of utmost importance to get the right rig up at the right time—never be over-canvassed in a storm.

The stormy seas gave sledge hammer blows to the main body of the boat, threatening serious structural damage. It was scary at times, with the boat heeling (tilting) by 60, or at times 80 degrees. After the storm abated, the swell and chop continued through the next day, making all of us thoroughly sick. I kept the limb on all the time, only able to give it a breather of a couple of hours every three to four days. It was too early in the voyage to let the aches and pains be taken seriously. This was followed by three days of constantly looking out for sudden squalls. Several of them hit us with virtually no reaction time: one saw it coming—and there it was, barely giving us the window to strike down the sails. Continuous sail changes, reefing up and down in the huge swell and the chop, kept us wet, cold, fatigued and sick. So we decided to put into La Coruna to get some respite from the storm fatigue, and used the opportunity for some victualling—procuring fresh vegetables, fruit and bread, and topping up on fresh water.

Mooring at la Coruna Sailing Club

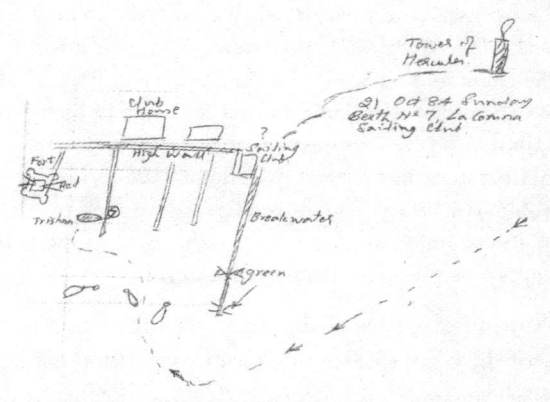

The Mooring at La Coruna Sailing Club

We reached La Coruna on 21 October 1984. It is an old, cobbled Spanish town, with castles, forts, a museum and a city square. The Spaniards, meticulous and conservative, were out in their Sunday best. The town was in the 'day of rest' mode and all shutters were down. The marina all-in-one, a person by the name of Roberto, agreed to post our mail on Monday since we could not get postage stamps on Sunday. We sailed out in the afternoon, slipping our moorings at about 1700 hours. Again, there were no winds as we passed the Islas Sisargas lighthouse on the Spanish coast, just west of the Towers of Hercules. The Spanish are obviously more meticulous with their outfits than their lighthouses—the lighthouse was flashing 3 in 12, when it was supposed to be 3 in 15 seconds!

Washed, rested, we were glad the Biscay storms had prepared us for some bad weather sailing. Seamanship is an evolving asset, with ever-increasing scope for upgrading skills. The head winds varying from zero to force five (on the Beaufort scale) caused us to tack all along the Cabo Finisterre (Cape Finisterre). This was a welcome change from the Biscay storms, though progress was very slow. Schools of dolphins with light grey underbellies popped out of the water now and again. We were in thick fog, with visibility at times down to less than a quarter of a mile. At night, a trawler frightened us by bearing straight down on us from astern (behind), turning away barely a hundred metres from us when we wildly flashed the searchlight on him, and also on our sails. Not satisfied with the encounter, he turned around barely 2 miles ahead, only to bear down on us again, this time from the front! The fog allowed us only a quarter of a mile before we could see him—the rest of it was an acoustic exercise, with all ears strained on his engine noise. Two close shaves with the same trawler, and the dense fog kept us on edge till it cleared, well into the next day—23 October.

Diary entry:

> Night of 23 October, off Port Viana
>
> Visibility down to zero. At times, the bow of the boat is lost in fog when seen from the cockpit. Everyone has a lifejacket close at hand, and the duty watch is flashing the

searchlight once every few minutes all around and then on the sails, and keeping a good ear out for the engine noise of any approaching ship. After a Diwali evening meal—tinned sweets were served, and a few flares fired as fireworks—Tipsy and Shekhar are fast asleep, fully dressed, lifejackets at hand. I am on mother watch—'mother of the day' everyone calls it. KS is at the nav (navigation) table.

The Rio Tejo-Lisbon

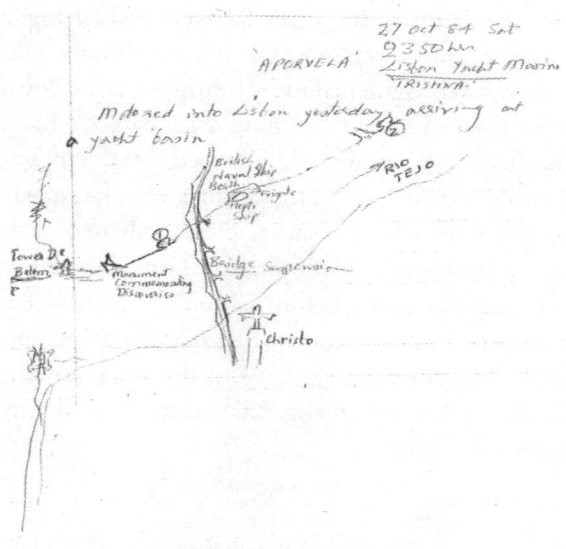

Passage up the Rio Tejo-Lisbon

We reached Lisbon, in Portugal, at the mouth of the Rio Tejo (Rio is river in Portuguese) on 26 October. The customs launch came up to us to complete formalities, directing us to yacht basin number one where we got grounded since there was inadequate depth. We waited for the tide to re-float us, then moved to basin number two—the very small but safe Aporvela basin—and tied up alongside a 1930 Swan class yacht. Here we got to wash and bathe in a pre-fabricated toilet-cum-bath.

An Indian Embassy representative visited *Trishna* at 10 a.m. the next morning. A lavish dinner was hosted at Hotel Palace Ajuda, by Mr Aditya of Air India, and Mr AND Haksar, the Indian Ambassador—what a change from the food on board! The Portuguese Army commando unit sent a van with officers, and we were hosted to a regimental afternoon, and a visit to their army centre. This was followed by a sumptuous Portuguese lunch with officers and men, served with good Portuguese wines, somewhat in the style of our Regimental *Bara Khana*. The Commandos presented us their regimental banner as memento, followed by hearty throaty salutations that seemed like their regimental war cry.

Trishna motored out of the Lisbon yacht basin, into the Atlantic, passing under the big suspension bridge with the gigantic statue of Christ—Cristo Rei statue, said to be inspired by the statue of Christ in Rio De Janeiro, Brazil, on our Port side—at about 7.30 in the morning of 28 October, again a Sunday. Here we were accosted by the small but fast customs boat, and told to go back again to the maritime police and obtain emigration clearance, which put us back by a few hours! They were kind enough to take Tipsy in their launch for the paperwork. We finally cleared the main harbour guard posts, old fortresses on either side, one of them—the Discoveries Monument—dedicated to the discoverer, Christopher Columbus. We reached the Tower de Belem at 10.30 a.m., and headed due south for Gibraltar.

Diary entry:

> Sunday, 28 October
> Heading southwest, 5 miles off the Portuguese coast
>
> Flat sea, lovely day, with sun nice and bright. Gibraltar is 250 (nautical) miles away. Limb giving some worry. Left condyle bone pressing down with all my weight on the limb socket all the time—even sitting causes a lot of pain. Loose rivets of the joint are causing the suction in the socket to leak, so the limb is not held up by suction, but keeps slipping in and out with a piston action with each step. Not comfortable now to get about the boat. Must stop that suction leak in Gibraltar.

After leaving Lisbon, there were the same calm patches, with some head winds making us tack upwind all day. The winds built up on the morning of 30 October. As I slept soundly (while on mother watch!), the crew struggled through two sail changes, down to storm jib, in a 30–35-knot gale and choppy seas. Constant sail changes and tacking in head winds were the main features of the 30th as well as the 31st of October, both wet and miserable days. The winds were high, the seas were choppy, terribly bumpy, and uncomfortable. I had a piece of cake snatched from my hand by a splashing wave as I was steering at the helm even before I could bite into it! It was not uncommon for tea, water, or any drink to be blown out of glasses as we held them on deck. The skipper deliberated over putting into Cadiz to give the crew some rest, as we approached it on a starboard tack. However, in the end we decided to sail on to Gibraltar.

Sailing to Gibraltar

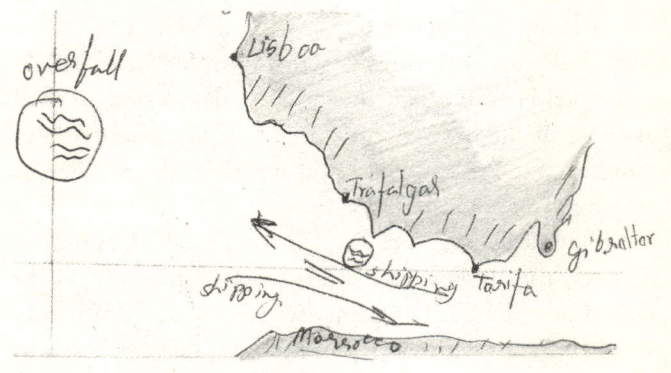

The Sail into Gibraltar

There are east as well as west-going shipping lanes from the Atlantic Ocean clearly marked as one enters or exits Gibraltar. Between them is a separation zone. We coasted along past the Trafalgar Light at about 9 a.m. on 1 November 1984. Then we headed across the shipping lanes to go across to the side with favourable tides. As we discovered, there are on-going as well as in-coming tidal channels just like shipping lanes! In the process, we crossed an area of noticeably choppy waters prominently marked on the charts (maps at sea are called charts) as 'overfall'. Thence we trudged bumpily over the 'overfalls', on to Gibraltar.

It was there that we heard the tragic news of Indira Gandhi's assassination. Initially, we could only hear the repeated mention of Indira Gandhi on the Spanish and Portuguese radio channels. All we could tell was that something significant was being reported about home. There was no way to know any more. It was only on approaching Gibraltar that we were able to receive the BBC bulletins that conveyed the shocking news of her assassination. We sailed in with the flags—ours as well as those of the host countries—at half mast, as a sign of mourning, and that is where they stayed for the duration of our stop-over at Gibraltar.

Gibraltar or the Rock, as it is fondly called, appeared through the haze on the north eastern horizon, as we tacked past the Tarifa lighthouse. Slowly, the dim shapes visible behind it turned into buildings, quite Spanish in their architecture. Soon we could see bunkers, soldiers' barracks, huge breast-walls and fortifications along the hillside, and a long and solid breakwater running all the way into the area of the marinas where the HMS Churchill, a nuclear submarine, was moored. Several aerial cableways could be seen connecting various points on the Rock and areas at lower levels. All in all, it appeared a small and lovely place.

A berth had been kindly earmarked for *Trishna* in the Royal Naval Marina area by the garrison, and the hot shower there was very welcome. We gave a farewell dinner to our sailing guru, Ron Gravells. We refrained from drinks as we were in state mourning to mark the assassination of our Prime Minister. On 4 November during Sunday mass, the pastor also called upon everyone to pray for peace unto the departed soul.

The naval workshop facilities at Coaling Island helped us deal with the (thankfully) minor consequences of the storms of Biscay, which had smashed some fittings and damaged the latches and sealing cowlings. Thankfully, there was no structural damage despite the beating the boat had taken.

The elementary comforts of an officer's mess can sometimes satiate all of one's worldly desires of the highest order; and for me gratification was complete with a hot bath, wholesome food, and a full night's sleep between clean sheets and a blanket on a real full size bed, and with the limb off! After a good night's restful sleep (such a blessing after the continuous four-hour-on-four-hour-off watches at sea!) I awoke to a gentle knock on the door, followed by Sarah, the stewardess's sweet call of 'tea please?' Moments later, a plump middle-aged Spanish housekeeping lady entered to do up the room. Hearing her muffled scream, I turned to find her staring in horror at the limb by the bed. I had to launch into laborious but unspoken explanations through varied gesticulations, nodding, and some benign smiling at the apologetic and helpful woman who finally figured out that it was indeed a separated limb but not a real one in flesh and blood. Peace was then restored!

A walk around the city centre and a drive past places of interest followed, courtesy our hosts, the Commander and staff of the Naval Base, HMS Rooke. They took us to the Spanish–English border post at the Catalan Bay. Huge iron sheets had been erected to create an artificial catchment area to harvest rain water. We were told that fresh water being in short supply, at several places, sea water was used wherever possible, to flush toilets, etc. We went through the famous Gibraltar tunnels running over 35–37 kilometres variously. We went on to the upper galleries in the Rock, with its long lines of gun emplacements—much like a ship's gun ports opening seawards for the defence of the Rock. We saw the 100-ton gun which had inspired the famous movie, *The Guns of Navarone*, and were also taken to the model room at the top of the Rock. It was a thrilling visit by any standards. We did not miss the Gibraltar apes, of which there were plenty on the Rock—and were much like our own Ayodhya apes back home!

Commander Hamley, a naval dentist by profession and a rocks-and-archaeology enthusiast by inclination, offered to take us on a personalized visit to the world famous St. Michael's caves. While the upper caves, with the then oldest human skull of the Neanderthal Woman, were open to the public, the lower ones—discovered by accident in 1942— were not. This was because earlier attempts at allowing tourist access had caused much damage to the priceless, ageless and unique rock formations because of people who wanted to take home souvenirs, or etch their names. I was advised to opt out of the cave visit and see the city instead. Everyone assumed that I would not be able to cope with all the descending and ascending inside the long and winding cave, essentially with the help of ropes and ladders. But I decided to give it a try instead, determined to ensure that I did not drag the rest of the group down. The elementary principle to follow in such situations is to keep going as long as you can be sure that you can retrace the ground you have covered, both in terms of ability and time allocated. Never go where you can't come back from! I managed the ropes and the crawling well enough to finish the tour along with the others, so no one could complain. Another small but meaningful confidence builder!

The good Commander asked if he could take a picture along with me. He actually rode me home pillion ('Oh, don't worry about the helmet!') on his motorcycle, to a kitchen-table dinner preceded by a couple of rounds of good Scotch whisky, with him and his gracious, though slightly taken-aback, wife. The next day he took me to see his dental clinic, and took jaw impressions to have dentures made for me as a personal gift.

'I will mail them to your home in India,' he promised. Hamley was true to his word and the dentures he made reached Asha in Gwalior by parcel—after we had set sail from India to go around the world. They finally reached me at Panama, brought over by the replacement crew. They fit me perfectly in the first go and were good for over two decades. Thank you, Mr Hamley, for the caves, the dinner and the dentures. I owe you one.

Gibraltar to Port Said

Rain and a cold front caught up with us as we slipped our mooring lines, and sailed out at about 1315 hours on

4 November 1984, setting a course of 080 degrees to round the Cabo Degata on the southern coast of Spain, 150 miles away. Soon, gale force winds from dead astern (behind) hit us.

Diary entry:

> Spent the night in constant vigil and uneasiness, apart from terrible discomfort and wetness after being thrown about. Winds over 45 to 50 knots for over 36 hours. Reefed 4, then 10, and again 12 reefs in the mainsail (one reef is one turn of the sail round the horizontal boom, taken while lowering the sail along the mast at the same time, using winches for the purpose, thus reducing sail area). Twelve reefs means there is hardly any sail left on the mast) with jib (foresail) down—*Trishna* has less canvass on than a windsurfer now! Even so we are doing 6 knots! Hard steerage needed to keep boat from broaching or rolling over. Huge seas—fascinating, frightful. Over 50 feet high—overtaking. Few broke over the stern.

This was our first big storm with winds and seas from behind us, and there were many boat-handling lessons still left to master about this point of sailing. It was good that our learning happened ahead of any tragedy, for any mishandling could easily have led to a broaching (veering upwind) by the boat, leading to possible flattening or even rolling of the boat if hit by an untimely wave.

The seas calmed down on the night between 5 and 6 November, giving us a quieter but faster sail for the rest of that night. On 7 November, *Trishna* sailed into Ibiza, in the Balearic Islands.

Balearic Islands–Ibiza

Diary entry (undated):

Sailed into Ibiza, in between the narrow channel marked by the North and South black-and-white banded lighthouses, between the islands of Ibiza and Formentera, at about 1630 hours GMT. Motored up to the yacht marina at Porto Nueva, Ibiza. Tied up alongside at berth number 708. Later walked up to the yacht club, chandlery (boat stores shop) and back to the boat. Got some sleep.

Mended the two foot pumps next day, and the wet suits locker. Washed out the toilet with sea water. Tipsy contacted Delhi on phone. We could afford only one call per port—I asked him to request Mrs Chowdhury to pass on our news to my sister in Delhi, who would then relay it by telegram to Asha in Gwalior.

First thing: boat repairs; after 4 p.m. we found time to visit the island, and I went off to explore the Museo Monografico Del Puig Des Molins, via Romana, at the base of the hill. It had burial chambers dating back to the Phoenicians. Excavations were still going on. The museum was full of artefacts dating back to 500–650 BC, and included impressive terracotta pottery, ornaments and stone engravings. We then visited the Dalt Vila area, with its famous cathedral that had over 250 steps—and I made it to the top *and* walked back without a stop! All along, there were old Ibizan stone and lime houses. The setting was very soulful. KS exchanged yacht burgees (small sailing mast-top flags) with the Yacht Club, as a symbolic and traditional goodwill gesture by a visiting sailor. We dined at the cheapest eating house, so no one had to cook, much less eat our own cooking! The final payment was made by 50 Spanish pesetas postage stamp, since Tipsy had no more local currency left!

Having taken the priest's blessings at the Cathedral in San Antonio, and procured water and fresh rations, we were ready to sail onwards—to Malta.

Heavy to medium seas in variable winds awaited us. For over three days, the crew suffered from seasickness, flatulence and an overall feeling of discomfort and restlessness. Although we were beating upwind in choppy seas, the general conditions did not entirely warrant these symptoms. After much wondering and questioning, the culprit was narrowed down to the water we had taken on at Ibiza. It tasted different and was probably hard water with some minerals that did not suit us. That particular water tank was then isolated; older water was severely rationed and used strictly for drinking. The hard water was used only for boiling tea or cooking, and the tummy complaints disappeared in a day or two.

The night of 11 November brought in black squally clouds, stealing up on us now and again, bringing stormy winds and rain, and we had to drop headsail and re-hoist it after the cloud passed. We decided to tack away to avoid the path of one such big black cloud, and managed to almost outmanoeuvre it. Its fringes hit us whiplash blows of winds about 30–35 knots (55–65 kmph) lasting about 90 minutes, thrashing us about in wind and rain before it subsided, and all was well again. We caught two fish weighing about 2½ kg each the next day, which were cooked jointly by Shekhar and Bharti, and relished to the last piece by all. Storm-less for a while, we rested and the morale on board soared.

CHAPTER 5

ONWARDS TO MALTA, CLOSER HOME
November–December 1984

Our cat-and-mouse encounter with tropical thunderstorms carried on through the next few days, as we sailed past Cape Bon, Tunisia, which we left 20 miles to our south on 15 November 1984.

Diary entry (undated):

At 2000 hours on the 14th, after the thundershower, which Bharti, skipper and I weathered on the deck, winds settled in from the south. Tremendous progress; frequently at 8–9 knots (nautical miles per hour) on the boat's speed log. That night and half of the next day, the huge 30-foot swell followed us in unbroken regularity, pushing us firmly homewards. The effect of the bigger ones is that of riding the surf—a surging, uplifting feeling as *Trishna* is pushed forward and upward by the huge following waves—the boat stays on the frothing surfing crest for a while, before dipping down into the long regular trough ahead, waiting for the next wave and the next big upward surge. The feeling is euphoric.

Contacted two Indian officers on two merchant ships yesterday on our VHF radio—*Mawan* and *Liwan* of Uniwan Shipping, Hong Kong, and what sounded like Barber Lines. We chatted them up for a while. One was from Surat, the other was probably someone called Sandhu...

Today, hit by squally weather, down jib, 6 reefs in the main, boat speed 8–10 knots, winds 35–40 knots on the speed log, with following winds, that makes true wind speed of 45–50 knots. Charging towards Malta. Must remember: safety first, last, all the time—boat lives, we live.

Changing headsail, sitting on the forepeak (forward-most part of the foredeck), the thumping deck caused a water spurt right up my storm suit trousers, wetting me where I least wanted to be wet and cold! Flying fish that fall on the deck make for easy cooking and good eating.

Winds turned into a proper storm by 1700 hours on 15 November—and what a storm it was!

Diary entry:

> 16 November 1984, 1245 GMT
> (almost 20 hours later), 70 miles WNW of Malta.

Storm still abating. Had to go down to 13 reefs, no headsail at night. Speedo at times pushing its max reading at 10 knots so actual speed was more. Doing that only with the pushing swell, and the windage on hull, spars (mast and boom), the wire rigging, and on our bodies—sail is almost nothing—only there for directional stability and steerage. If conditions before were bad, yesterday they were awe inspiring and a bit frightening. At the mercy of Mother Nature. Boat behaves beautifully and easily. Wave after huge wave, roller after seemingly even higher roller, taking our breath away as we look on. It would either break in a cascading, phosphorescent, bubbling frothing, foam of ethereal beauty, or would push us homeward with a gigantic shove without breaking. An occasional wave even broke over the stern and into the cockpit, flooding it with frothing foaming sea, threatening to swamp us. All except the two crew members on watch—themselves harnessed and tethered to the boat by lifelines—had to be locked into the protective body, that is, the belly of the mother-boat. The companionway hatch and weatherboards kept the fury of the waves out of the cabin and prevented them from flooding the cabin and sinking the boat. An ugly, powerful, rain bearing, scary looking cloud followed an even blacker and larger cloud, as a front followed another front and the depression moved over us, heading east. Every grey brought hope that the storm would abate—only to turn black again. Moonrise was well past midnight—a bit of celestial light does wonders to dispel the gloom and raise the spirits. Each time a big one broke over the boat, the skipper, at his post at the nav table would yell 'OK?', and each time the man at the wheel yelled back: 'OK!' Meaning situation under control. Though merely four or five feet from each other, it needed all the lung power one could muster to be heard over the roar of the ongoing thunderstorm. No one got any sleep—for some it was the second night running. Most could not retain any solid food, managing with a sip or two of juice or water to stay hydrated. At about 1 a.m., a Greek ship, calling herself *Falahope* I think, overtook us in the pitch dark. Seeing only our lone tiny masthead light in the black stormy night concerned her communication officer enough to first flash a morse code on his aldis signalling lamp to us, then come up on VHF radio and inquire if we were in distress and needed help. 'What ship?' he inquired. To which we replied with a more than justified tinge of pride: 'Indian sail boat—and no thank you—we don't yet need any assistance.'

Seldom has there been a more welcome glow than the dull morning sun the next day. With the storm's fury spent, the swell took the better part of 24 hours to subside to a level of comfort. We removed 4 reefs, while getting on at over 5½ knots only on reefed main. Malta was close by, and home a bit closer than before the storm.

Diary entry (undated):

Humour and cheer are balm to frayed nerves—abundance of both on this ship—as we move over this eternal solvent, the sea.

Gozo light—also called Gwadtex—was sighted, followed by a night-long sail along the Eastern coast of Malta on to Valleta harbour into which we sailed at daybreak. A friendly face waved at us from his yacht, inviting us to tie up alongside. It was Donald Milley and his yacht, the *Avalon Venturer* welcoming us.

We learnt that nothing happens in Malta in a hurry; and nothing at all if it is a Saturday or Sunday. Hence, no running water in the dock-side toilets on a weekend! But, we did manage a wash, food, rest and letters.

The Grand Master's Palace with its tapestries, offices and stateroom were over two to three hundred years old; the armoury had Turkish and pre-Turkish weapons, and was very impressive. Walking up and down the Main Street in Valletta felt good, though it took a while to find our land legs again. My quip was: 'Sometimes it doesn't listen to me!', as I wobbled along. We walked to St. John's Cathedral, and later to the local yacht club—the Royal Malta Yacht Club—for a burgee exchange ceremony, some well-earned beer, and Maltese food of mashed beans in garlic, garlic bread, and shellfish.

Malta is a mix of the Orient and the Occident, with European and Asiatic values, cultures and habits. Some things were very inexpensive, others exorbitant—typical of an isolated economy. Bus travel was very cheap; people were very well dressed, and no one was in any hurry. Automobiles were mostly old but well-maintained. When I asked, 'On which side of the road do people drive?', the reply was, 'In Malta we only drive in the shade!' Inducements expected by port and customs personnel were demanded with impunity—wines, tobacco, chocolates, anything.

Every house in Malta has a history; and every square has a dome or a cathedral—each more beautiful than the other. The cities of Valletta and Mdina were built using rock quarried out from under them. Thus, the lowest floors are basements or dungeons, many over four hundred years old! Roofs are invariably stone arches. We saw many sound old buildings lying in disuse, while new buildings were coming up all over the place. I was told that the people were now keen on modern structures. There were several pre-historic temples, like the Tarxien Temples built between 3600 and 2500 BC. The Hypogeum—literally meaning 'below the ground'—has more than three subterranean stories. It was also built between 3000 and 2500 BC, and is among the oldest temples and buildings in Europe.

We visited the home of the gracious Mr and Mrs Walters for tea—Mrs Walters' sister is married to a good friend from my hometown Lucknow. Mrs Walters had made samosas and *gajar halwa*, which we gleefully ate in large quantities.

The Addolorata Cemetery at Paola, and the Mosta Dome—the fourth-largest in the world, were also impressive. There was time only for a hurried visit and a mere glimpse of the places mentioned, also considering that our pockets were too strained even for the entry fee for each of these.

Geographically located in the middle of the Mediterranean Sea, Malta has been overrun several times, and has borne the brunt of the two great wars. It was bombed out heavily during World War II. The entire population was so deeply involved in the war effort that the British government conferred the St. George Cross for bravery on every living citizen after the war ended.

Having paid port charges of Maltese pounds 20 (a Maltese Pound was then equal to about one pound sterling and forty pence), we slipped our moorings on 20 November 1984, at about 1640 GMT, and set course bearing 090 degrees, for Kriti (earlier Crete), after clearing the outer entrance of the Grand Harbour at Valletta.

We continued to get our share of moderate to strong winds, with fairly rough seas. Progress was respectable, at about 4–6 knots all along.

Diary entry:

21 November 1984

Last night, played chess with a storm to our north, trying to outmanoeuvre it by studying if the wind was backing or veering, which gave us the probable location of the eye of the storm. Passing Sri Lankan ship, *Lanka Ratna* kindly gave us the weather forecast on the VHF radio. As we headed on 110 degrees to keep the storm to our north, it also began moving on a parallel course, so we gibed (swung the sail around) and set the new course of 080 degrees to pass to its north, finally clearing it after daybreak. Lightening, thunder and light shows all night along with the gusts.

After hoodwinking the storm, the winds were steady, with a fair sprinkling of clouds; but it was not cloudy enough to hide the sun. We had become quite good at reading the approaching clouds for what they were about to deliver to us, hence being able to execute sail changes before the squalls struck. Steady sailing.

Diary entry:

23 November 1984

If ever a voyage can be romantic, it has been for these past two days and nights, spent in watching the clouds fleet past, continuously changing shapes—here is a flying horse, there a praying priest, a flying carpet with a mullah on it, a lion with a horse's body and wings, an angel flying, now a threatening demon. Man's imagination is boundless—no two clouds or two ripples are exactly alike. No two sailing days are the same—each has its own flavour and tang. Looking at ripples off the boat's bows and also the wake of the boat off its stern is an endless exercise in imaginative tomfoolery. Frothing foam, forming a wave, then gently nudging the boat, breaking foam upon more foam before floating away in all directions and in all shapes; air bubbles being trapped under water, giving the sea various hues from deep green to sky blue—and in between, the foaming white. Yesterday was maintenance day for my stump. I aired and sunned it—once every three or four days is a must; on its health depends the success of my sailing.

We reached Iraklion, on the northern coast of Crete, at about 1530 hours on the 24th, sailed into the inner harbour, past the breakwater wall, keeping it to our right, to tie up alongside an old 40-footer barge at the jetty. Iraklion is a small place, with a romantic restaurant where people in colourful clothes sat in the sun enjoying tea. A 38-foot, rather racy yacht named *Uccello* (Italian name for a bird, we were told) sailed into the harbour with three girls and a boy, arousing considerable interest in our all male crew.

Prolonged sailing at sea without the company of the fairer sex does odd things to the mind.

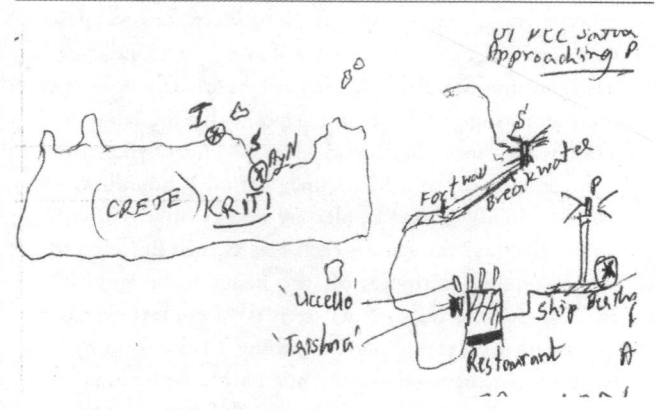

Island of Kriti and Iraklion Port

Note: On the map, I is Iraklion, S is Spinnalonga & AyN is Agios Nicolos

Crete is a tourist's island. It was still summer here, warmer than the rest of Europe, where winter was already setting in. The tourist season was receding from here rather late. Tourists interested in the Minoan civilization throng the place, and can be seen all over on bicycles, hitchhiking, or on yachts. The Knossos Palace (parts of which were constructed between the 19th and 17th century BC) and the Knossos Museum are a big draw. Souvenirs are a big industry here. The phallic symbol worshipped as the genesis of creation and power (not unlike the representation of Shiva in Hindu mythology) and the half-man/half-bull monster, the Minotaur, inspire the vast majority of souvenirs.

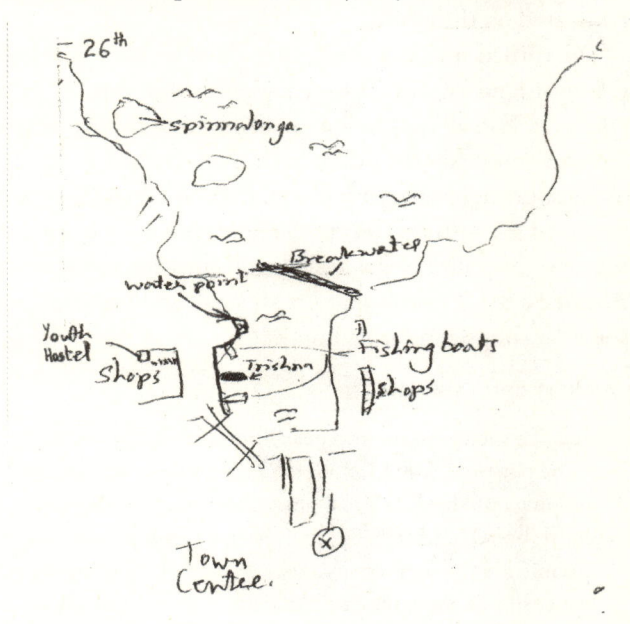

The Port of Agios Nicolos

We sailed out to the neighbouring port of Agios Nicolos, or simply Ay Nicolos, further east along the northern shores of Crete, in the wee hours of 25 November 1984, in very low winds, forcing a slow passage over the short distance. We could see the American air base, with Nissan huts painted in camouflage colours. There were plenty of greenhouses dotting the landscape. The countryside was rocky and hilly, with olive shrubs growing all over. We learnt that picking olives could fetch a rolling stone tourist as much as US$

20 per day, and that no cooking medium besides olive oil is permitted on the island.

We turned into the small port, past the erstwhile leper colony island of Spinalonga and into the tiny harbour, where at last we reached a small homely fishing village. *Trishna*'s mast was the tallest in the harbour!

Each gracious villager had a kind word for us. They were a relaxed lot with no rush to get going! Many gathered on the jetty in polite curiosity. A stroll into the town centre revealed a small town square, with small and narrow alleys, souvenir shops and eating houses.

Diary entry (undated):

In all, a very pleasant and peaceful place—small enough to be personal. Dined at a local eating house, on limited helpings of sheek kebabs, pork chops, meat balls, with local bread and sauces, and beer—finances did not permit a very sumptuous meal. Food is becoming less expensive as we move east. Another night of eight-hour sleep!

Mythology has it that the great volcano of Santorini, in the southern Aegean Sea, destroyed the ancient Minoan civilization on Kriti, possibly due to a resulting tsunami, and was responsible for sinking the mythical city of Atlantis, and that the entire earth was covered in a haze caused by volcanic ash for over a year. Santorini has also been made famous by Jules Verne in his book *Twenty Thousand Leagues Under the Sea*. We could see the twin volcanic islands created by the repeated volcanic activity in the area.

After regular boat checks, and loading water and fresh food, we slipped our lines at about 1500 hours on 27 November, heading northeast at a bearing of 60 degrees for about 20 miles before rounding the two islands, and setting course of 130 degrees for Port Said, about 400 milesaway.

There was not much wind for three days, but the good Mediterranean weather was great compensation, and no one complained! The clear sunny days, clear night skies, flat seas made for gentle progress.

Diary entry (undated):

> Tipsy caught up with paperwork—he is really good at his paperwork, and mothers us along. Without him, our shore administration and personal administration back home would have a lot lacking. Shekhar and Bharti write a bit, listen to music and we all generally soak in the bliss of the Mediterranean.

Respectable winds picked up towards the end of the 29th, and for the next two and a half days, we made good progress. Flat seas ensured that we were comfortable below deck even though we were tacking in head winds.

Diary entry:

30 November 1984

> AP and I found ourselves absorbed in star-gazing during night watch. We watched the celestial sphere (night sky with stars) pass overhead, the soulful evening twilight turning the beautiful day into an equally beautiful night, with the constellations of Andromeda, and later

the Belt of Orion, the Canis groups of Canis Major and Canis Minor, and Gemini rising from the eastern horizon even as Hercules, Ophiuchus and Sagittarius set into the western horizon, one after another, moving with the divine hand—slowly, imperceptibly, and Venus making its dramatic descent in all its glowing majesty. Early morning brings up Virgo with Spica, and Arcturus in the Boötes constellation, rising out of the eastern horizon as their predecessors set on the opposite side of the earth. In the day, large schools of dolphins, probably thinking the boat to be one with them, playfully swim right next to us, jumping in and out of the water. The water is clear enough for us to watch them swim away gracefully with speed, ahead of our bows, preparing to jump up majestically in a graceful motion—and we go click, click, click. In all, unbroken peace and tranquility. The power and peace Nature offers slowly permeates the mind. Modern day education could do well by bringing this simple closeness to nature to every man; it would do a lot of good to all. Enough of this runaway babble; must catch up on some letters since I am on mother watch and it is a peaceful day today.

Various mother watches found their own ways of being creative: Tipsy cooked *aloo-gobi-ki-sabzi* served with rice *pulav*; AP made a phenomenal effort to turn out *chhole-bhature* using pre-cooked pita bread taken on at Kriti as a *bhatura* substitute; Bharti made what he had been pining for for a long time—rice, *daal* and *sabzi*.

All in all, our approach to Port Said was comfortable. We were looking forward to meeting Soma Pillai who was to replace Tipsy there, for he would bring first-hand news from home.

We put into Port Said at about 9.30 or 10 a.m. on 1 December, led by a pilot patrol boat, and finally tied up at Port Fouad at about 11.30 p.m.! Egypt was giving us a taste of things to come—the helper on the pilot scouted around our scruffy little boat for something he could pick up and ultimately had to reconcile himself with some tea bags as nothing else seemed worth asking for! This was our first taste of Egyptian ways. We parted with half a box of tea bags in disgust and embarrassment. It was the done thing, we were told. Corruption and lethargy were apparently routine aspects of daily life in Egypt. The officials we met while getting our paperwork and permissions done were an expressive lot, gesticulating and talking nonstop. Much of what they said was superfluous and often untrue, contributing to the overall inefficiency. They behaved authoritatively at first, and gradually warmed up to us in a display of chumminess that transformed without fail into a list of demands—cigarettes, chocolates, soaps, even the sailing caps off our heads!

2 and 3 December were spent in boat maintenance. The auxiliary engine was overhauled; the sail reefing mechanism was washed with fresh water and greased; the rigging shroud turn-buckles were inspected, and the tops were re-taped so that the split pins would not slip. Bharti and Shekhar spread out, washed, and dried the twelve sails after inspecting them for damage. AP and KS packed all charts and navigation publications used so far to be sent back to Mumbai, and opened the yet-sealed container with the charts needed for the second half of our voyage

to India.

Tipsy tried to tackle the shipping agent, one Mr Abood, a Libyan who was working for Ameaster—the American shipping agents' company referred to us by Ashok Tawade, the Consul General in Port Said. The rates he was quoting were unbelievably high, closer to those applicable to ships rather than for a vessel barely the size of a lifeboat. However, we ended up paying most of it since he had already been hired on our behalf *without* prior negotiation—a strict no-no in Egypt. Tipsy had quite a harrowing time; even the visas for us to step ashore took over a day to come through. This was despite the fact that the Indian Embassy, the Military Attaché (MA) Colonel MC Gautam (a Bengal Sapper officer), as well as Soma Pillai and others had already done a reasonable amount of leg work before we sailed in. No work in Egypt is done on the quick. A request for getting a job done is usually answered by '*Insha Allah, bad bokra*', meaning 'God willing, after tomorrow'! We were also told it was a rule that each of us must change at least US$ 150 into local currency before being permitted to step ashore!

It was once again time to shower, launder, wash and air out the boat, clean and flush out the toilets and the bilges (the lowest area inside the boat where water and sludge invariably collects), check the gear and rig, rest and recoup. The first few days passed as an epilogue to the previous leg of the voyage, and a prologue to the next half of our sail back to Bombay.

The mooring at Port Fouad in Egypt had extremely limited facilities for washing or bathing—the first things a sailor looks for once in port. So, when the Indian consul, Mr Tawade, along with Colonel MC Gautam, Mr Abood the shipping agent, and Ms Sonia the personable Egyptian interpreter came to look us up, we were caught unshaven and seriously underdressed. Those of us who were not wrapped in their towels were only modestly clad in their jogging suit lowers, washing clothes in the open. They stood aside, slightly embarrassed, trying to make polite talk with a bunch of scruffy bare-chested men when Tipsy chose to emerge from the battered wooden bath, dressed only in his long wet hair and dripping beard with the true aplomb of the full-blooded Sikh that he was! The conversation became distinctly more laboured.

Later, at a dinner party also attended by the Indian Ambassador Alfred Gonsalves, the Consul revealed to us that after that first encounter, he had had his misgivings about inviting us. He seemed genuinely relieved to see us turn up for dinner in smart going-ashore suits, complete with neck ties. The gracious hostess fed us excellent home-cooked Indian food, which we tucked in gladly.

The Ambassador visited the boat next day, and spent the better part of an hour on board, putting down his hand in our log book. Colonel Gautam, arranged for two cars and packed us off for a day long visit to Cairo.

'Of course, your boat comes first,' he said, 'but you simply can't come to Egypt and not see Cairo!'

Thank you, good Colonel!

Off we went to Cairo, over 200 km to the south west, where our board was shared between PR Rao, a representative from the Shipping Corporation of India and Colonel Gautam, whose house was on the island of Zamalek, in the Blue Nile River.

Diary entry (undated):

> Our gracious hosts deserve heartfelt thanks for putting up with scruffy blue-water sailors fresh from the sea—a dinner to be remembered for a lifetime—open hearted homely friendliness, so far away from home. Deep, restful sleep.

Cairo, the city of a thousand mosques, along with its world famous sites, offered enticing fare in terms of tourism. Petrol was cheap—probably the cheapest in the world, and food heavily subsidized by the government. Cars almost choked the roads of Cairo, and it was difficult to find one that didn't have a dent or two.

We saw the Tower of Cairo (made in the shape of the Pharaonic Lotus), and the Cairo Citadel with the Mosque of Mohammed Ali, where, it is said, that Mohammed Ali Pasha, the grandfather of King Faroukh, invited all rival kings and chieftains, the Mamluks, to a meal—only to gun them down later. We also saw the Al Rifai Mosque where the last two Shahs of Iran lie buried. Sightseeing was followed by a typical Egyptian lunch at a roadside eatery much like our *dhabas* in India.

We also visited the Pyramids, followed by a double quick look at the Sphinx. After that it was the Sahara City entertainment hall, and some belly dancing and African acrobat shows over a sumptuous Egyptian dinner!

CHAPTER 6

PORT SAID TO BOMBAY
December 1984–February 1985

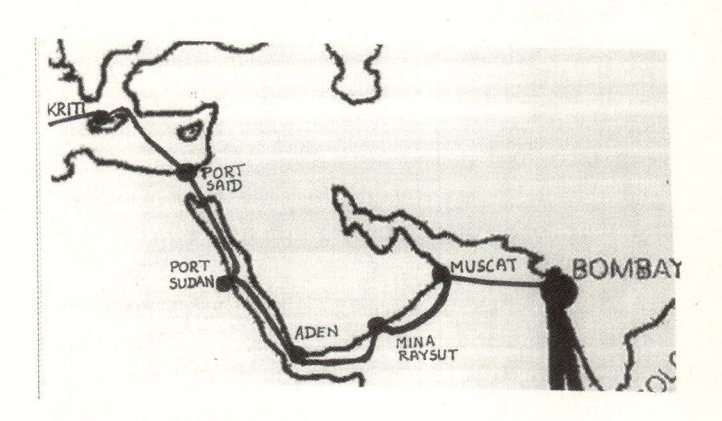

RouteMap: Port Said to Bombay

Diary entry:

5 December 1984

Off to Port Fouad and back home on board the *Trishna*.
Wrote letters almost all night...got the ship ready to sail...an hour's sleep and we slipped our mooring lines at 7 a.m.

All boats and ships can only traverse the Suez Canal under compulsory pilot-care for which one has to pay, depending on the size of the craft. So off we sailed, as soon as Mr Ali, the designated pilot came aboard.

Tipsy bade us goodbye; we knew we would miss him. Soma Pillai joined us, bringing with him news and letters from back home, and home-made goodies for all. We sailed down the Suez the whole day, gazing at both banks in the flat channelized waters, sailing at times a mere ten or twelve metres off the banks. We passed by Al Quantara, and the surprisingly narrow channel, later dropping anchor for the night at Lake Timsah, off Ismailia. A new pilot came aboard at 5.30 a.m. and we reached Port Suez at about 5 p.m. Having escorted us through the 'pilot mandatory' zone, the pilot departed, carrying with him a tin of meat— the inevitable 'gift'.

Tipsy had a hard time trying to clear the few goods that had come from India for us—a replacement VHF radio set, some souvenirs to be gifted at ports to hosts and/or authorities and the sailing fraternity in general during the remaining voyage, etc. He regularly hounded the customs and other officialdom to permit him to take charge of what was rightfully ours. His constant badgering of the Ameaster

Shipping Agents and Mr Abood regarding our VHF radio drew the inevitable reply: 'Inshallah bad bokra'...'God willing-after tomorrow!' Finally, with a lot of help from the Indian embassy, Tipsy managed. This was at about 5 p.m. on 8 December 1984, and his flight to India was at midnight, and that too from Port Said, two hours away! He was not allowed a visit to say goodbye to us, which he finally did on the VHF radio. He had added some electric spares, and a small bag of very few fresh rations—more would have attracted export formalities and customs duties! Our goods reached us at about 3 a.m. the next morning. Tipsy must have finally found some rest only on the flight. A floating water bowser tug came along, and we filled our tanks and containers with good water for the cost of two pounds—earlier Mr Abood of Ameaster had told us that getting a few jerry cans of water while alongside at the pier would have attracted export formalities! A dhow carrying oranges came along, and we bought some, though they were expensive, to add to our meagre stock of fresh food.

We weighed anchor at 6 a.m., and set course for traversing the Gulf of Suez through the Gulf of Gubal, and into the main body of the Red Sea. The sail upto the junction of the Gulf of Aquaba was rather uneventful—the seas were oily and filthy, with heavy to and fro shipping of which we steered clear.

Diary entry:

13 December 1984

Good winds along the western side of the Red Sea, past the Two Brothers islands with the light—and the

Daedalus Reef, also called the Abu el Kizan light. We are doing fine—averaging 6 knots. About 300 nautical miles to our next port of call: Port Sudan.

There is a longing now for all that is dear—home and family; it has been five months now! The feeling lingers.

The wind gods were with us, and we made phenomenal progress on the passage to Port Sudan. The speed log indicated that 700 nautical miles had been covered in just over five days—making it an average of over 140 nautical miles a day! Winds were northerly, a steady force four.

Diary entry (undated):

One or two more runs like this, and we should be home in good time.

It was a happy crew that sailed into Port Sudan after a fast and comfortable passage, on 15 December 1984. Mr Mithani, a much respected local businessman, was also doubling up as the Honorary Consul General of India since Khartoum and the Indian Mission were over 1500 kilometres away. Our bathing, cleaning, washing, and resting routine was executed at the kind gentleman's house. Along with his friend, Mr Yogesh Bhai, he drove us around, got our gas bottles filled, helped us buy food, postage, etc. He also fed us a hot lunch, and played our kind host in Port Sudan. We gorged on the cheapest food around—mutton *kebabs* and *naan*.

Colonel Yusuf Bin Mohammed Bin Yusuf of the Sudanese army had undergone a professional military course in India with the Indian Army. He took it upon himself to host us to a lavish spread of Sudanese food at a memorable dinner at the gracious gentleman's house, which we were more than happy to enjoy. We ate it the Sudanese way—from one common big round metal plate. His uninhibited friendliness and the variety of delicious meats vied for top honours as we savoured new environs, friends and food. And of course, we were grateful for it all.

The next day was spent on routine boat readiness drill, and we set sail for Aden on 18 December. The sail down the southern half of the Red Sea was stormy all the way to Aden, with head winds bang on the nose. Sailing in waters with innumerable unmarked reefs and atolls, especially on dark, moonless, stormy nights with strong adverse currents, was a new and frightening experience.

'No yacht should sail southbound in these waters of the Red Sea in December/ January.' This is what I was to write in my diary later, after reaching Aden.

Persistent stormy head winds and huge seas continued for all of the ten long days, and ten even longer nights. The boat and crew took a beating, getting knocked about at odd angles of heeling and pitching in the steep, choppy seas, with big waves washing overboard all the time. Everything was wet. There was water dripping in the galley area, the navigation table, and behind the main electric panel, increasing our fears of a short circuit and consequent electric fire. Sea water seeping into batteries was also a source of worry—it could produce explosive hydrogen gas inside the closed boat. We hoped and prayed for the water not to drip in through the seams and fittings of the hull as that could indicate serious structural damage to the boat.

There was water entering the main air vent holes on the deck every time it was washed over by a wave, sending cascades of sea water right on to my bunk—so my sleeping bag and foam cushion were always soaked. There was water inside personal lockers; the bilges were always full of sloshing, oily, mucky water, at times overflowing on top of the floor boards, making any movement slippery and hazardous in a jumping boat. We lost one air vent cowling to the stormy seas, and barely managed a timely retrieval of the other one, just as it too was about to disappear overboard having come loose with the constant thrashing it had received. Since we did not have blanks to close the air vent holes, water was relentlessly pouring in through them. The threat of capsize was palpable and were it to happen, we knew that the water would then rush up through these vent-holes into the upturned boat. The prospects were daunting. The severe thumping as the boat got tossed about in the steep and choppy waves caused the foresail to lose three hanks, increasing the strain on the remaining ones.

The waves in themselves were not the biggest we had experienced so far—there had been the over 50-footers in the Biscay and the western Mediterranean. These were 30–35-footers. Similarly, the wind wasn't much in excess of what we had been through earlier, being 30 gusting to 40 knots. But, since the storm was whipped up across a relatively short distance across the Red Sea, as compared to the earlier ones across the Atlantic Ocean or the Mediterranean, these were short and viciously steep, choppy seas, into which we were hammer-heading. Also, the never ending storm was wearing us down. It was tiring and demoralizing to constantly battle such a strong opposing current.

And, it lasted ten continuous days of twenty four hours each, half of them a shade less depressing with a grey hint of day, the others, ominously black nights. We called Red Sea 'Laal Singh'! Progress was depressingly slow—at times a mere 5 nautical miles over an entire dark, stormy, wet night, tacking against a strong current. The helmsmen battling the dark choppy seas were being constantly washed over, and had red eyes full of salt water, salt caked around all the creases of the face and eyes, around the neck, and deep into the nostrils and throat. Even our tongues were swollen with salt, lips were white and salt-encrusted; there was salt in our hair and behind our ears. In other words, salt was *everywhere* imaginable!

And all along, there was the constant danger from shipping, since the passage through the Red Sea is amongst the busiest shipping lanes in the world. There was also grave danger from the unmarked reefs and shallows, some submerged in high water, only to re-emerge during low tide. Several yachts have foundered on these nasty hidden rocks, and eventually sunk. Utmost care and vigilance was needed if we were to avoid a close brush with either ships or submerged reefs and rocks.

Making no progress in such seas had a devastating effect on the spirit. As we gritted our teeth and set about to face the seas, watch after watch, day after night—again, and yet again—to crack the deadly deadlock. On the night of the 28th we tacked the whole night in the storm, only to find we were again heading to the lights of the same township of Mocha we had seen the previous evening. In other words, we had not made any progress in the storm the whole dastardly night! Mocha marks the turning point in the Red Sea, and is the NE sentinel to the Straits of Bab-el-Mandeb. The night saw our main sail blowing out, necessitating a main sail change in the pitch dark of a moonless vicious storm.

Our appetite was down to almost zero—a half kilogram tin of fruit cocktail was often sufficient for the crew of six, each preferring not more than a teaspoon or so, for fear of throwing up what little one had had. Chocolates, sips of re-hydration drinks, fresh lime and suchlike kept up body sustenance levels.

This part of our journey included my first really dangerous fall on the foredeck. My limb's left knee-lock also gave way. The right one had broken in the UK itself before we set sail, limiting my foredeck stability sharply—particularly on a jumping and jostling foredeck. I would move on all my fours, or three and a half if you wish!

A fresh sail was needed to be brought up, and the one removed needed to be lowered into the fore-peak, down the fore-hatch. Moving up to change a headsail, as I grabbed the fore-hatch slides, the bows began to rise sharply over an oncoming huge wave. Suspended in a tricky balance of forces, I found myself buckling over with the foredeck coming up sharply to meet my face with a loud crack to my jaw. For a moment I thought my jaw had given way again, wired together as it was in seven places. But Colonel Anand, the orthodontist at Pune, had done a sound job, and the jaw wires held. As I found Bharti's hand grope for my storm-suit collar to try and lift my head up, I signalled with my right hand that I was alright. The night also saw Bharti go for a good toss as his feet found the foredeck below dip sharply, and slip out below him. Thankfully, he too was not seriously hurt. Lifelines did what they were meant to do, and no one got washed off.

The mast housing—where the keel-stepped mast goes through the deck, to rest on the keel below—was taking a beating. A grey mixture of sea water, aluminium from the mast, and epoxy from the mast housing, ground together into a dirty paste, was bleeding down the mast and into the bilges all along. The cushion- rubber pads there had slipped out, and were refusing to be put back in place. The boat was bleeding and we were unable to do anything. I resolved not to leave the next port without fixing it.

That is precisely what I did later, at Aden.

By short tacking close along the eastern shores, out of the main strength of the central currents, and carefully playing the wind shifts, we finally broke through the worst of it.

During those days of trial and troubles, some of the *Trishna*'s log book entries, made hourly by the watch on deck, read as follows.

Diary entries:

...Seas rough. Close encounter with a container ship.
...Bright clear bumpy day.
...Seas improving. Still rough.

We had raised many ships on the VHF radio, requesting them for regular weather reports since we did not have any such facility on board. Not all responded. We also requested a few others with Indian crew, to pass on our position to India.

On the night of 27 December we had a close encounter with one of the well reported and much warned-about reefs of the Red Sea. Several unmarked and unlit ones abound along both banks, and the chart is littered with markings of shipwrecks on several of these. The sight of these wrecks, clearly visible in daylight, can send shivers up any seafarer's spine. One dark night, we had to suddenly alter course by 90 degrees to avoid one such rock called the Avocet Rock. On another occasion, we had to throw the wheel right over as the depth suddenly dropped to only three fathoms.[1]

In retrospect one could say that the Bay of Biscay was the breaking-in of us new yachtsmen. The Mediterranean and its stormy seas, the Red Sea with its short, choppy stormy head winds, strong opposing currents, unmarked reefs and rocks, and narrow shipping lanes, provided the context for our maturing process. Needless to say, we felt proud of having emerged successfully through these varying conditions, and the changing moods of the seas and the winds—but only once we were through with it all! After ten days of hard sailing, the actual approach to the Straits—the last 30 miles or so—became suddenly very easy to negotiate. It was as

---

[1] A fathom is a measure of the depth of the sea and is equal to six feet.

though the Red Sea had acknowledged our persistence and given us passage finally. The Gods had said: 'Ok, you pass the test; you may pass in peace now.' And really, the winds reduced, the seas eased, the opposing currents reduced to almost none, and we sailed right past the Perim Island in the early hours of the morning of 29 December. Much relieved, we decided we could afford to raise a quick toast to our crossing the Straits of Bab-el-Mandeb safely—more or less the last challenging stretch we had foreseen on our voyage homewards.

Diary entry (undated):

...endless beautiful ripples ahead lies Bombay.

The rest of the 29th and 30th saw us tacking upwind in a calm Arabian Sea, in and out of the Ghubbat al Haika Bay, and towards Aden, which was reached with an accompanying school of dolphins on the afternoon of the 30th.

Aden Radio was quick and efficient, appearing more so after our recent experience in Egypt. A motor launch manned by young cheerful lads approached and handed us a form which was filled and returned with the usual details of the ship and crew, purpose of visit, number of days we intended to stay, etc. They showed us where to drop anchor since there was no marina. The last marina facility we had enjoyed had been in Malta. We anchored in good holding seabed conditions, in three fathoms of water, about a hundred metres off the immigration office.

Aden had a strong party government and a tight security system. The people were nice and friendly, but we learnt that they were not supposed to socialize with foreign visitors. Immigration formalities were quick and easy—passports were taken away, and passes issued.

In Aden we washed and cleaned out all the Red Sea salt from every inch of our bodies at the Seaman's Club. We also took a stroll on shore through the small town, to feel the walk after a rough sail, and ended up eating at a roadside eatery not unlike our Indian *dhaba*. We had our fill of two super-sized *paranthas*—locally called roti—and chicken. All this cost us 700 fils (1000 fils were roughly equal to a dinar, or the equivalent of about a US dollar). This was followed by a knockout sleep on board, while anchor-watch was kept by rotation.

Rajinder Paul, the First Secretary at the Indian Mission, paid *Trishna* a visit the next day. He gave us a rundown on life in Communist-controlled South Yemen. Food, drinks, houses, jobs, education, transport were no problem as long as one did not get involved in politics. Jailing on mere suspicion was common: 'No one comes out of jails here!' When we asked him, 'What happens to old inmates in jails', the answer was: 'There are no old inmates in jails. They don't last that long!' Even vegetables were sold in government shops. Women had special rights, and could get their husbands packed off for any reason whatsoever—so much for male dominance! We were invited for a glass of beer at Paul's house, where Mrs Paul fed us plate after plate of hot home-made *pakoras* which were polished off in utter disregard of social propriety!

The New Year 1985 was welcomed on board *Trishna*, riding anchor off Aden, listening to some music on our music box, and relaxing. General party noises were audible from the township close ashore, and we could see fireworks. The crew rambled till midnight at which hour the VHF channel 16 began crackling nonstop New Year good-wish messages from every ship or craft afloat within range. One Bangladesh ship repeatedly kept up an 'Any Bengali, any Bengali, over' message, and there were lots of blaring ship horns, and general merriment and cheering—and we were in 1985! Mr and Mrs Manners, the Indian Ambassador and his wife, visited *Trishna* on 1 January 1985.

Mast shroud looked into, packing in place, it was now time to move on. We heaved anchor at about 6.30 a.m. on 2 January, after the immigration officer came aboard, looked us over physically, and made it clear that we were to leave immediately since our passports had already been handed back. In fact, we took about twenty minutes to stow our spare anchor, which was delay enough for the Aden Port Control to call us on VHF radio and ask why we were not leaving!

Only Russian and Chinese ships seemed to be visiting. Russian ships came in at the rate of about two a day. One Chinese vessel was bringing in rice—or so we gathered from the exchanges between the ship and Aden Port Control on the VHF radio Channel 16. While leaving harbour, we saw several tugs moored at the entrance. All had dates for names —*20 June, 24 September, 16 October*... An old hotel in town also had a date for a name as did a local petrol pump. Since there was no news yet if AP's newborn was a boy or a girl , we suggested names like, '1st January Singh' or the inevitable 'Laal Singh' (for the Red Sea) if it were to be a boy!

The seas were flat; medium to strong winds blew from the east and the north east, 10–20 knots; but strong currents impeded good progress. We covered merely a little over 50 miles on the first day out of Aden. Pillai turned out corned pork with Aden bread for lunch, and tinned chicken and mushrooms with rice for dinner.

The average distance covered per day remained a meagre 50 nautical miles from the 3rd through to the 5th of January. Then the currents began to abate as we left the Gulf of Aden, but the winds dropped too, so we were becalmed at times, slowing down progress.

The flat and calm seas yielded us a ringside view of a school of at least five whales spaced about twenty to fifty feet apart, their submerged heads, spouts and humps clearly visible. The closest one passed to within thirty feet to our starboard side. It must have been longer than twenty feet; it was barrel-like, greenish and brownish black in colour, and floated away with its hump barely above water line. Having passed us bye about two hundred metres, they began jumping clean out of the water playfully in the overcast weather. They jumped at least a clear eight to ten feet out of the water, before splashing back into the sea. Soon, another school of three passed about a hundred metres to our starboard. It seemed as if Nature had specially laid out the grand spectacle for us.

Indeed, it did seem that the Gods also wanted us to have a pleasure cruise—with flat seas, 8–10 knots of head winds, we ambled along covering not 60 nautical miles a day. If mood be right, here was a perfect holiday at sea to soak in the pleasures of cruising. But we wanted winds; we wanted to move on to cover distance. I had my own reasons too: Asha was expecting our second baby, and it was due on 10 February.

A miscalculation of our drinking water reserves led us into the small harbour of Mina Rayasut, adjoining Salalah to take on water. Salalah was dry and desert like, dusty, hilly and rocky with only shrubs to show for greenery. The little city appeared to be spanking new—all the roads, houses, shops, and even the palace walls of the two palaces of the Sultan were brand new. The breakwater (made of quick-to-place concrete tetrahedrons) and the jetty were new too. We were told that Salalah had been developed recently to consolidate the Omani border areas, which were till recently being ravaged by South Yemeni intrusions and local rebels. Development was of good quality. No Omani was out of a job, we were told.

It was only when we were already in the harbour that we realized we had been mistaken; we actually had enough water, and need not have called into the harbour at all.

Having topped up water since we had come along anyway, we met several Indians who each extended a warm hand of friendship. Many Indians were in government jobs, including the police officer in charge of the Port Police, as well another ex-NDA and ex-Indian Navy officer,

Randhawa. He was commanding an Oman Navy coastal patrol boat.

Water topped, we cast off for Muscat. In less than a day these newfound friends had won our hearts with their spontaneous warmth. At Salalah, the official time was advanced by an hour since we were progressing eastwards.

Variable winds on the nose continued to dog our progress towards Muscat.

Diary entry (undated):

Sailing conditions have become Arabian Sea-ish.

It had to happen! On the night of 12–13 January, at about 1 a.m., there was a huge *whoosh*! It was so very close that we all got up to look and lo! *Trishna* was sailing bang in the middle of a pod of nine whales! They would squirt water with great big *whoosh* sounds, some barely twenty feet from the boat. The whales looked like huge, dark, floating logs. The sky was overcast with clouds, and there were winds. The ethereal procession floated with us for over five minutes, and our friendly investigators disappeared as soundlessly as they had come. Were they checking out a big fish? I wonder!

The next day, probably induced by the flat seas and cloudy skies, dolphins appeared in large numbers. There were two schools—one to the port side, the other to starboard side—each of over forty to fifty dolphins! At times, over twenty of them would jump clean out of the water at the same time—some as high up as six to eight feet. It was a sight fit for a king of all that he surveys—the yachtsman!

The ship's transistor radio-cum-cassette player, popularly called our music box, was our window to the world. We could tune into the BBC, the Voice of America, and now we had begun to catch All India Radio too, getting to hear news in Hindi or Urdu occasionally. Rajiv Gandhi's formative days as Prime Minister were the main focus of our news interests. Listening to news at sea keeps one connected, giving one a sense of belonging and involvement in an otherwise disconnected existence at sea, which can be extremely disorienting.

The high points of the news from the rest of the world, from the time we set sail had been: Operation Blue Star at the Golden Temple, Indira Gandhi's assassination, the election of Ronald Reagan as POTUS, the Coal Board and the Union strife in the UK (Margaret Thatcher versus Arthur Stargill), India's election campaign news, the Bhopal gas tragedy, Rajiv Gandhi's clean sweep at the polls, Sri Lanka–India relations, the signing-off of Hong Kong to China. We had sailed through it all.

One night, there was a lot of jet aircraft activity lasting over two to three hours, with the dropping of flares, some of the floating variety. It appeared to be some form of air force and naval joint military exercise. The next day, several distant booms—like big naval guns firing—were also heard. We never figured out exactly what we had been witness to.

The ship's log has repeat entries (by the duty watches) of flat seas and variable winds: 'flat calm', and 'winds dropped', or 'no winds—flat calm' were some of the entries made through 15 and 16 January. Shipping traffic increased as we progressed towards Ras Al Haad, the eastern most point of Arabia. The Al Masirah Island was passed on the 15th night, and by dawn, the 35 mile long island was well astern. On the 17th evening, we sighted the Ras Al Haad light, and went around it, hopeful of being able to put into Muscat by the 18th night. But it was not to be. Light winds and a knot strong opposing current was to slow us down, and we finally put into the picturesque Muscat harbour of Mina Qaboos at about 8.30 a.m. on the morning of 19 January.

Even as we approached, we were charmed by the contrasting beauty of old stone fortresses against the colourful Sultan's Palace, as it slowly emerged from behind the maze of rocky islets on the one hand, and the modern multi-storied buildings on the other. We made our final approach towards the harbour, with its harsh yet serene, rocky, bare and jagged backdrop. A huge rock had names of visiting ships, laboriously chalked out by some very keen and hard-working seafaring crew decades ago, the manner in which one finds names scratched out on old tree trunks, or cinema walls.

Trishna was well received by the Harbour Master on making the customary radio contact on the VHF radio Channel 16. He actually asked a 60–80-footer gleaming white sail training ship leaving the harbour to give way to the puny *Trishna* as we sailed in. Later, he himself came out in a motor launch to receive and guide us in. After berthing alongside berth no. 7, we were quickly cleared by customs and immigration. Only then could we meet the waiting Mr Toor, the Second Secretary in the Indian Mission here, and Mr MS Rao, our skipper Major KS Rao's father-in-law, who had come to receive us. Here again, we met several people retired after service with the Indian government and the Indian Navy, who were presently in charge of several port, police and coast-guard operations there. We were given permission to stay ashore till 7 p.m., which we requested and got extended to midnight. After passing through the only gate for persons going ashore (where police, with sniffer dogs at hand, frisk and search at will), we were off to the house of Mr Rao, after a quick meeting over tea at the Embassy, with Dr Ishaqe Ahmed Sajjad, the then Indian Ambassador in Muscat.

We really made ourselves at home (it was becoming quite a habit...and why not?) at the skipper's in-laws'! Vani Rao (Mrs KS Rao, skipper's wife) was also there. It was wonderful to see her face awash with joy and relief on meeting KS, as was the skipper visibly delighted to meet her.

Vani undertook to run all our clothes through the washing machine—an unpalatable job at best, since the dirt on a sailor home from the sea is proverbial! We had been at sea, unwashed and un-bathed for over eight days. An endless stream of home cooked food flowed in—*idli*, *upma*, tea, coffee, *gulab jamuns* and what not!

Several Indian families took turns to invite us home, and fed us good home foods. We drove around the shopping area called Ruwi, as also past the magnificent domed Sultan Qaboos Mosque and the Sultan's Palace—breathtakingly beautiful buildings.

The son-or-daughter mystery was also solved here, as AP finally learnt that it was a daughter, two months after the baby had graced the earth! And no—he did not name her '1st January Singh', or 'Laal Singh'!

On 23 January, we picked up water and provisions, took a look at the boat and its fittings, and were all set to leave.

With packed home food carefully stored aboard, we set sail in a flurry of waving, photographing, and good byes, finally to Destination Bombay!

Arabian Sea conditions continued, and our progress was unexciting, though we did get the opportunity to see a wide variety of sea-life up-close. There were flying fish and dolphins in large numbers; kite or ray fish would often jump out of the water only to flop back with a smack as often their flat sides landed on the sea with a slap.

Diary entry:

25 January 1985

> The moon is in the first quarter, and dark nights with flat seas bring out the beauty of the shimmering bow wave as well as the wake generated astern by the moving boat—a deep green phosphorescent glow—a rich silken shimmer, actually giving off bright light in the dark moonless night. At last, direct course for Bombay! And how time seems to have flown! Years now seem telescoped into minutes, while this very same time used to feel as though each minute was a year in passing.
>
> Tomorrow is our fifth marriage anniversary—here's to Asha—the greatest wife in the whole world!

26 January passed like any other day. But being Republic Day, Bharti hoisted the tricolour on *Trishna*'s yard arm as

we looked on.

The next three days brought gentle seas and a steady breeze from between 30 degrees to 60 degrees east of north, pushing us homeward at a good boat speed of 5–7 knots, putting us within 240 miles of our destination.

The nights of 27 and 28 January were cloudy and overcast. The moon, being in the first quarter, set early at about 9 or 10 p.m., and it was a dark peaceful night. A few flying fish began appearing on our side decks, which we picked up before they could wriggle back off the boat and into the sea. They were our breakfast next morning! Soon, the few became a torrent of flying fish—it was like a flying fish attack by the hundreds! They leaped in their characteristic flying glide all around. It was a swarm which came on, hitting mast, shrouds, sails, dodgers and spray hood. Everything above the waterline was under attack. In the cockpit, I had to protect my eyes with one hand while steering with the other, for these flying missiles could cause serious injury with their hard jaw-bone!

It was nothing like we had ever seen before, or have seen since! These fish, 8–10 inches long, darted out of the water in schools, hit against something or the other on the boat, and rained on the deck in large numbers. Was it a predator attack by whales on them that caused them to dart out of the water and collide with our white sail standing out against the dark of the night? It was quite possible. Or was it mating season? I wouldn't know—I am no fish expert! This phenomenon carried on for the better part of an hour and, by the morning, we had collected eighty or ninety of them in a bucket. They were cleaned and served for breakfast as well as for lunch—and we still had plenty left over.

As if sensing the anticipated homecoming, *Trishna* was charging homewards with gusto. Not far now!

Trishna entered Bombay harbour on the night of 31 January 1985, waiting overnight at the outer anchorage to sail into the Naval Sailing Club area the next day. On 1 February 1985, *Trishna* sailed in, and onwards to the mooring buoy, and tied up.

We were the first Indians to have sailed a sailboat all the way home from England or anywhere in Europe!

Diary entry (undated):

> A haze of mixed feelings and events. Extreme relief at having sailed home safely, at having found our plan has worked!—so far. The voyage around the world is yet to come, but there is this confidence of being asure-footed yachtsmen now, and an eagerness for the seas.

I telephoned Asha on 6 February, and flew out to Delhi, and on to Gwalior the next day, to be with her.

The National Defence Academy

Ronnie

None of the cadets really took much note when Commodore RL Pereira of the Indian Navy took over the reins as Deputy Commandant or Dep-Com. It was not common for cadets to even see the Dep-Com unless one was marched up to him either for consistently poor performance in physicals or academics or for committing an act of grave offence and indiscipline or 'moral turpitude'—whatever that meant. In general, we were made to see him for not possessing OLQ or Officer Like Qualities. And once marched up to him, one seldom came out without being relegated to the next term, thereby being put back six months, or—and this was really the last rung—being withdrawn from the Academy and losing a future career in the Armed Forces as a Commissioned Officer. So, unless one had performed some serious act of commission or omission, one could normally rest easy. One would seldom set eyes on the Dep-Com except at functions where he would lecture all the cadets from the podium; and even more feeble were the chances that the Dep-Com would ever set his eyes on you.

Not so with Ronnie. Ronnie soon made it clear he was

as much part of the Academy curricula—through day and night—as all of us, and that he was going to live the Academy life with the same ferocity he was determined to make us live it. Ronnie the enigma, Ronnie the hero we worshipped, Ronnie the devil we feared, who would catch our every wrong-doing day in and day out, who was high on the dos-and-don'ts routine, and above all, the Ronnie we loved for what he was, and what he was committed to do—his dedication was as unmatched then as it is even now, over forty-five years later. Ronnie was afflicted with burning passion for everything he ever set out to do—or did not do. Above all, he was determined to be God and godfather to each and every one of the fifteen hundred cadets, and to turn them into the fittest and finest human beings on earth. It was his obsessive dedication that actually managed to make both work.

Ronnie was everywhere at the same time. If that sounds impossible, just ask any of us who was there. He certainly was at the most unlikely places at the most unpredictable times. He could be in the tea queue at 5 a.m. or appear behind you to catch your smart-alecky moves to cut corners! Suddenly, who do we see but Ronnie! In fact, he saw us before we saw him! And off we were on a punishment hike, or subjected to a few day's 'restrictions', which could include regular reportings in battle dress while others had time off to watch movies. He always smiled gently while shooting off punishments. Though most of the time he sported a stern look, if you looked closely, his eyes, always had the kind twinkle of a man who meant well! You see, Ronnie had the capacity to mean it—and to do it. If ever, anywhere in the world, any group of fifteen hundred young men, with all senses at full alert and energy levels at an unbelievable high could lay claim to collective foster parents, they would be speaking of Ronnie and Phyllis Pereira.

For every stern look of Ronnie's, there was an equally benign and kind look from Phyllis. Phyllis was mother to all fifteen hundred of us. To that if you add five hundred new recruit cadets for every six months they stayed, that made her foster mother to over four thousand hyper-charged boys! But it was easy for Phyllis! You see, she had a heart that was really big—and she loved with a protective force that would let no harm come to even one of us.

Ronnie and Phyllis made sure that the biggest and the smallest components of the plan at building our lives, during these formative years stayed in place. These were executed by the bevy of staff of all ranks, from Brigadier down to the Drill NCOs, the equivalent ranks in and out of uniform that made up the NDA training staff, as well as professors, readers, lecturers, etc. They helped us maintain the high academic standards required of us. Our days were hammered out into weeks, precious weekends, months, and terms, till it was our turn to step in slow march past the quarter deck, with the Academy band playing Auld Lang Syne, and pass out of the Academy we had grown to love, to hate, and to move beyond, towards being commissioned into the Army, the Navy, or the Air Force.

Fourteen years later, our iconic Dep-Com and Godfather to all, Admiral (Retd.) Ronnie (RL) Pereira, was to write in his letter to me dated 16 June 1986, from his home which he and Phyllis had aptly named 'AT LAST':

> Both of us are really very privileged people, in that the Service gave us the singular and unique opportunity for a two and half year spell at the Academy, and this gave us the best part of 1500 sons, the very cream of the Lord's creation, and made me realize, so profoundly, that this great country of ours just must go from strength to strength, with such magnificent youth. I have some favoured ones, among whom I count you, but that is really the selfishness of old age, for the others are not entirely the second string, for they were all excellent. My joy was in moulding all of you as I thought best, and I hope I failed in only a few.

Kanshi Ram

The action and energy on the drill square exuded both by the drill *ustaads* (instructors) and cadets were phenomenal. Drill periods were 40 minutes of sheer hell, during which cadets were made to do all kinds of monkey movements like jumping up to touch knees-to-chest, double time march, etc. Basically, the idea was to keep the cadets and the drill square energized to a degree probably humanly unsurpassable. Both the intensity of cadet hyper-drill-activities as also the continuous high decibel commands of the twelve drill *ustaads* would be widely spread across the large drill square so that one squad-and-instructor group did not clash with another—at least not too often. When that happened, one simply followed one's own drill *ustaad*'s command—even if it meant marching straight into the oncoming drill squad! All this eventually made for good (meaning excellent) drill individually, as a drill squad, and finally as the Academy Drill as a whole. Drill is the basic building block of the Army—the immediate and unquestioning obedience of orders; the 'Theirs is not to reason why/ Theirs is but to do and die' stuff. The loud and rapid-fire orders of our highly dedicated drill instructors still ring in our ears. They were a motivated and dedicated lot, psychologically screened and drilled to transform us from youthful ordinary boys from all walks of life into stereotypical unerring and unfaltering officer material. Looking back, all of us, to the last man, feel they did a damn good job.

The drill *ustaad*s were also a feared lot, best avoided at all times when off the drill square. This was hard to do since they were positioned strategically across the length and breadth of the Academy to nab erring cadets cycling out of squad, or committing any of the thousand improprieties that fell under the banner of 'just not done'. Cycling out of squad formation (in twos abreast, with one leader) was not allowed; otherwise, one simply ran on the double, cycle wheeling in hand as one ran. They nabbed cadets talking while in squad, or not swinging-up (marching with hands swinging up to shoulder height both forwards and backwards!) if marching in squad. The slightest divergence from the perfect straight line or the tiniest flaw in the way one was turned out—say with a button out of place or even discoloured, or not having a mess-tin hair-cut (only a slight stubble of hair was allowed on the head as would fit into the imaginary lines of an upturned mess-tin) would draw their ire. Any one of the dozens of such misdemeanours could get a cadet into varying degrees of trouble: from 'lift up your cycle', to haunching, or front rolling to the next class or next activity, or even restrictions, or Sinhgarh Hikes. A shoelace with a missing aglet or an unclean (clean means fresh-washed clean!) handkerchief, or even a handkerchief being produced from the wrong pocket (the left pocket was the right pocket, dumbo!) was also reason enough for the poor offending cadet to get into trouble.

If Ronnie was at the top of the stack of our idols epitomizing 'The Ideal', then Kanshi Ram, the Drill Subedar Major brought up the rear—quite literally as well as figuratively. We feared, and hated, and—yes—idolized him. He represented the 13 hob-nailed and horse-shoed drill boot planted firmly on our collective bottoms, pushing us ahead into the pyre of drill and discipline training with the hope and aim of turning out well moulded Armed Forces Officer material—the best anywhere. It was all done in the same manner as a factory turns out stampings from a high quality die—each an exact copy of the other. Physical attributes apart, the Academy manages to achieve a lot of drilled and even psychologically similar responses, from those of us who have gone through the mill. To be clubbed forever as 'typical ex-NDAs' is a stamp worn with pride for the rest of our service lives in the Army, Air Force, or the Navy.

We all firmly believe that what the Drill SM achieved was

what he had set as his particular goal. The Drill SM was the single most feared man in the Academy, since compassion was not a virtue he allowed himself or his drill staff. You see, drill was drill, not to be corrupted by mundane things like compassion, logic or reason. Yes, ask anyone trained during his time, and he will tell you that we are all individually and collectively proud today of what Kanshi Ram did to make us what we are—and this despite the fact that he was despised at that point in our lives.

There were, of course, jokes about the Drill SM and his Hinglish, as he tried to beat the cadets in their last bastion—English. This was, understandably, his weak point. There was the time the Drill SM almost caught a cadet late for his academic class, but since the cadet had just managed to enter the class room and was thus in the jurisdiction of the concerned academic instructor, the Drill SM excused himself in, and barked the order (drill orders are, for some reason, always barked): 'See me behind the class when I am empty.' Then there was the time when the Drill SM, finding two cadets sharing a single rain-cape during a monsoon shower, barked out this order to his accompanying drill staff: 'Saab, make out a charge against these two understanding tree, sharing rain one-in-two'. Or the time when he approached the drill squad—cane firmly clutched in both hands behind his back, up-curved proud moustaches, head held high, scornful and suspicious constantly searching for flaws. He ordered the front line to 'right foot up'. What he meant was that the right foot be up-turned backwards for him to inspect the mandatory 13 hob nails, and a horseshoe on each drill boot sole. One cadet made the mistake of turning up his left foot instead. True or false, the Drill SM is attributed with having said: 'Who this cadet with both foot up?' But then, his drilled-to-dullness mind lit up, and he made haste to march off in his quick-step, aggressive style, trying to salvage his honour as best possible under the circumstances!

Man-handling

The age old method of lashing out, or the use of physical force to resolve disputes, had a new meaning—that of putting in place an errant junior. Often, the only face-saving defence put up by the victim was a feeble 'Don't man-handle me, sir!' Incidents like these were soon forgotten, and normal life resumed, unless one of the two carried a grudge which surfaced later. During a rehearsal for the passing out parade (POP), a course-mate and friend from my RIMC days, fidgeted ever so slightly on the drill square. He moved at a particular moment when the parade was to stand motionless, without a single muscle stirring. A drill *ustaad* detected the minute movement, and went on to hold the cadet by the belt, and give him a shakedown physically.

In an attempt to preserve his honour amidst such a public assault, the cadet objected saying '*Ustaad, haath mat lagao*' (*Ustaad*, don't touch me, don't get physical). In this no-win situation, it was now the drill *ustaad's* turn to defend his honour upon being publicly told off, however feebly, by a cadet. He did so by asserting loudly '*Achhaa, haath mat lagao bolta hai*!' (Oh, so you are telling me not to use my hands!). At this point, the Academy Drill SM, Kanshi Ram, witnessing this commotion from afar, standing a hundred metres ahead of the fifteen hundred strong parade, interjected in favour of the great oppressive training system. A loud holler shook the parade ground, which must have been audible from all the four corners of the Academy. He shouted '*Ustaad, haath mat lagao*!' And just when the sheepishly gleeful cadet thought he had won the day, a booming repartee followed: '*Ustaad, kick lagao*!' (*Ustaad*, use the kick instead!)

NDA! Oh NDA!

Life in the NDA was a treasure trove of humour. After all, humour was all we had. Everything else belonged to the Academy instructors, in a large measure to the drill instructors. Whatever was left over belonged to Ronnie. We were fair game for any and every staff member. I suspect the general philosophy was: harass them day in and day out! It certainly is an unbeatable way to make one mentally tough. In equal measure, so was the staff fair game for us! Of course, this was limited to our fabricating and sharing jokes about them—some true but mostly half-true.

The Academy was full of lesser versions of Kanshi Ram and Ronnie. Several of our Academic instructors, we hold in very high esteem today: Mr Savardekar, Mr Keshwani, Mr DD Agrawal, Mr 'Pondy' Sinha, and many more, along with our Squadron Commanders, Divisional Officers, and PT and Games Staff. But that did not prevent us from making them the protagonists of most of our jokes. You see, jokes kept us going through the madness of it all.

For instance—and this one I know to be true—one day, on enquiring about a certain cadet during the afternoon games parade, the Div-O (Divisional Officer of Captain rank[1]) was told that the cadet had gone to attend extra swimming coaching to sharpen his breast stroke needed to pass his higher swimming level test. The Div-O barked loudly: 'Why the bloody breast stroke? Why not the bloody chest stroke? Is he a man or a woman?' Hinglish and the Army go back a long way together—and May God bless them for these gems!

What's in a name?

During our first few days at the Academy, it was *de rigueur* for the seniors to make us remember in an instant the names of the who's who of final term appointment holders. These included the Academy Cadet Adjutant (ACA), feared by one and all since he was in charge of cadet discipline, or the Academy Cadet Captain (ACC), normally of a gentler variety. Similarly, the names of the Battalion appointments, like BCA and BCC, were also demanded. One forgot at one's own peril. If you didn't blurt it out instantly, you would have to do push-ups or front rolls in the dusty squadron parade ground—each

---

[1]*The NDA was divided into 12 squadrons, and each squadron was further divided into three Divisions each having an officer of Captain rank in charge, or equivalent rank from the Air Force or Navy, much like having 'houses' divided into 'sub-sections' or dorms in a school.

push-up or front roll punctuated with hollered letters spelling out the forgotten name.

Battalion Cadet Adjutant Neelakantan Jayachandran Nair—God, why don't we simply say NJ Nair? We were often asked to call out every letter of his name loudly, with a ground-push-up accompanying each announcement. Every one of these push-up sessions made us memorize the spelling of his name, never to be forgotten for life. And what a name! Did his folks name him with us first-termers in mind? I often wondered how his name was spelt in his native language. Did it mean more ground push-ups in Malayalam or less? The only other such obnoxiously long-winded name—evoking the seniors' glee and the freshers' dread—was shared with me many years later by my friend Captain (IN) Kureel. Would you believe his luck? He had to do push-ups while spelling out the name of a senior cadet appointment holder: Chandroth Kunnilmel Suchindra Sabu! This was another reminder that one must always be grateful because things could always be worse! As must surely have been in the case with the first termers who had to remember my friend Soma Pillai's full name: Manickawasagam Somasundareshwaran Pillai!

Survival instincts dictated that to get through each harrowing day of uncertain trauma full of unending front rolls, haunching and 'lift-up-your-cycles', one stayed constantly on the lookout for a reasonably senior cadet appointment holder, say a cadet Vth term Sergeant, who one could somehow associate with. An ideal candidate would be a senior from one's school or hometown, who one could lean on, find solace in or turn to for a 'lift', that is, plead for support in order to bail out of a 'situation'—of which there were plenty each day.

The 'Undies'

'Undie' was short for 'understudy'—meaning a capable junior selected to be helper and odd-job man to a senior appointment-holder cadet. The undies of senior appointments like ACAs or BCAs obviously had unspoken privileges—like being excused routine punishment fall-ins for their course, etc. It was always a snooty and smug undie who was ordered to break-off from a punishment fall-in by the call: 'Cadet so-n-so, carry on!' In return, his job was to get the senior's mug of tea and eats, both in the morning and evening, fetch-and-carry for him, which could mean conveying or ferrying his messages, orders or instructions, verbal or written. All this made him a kind of a semi-official adjutant to the senior. In fact a senior was also judged by the undie he selected—whether he had picked a smart and capable young lad or not. So it was always a mixed kind of a feeling if you were selected to be an undie since the undies really had no choice in the matter. Also, one always had to weigh the fringe benefits against the added responsibilities, and the fetch-and-carry.

All in all, an undie always carried a chip on his shoulder. My shoulder got the chip when NJ Nair, the Battalion Cadet Adjutant, picked me out of the first-termers to be his undie. Among other things, he also asked me to help him brush up some of his physical training moves on the wooden long-horse, since I had already perfected these moves at RIMC before joining the Academy. So now you can see why we from the RIMC were generally referred to as the 'RIMC Crooks' or 'certified crooks' at NDA. Some even called us 'Kennel Club of India! KCI registered, highly pedigreed!' We were supposed to be the 'crooks dela crooks' of the game. These descriptions were normally used with a degree of envy and respect, though some also said it with loathing. It all depended on the situation and the particular person.

NJ Nair was curious how I managed to get the doctors to give me so many days off to rest in my cabin, or told to 'Attend-C'—Attend to your Cabin—being sick or unwell and in need of a day's rest. 'No AK, seriously, tell me the truth! I'm not going to hold it against you. How do you do it?' he would often ask. I reminded him that I was from RIMC, and he seemed satisfied with the answer.

I didn't feel like a crook though.

Moral lectures

After a movie, punishment sessions, or pulling up sessions (generally called MLs or 'moral lectures') were the norm. A clarion announcement was made at all squadron locations that the Academy (meaning all cadets from the 1st to the 5th terms, leaving out the passing out course 6th termers) was to fall-in (fall into ranks and files in a squad) outside the mess after dinner. We knew immediately what the ACA (or the punishment-giving guy) had in mind for our post-dinner digestion process—a session of front rolling, haunching, push-ups and of running around trees and posts—in general sweating it out and rolling in the mud for a few hours or so.

A particular ACA is on record as having said, 'You guys …(threatening pause)…Don't you get on my wrong side (the same pause). For that matter, don't get on my any side.'

Another one was more explicit in conveying the point, 'Remember, your souls may belong to God…(the same threatening pause)…but your hinds belong to me. So no one should be caught out of squads, ill turned out…(etc.)'

Another such ACA, particularly good at cross-country running and boxing, was asked by his squadron commander to advise the squadron on how to improve their cross-country running performance. He had the following advice to share, 'It's simple! For the first five hundred metres just sprint! For the rest of the race—just step out!' Now, if only one had the stamina to sprint for the first five hundred metres, and step out for the rest on a 28 kilometre rough cross country route over hills and nullahs in the scrub, one would *be* the NDA cross-country champ, and wouldn't need any such free advice! The secret mantra of cross-country running seemed to be the same as the secret of general success in life—keep your nose to the grind—and success will *never* elude you! Sounds so simple. Needless to say, ACAs and such appointments have always been the butt of jokes—each scored out with undiluted vengeance. That was our training at the Academy, and we bore it with a smile, always. The second half of every term had the words

DLTGH (Days Left to Go Home) scribbled on the class blackboard followed, of course, with the figure depicting the working days actually remaining in the particular term.

Time

I first saw him running—if his disjointed, out of sync movement could be called running at all—towards the cycle stand at the PT Grounds. He was obviously late for his next class, late enough for him to have given up hope. Why was he crying? Or was he? 'Doesn't it hurt your bones to run like that?' I asked. 'My mother never allowed me to run or play with the neighbourhood boys. She was paranoid about me getting hurt or bruising my shins. A servant took me to school on a cycle. I have never really run at all! And here I am, always last...always late...and always in pain!' he said. His face had regained composure, and with it a wry smile. But his eyes had a haunted look, alternating between the hunted and the faraway. Sometimes a steely resolve shone through.

> Soft, effeminate kids, just out of mom's laps, were referred to as 'chikoo', a generalized nickname, uttered behind their backs, often with a smirk. I suspect, to make the rest of us feel better and bigger in some way. Particularly since 'chikoos' were generally very handsome boys. He was, what cadets generally referred to as, a 'chikoo', a smooth one.

If there was any one thing one was forever short of at the Academy, it was time. I suppose it is the only way to keep

16 to 20-year-old highly charged bodies out of as much trouble as possible. Yet, there is always trouble brewing at some corner of the Academy or other. It could be a challenge thought up overnight to hang a pith hat on top of the Sudan Block dome, or a group under a punishment round after dark suddenly scooting off at full speed in a fraction of a second as the Cadet Sergeant's attention was diverted by one of them. And God help the Cadet Sergeant if he were to follow the belligerent lot into the darkness where he would never be able to identify who really landed those punches! At the end of it all, there was no offence meant—it was nothing personal.

There is never a dull moment at the Academy.

Sneak-peeks

The other thing (besides time) that is always in short supply is a sneak-peek at girls...any girl! And if you ever got to talk to one, 'your day is made', as they say! That could only happen during the very limited number of social functions, or selected events—like some sports finals, prize giving, or suchlike. It could also happen on the road while a particular member of the teaching staff was dropping his daughter to the bus stand to go to college. Even the tone of the leading cycling-squad member would change as he called out the mandatory '*Saavdhaan chal!*' (This was an order to 'go-to-attention', a form of salute as you ride in a closely packed cycle-squad from one class to another, whereby one straightens the arms and torso to a stiff upright attention position). There would be an obvious quiver, or extra oomph in his call if the particular officer he was saluting was accompanied by his daughter. A particular staff member was well known for saying, 'I know you say a louder "*Saavdhaan chal*" when you see my daughter, you rascals!'

And of all such young ladies at the Academy, there was one who was the loveliest of them all. We had named her 'Miss Pretty Face'. At every chance crossing, our eyes would be glued to take in all possible details. But she was always looking demurely (angrily?) away, avoiding eye contact. After all, fifteen hundred (give or take a few) pairs of probing eyes were hard to withstand on a daily basis. Eye contact had to be avoided each time she traversed the badlands of heavy cadet traffic, before she could reach the Academy exit gate, and proceed to her college. Any chance eye contact brought on a severe blush.

But things changed as we grew up. As we crossed the higher thresholds of physical, academic and emotional maturity, we also grew from gangly sixteen-year olds into tough, responsible, disciplined young men, driven by the ideals that are embedded in the three Services that we were to be commissioned into. The Academy successfully turned us into the best young men ever (without us realizing it then), each a clone of the other. We were assets that the nation could be proud of. The country could be certain that the investment into these youth would pay good returns. All this was achieved without our explicit realization at the time.

Back to the present...and thus it was that a louder-than-usual '*Saavdhan chal*' made all eyes dart in search of the precious sight. This time, instead of avoiding eye contact,

Miss Pretty Face clearly peered searchingly into the cycling squad of cadets—and what was that? A fleeting hint of recognition and a smile before it was quickly masked again. I quickly looked back into the ten faces in the squad. Who was it that had the power to evoke what I thought I had seen? Or was I mistaken?

There he was, just behind me, his face wearing a gentle smile. Did he always smile like that or was this one of a different kind? His movements, too, seemed definitely less disjointed now, more gawkily graceful than before.

The Freedom Train

The Academy ran two special trains, with an arrangement with the Indian Railways to carry cadets to and from their vacations twice a year. The bunch of cadets, tearing at their leashes to be released from the straitjacket-like discipline rigidly enforced during term days, were bound to get a bit wild when together in large numbers, and with a weakened hold of the limited staff accompanying the trains. Stations were warned in advance of the NDA Special Train coming in, and all vendors that could, would down shutters and close shop. Some, like *chai walas* (tea vendors), *samosa* sellers, or fruit *walas* who carried their wares in baskets were fair game. Once a sale was made they could never find the right guy to claim their money from. All the chaps were the same age, wearing identical uniforms, with hair shorn in the mess-tin cut! Which one was it? There was a fair amount of chaos—as also the glee of the hyper-charged cadets. After all, if all has been taken away from you, there is nothing to lose!

'Catch me if you can!' shouted one to the *samosa wala* running after him. Then someone pulled the emergency chain, just as the train was easing out of the station. The Station Master was livid. 'I won't let this train go!' he shouted. 'So who wants to get back to the Academy in a hurry?' His threat elicited a loud round of cheer among the army of cloned cadets!

But reach the Academy we willy nilly did, to face an livid Deputy Commandant. Unlike the poor helpless Station Master, the Dep-Com was neither disempowered, nor were our faces unrecognizable to him. He had each cadet's Academy number, name, along with the name of the relevant Div-O in instant recall.

'All of you—six Sinhgarh hikes each!' he thundered.

Smelly punishment

Sinhgarh was the distant, ancient fort built by Shivaji. Well, for six consecutive precious Sundays off we were at 8 a.m., with bottles full of Coca Cola bought at rip-off prices from the on-campus Kapoor Café. We were flagged off, to foot it—that is, jog it—in battle dress to the top of the old fort. Tourist attraction it may be, but we were no tourists! We hated it. And if you were not back in time, you had to do an additional circuit.

'There must be a smarter way to do this,' said a cadet just before the sixth and final hike.

And so it was that Amarjit Minhas and I decided to take the 'smarter' way. Half an hour before being flagged off, we hid our cycles in the bushes on the way leading out. As soon as we were flagged off, we ran ahead, picked up the cycles, and cycled all the way to the base of the old ruins. We left the cycles with an old toothless dame running a tea-stall at the godforsaken spot at the base of the hillock, with the promise of payment, and up we scurried—but only after several of the genuine hikers had already reached the fort (to give the appearance of honest effort). We then reported to the accounting staff who dutifully ticked off our names. And we ran down again, picked up the bikes, scrambling and making haste to reach the Academy—the earlier the better! Who wanted to get caught!

As we sped through the narrow lanes of the crowded Sunday vegetable market in the village on the way...what the hell? The 'Bravo' Squadron Commander was spotted right ahead! The Major was out on his Sunday vegetable shopping mission! Damn! Damn! Damn!

He slowed his scooter down, resting on one foot and turned back, trying to recognize us. We had already raced past him down the narrow lane for there was no other way. Zip! Zip! And off we turned into an even narrower lane, rushing down to where it ended in grass, bushes and soil. We threw down our cycles, and crashed prone, faces down into the soil, hearts beating fast, trying to lie as quietly as possible.

But what was with the funny smell? Oh shit! Quite literally! Land mines! We were in the area which had received the morning load off from the squatting villagers and by God, did it smell!

'Don't move, not a breath!,' we whispered, reassuring each other. If discovered, we could easily face expulsion from the Academy or the loss of a term at the very least.

'Hang on...it will soon be over!'

Waiting cautiously, we gave it the right amount of time before mutually deciding it was safe. It seemed we had got away so far. With the stuff still sticking to our battle dress, we jumped on again, and cycled with the speed of the Devil himself.

> But who was this third person who we hadn't seen, now cycling with us? Agile, fit and muscular, his disjointed running was gone. So were the jerky movements. The once soulful eyes brimmed with confidence—the boy who had been mocked all the time had vanished. He had come a long, silent, lonely way, battling odds to redeem and discover himself. The Academy had put him through fire and moulded a soldier out of him. The confident eyes said it all. No more pain, no more melancholic helplessness alternating with an urge to be as good. He *was* as good—Bless him!

Yes, we got away with it. We actually got away with it *all* only after a good bath back in the Squadron with the scrubbing of our lives to get that horrible smell out!

ಌ ✥

Soon the terms passed. We were fifth-termers now. Many of us were appointment holders, being Vth Term Sergeants, or Corporals, and so on. Life was fairly settled, though not a bit less busy. There always seemed more to be done than the time given to do it. It is a good recipe to keep everyone out of trouble. Even so, trouble does have a way of coming up when so many cat-and-mouse cadets and instructors are in such close proximity, trying hard not to be outdone by each other.

It happened once that I, with all my authority as a Fifth Term Sergeant, ordered three cadets to pick up their bicycles over their heads, get down on their haunches, and leapfrog forward as a punishment for being out of a proper cycle squad (a squad consists of a minimum of five cyclists; less than five and you have to run with the cycle from one class to the next without riding it). These three were cycling furiously, hoping to avoid detection and reach their next class on time. I had done it a dozen times myself, as a first and second-termer. But then, so had the Fifth Term Sergeants then ordered punishment just as I had done now. On a cue from one of them to the rest, the three, now at a bit of a distance from me and judging they may be out of my tangible reach, got up, put their cycles down, and scooted—cycling for their lives to get away from me and their meaningless punishment.

'How dare they!' I thought.

So, off I went, chasing them with all I had, on my cycle. The honest truth is that first and second-termers running from a sergeant are a far more energized bunch than a sergeant trying to regain his pride.

As I turned the corner, they were nowhere in sight. Giving up the chase, I slowed down, and made the turn back. But...who was that behind the rock? Whoever it was was not alone. Sitting on the steps, the two made a pretty picture—though it was a bit out of place at the Academy.

I startled Him and his companion—Miss Pretty-face. The 'saavdhanchal' girl, our Academics Instructor's pretty daughter, and our now metamorphosed 'disjointed' runner!

Both were speechless—and so was I.

They had been merely talking.

Something on their faces said it all.

'I'm sorry. I didn't mean to disrupt anything,' I said apologetically.

'But there's nothing to disrupt,' both said together, like bells chiming.

'See you later,' she said, addressing him, and ran off.

We cycled back to the squadron in silence.

CHAPTER 7

FOR THE UN-INITIATED

The *Trishna*

Trishna was 37 feet long, and just over 10 feet wide at its beamiest (its widest-part), had a clear 6 feet headroom in its cabin centre, needed a minimum of 6 feet of water depth to stay afloat, and weighed 10 tons. The cabin was designed critically for maximum space utilization. Not an inch of precious space was wasted. The space capsule-like design below decks included a mini-navigation table on which a full sized navigation chart (maps at sea are called charts) could be spread out, with a seat for the navigator to sit on. The seat was built upon the housing for two 12-volt batteries. The area to the port (left) side, approximately at the same height as the head of the seated navigator, had the electric panel, the very high frequency (VHF) radio (a short distance line-of-sight radio capable of making

Beyond Horizons

immediate contact with nearby ships, other yachts or shore authorities), and the newly installed music cassette player—the sole source of desperately needed entertainment over many hours during those inevitable patches of monotonous windless sailing. The cassettes were repeated so many times that every crew member knew the sequence of songs on each by heart.

There was also a small storage area for navigational instruments needed to convert sun and star 'sights' into 'plots' or positions on the chart using the sextant. There was space for the sextant box to keep the precision instrument safe from harm. The slightest damage to the instrument would virtually render it worthless, since accuracy is the soul of a sextant.

Throughout our voyage, the ship's log book was kept in a drawer below the chart table, and was filled every hour by the 'watch'. This meant that when the crewman at the wheel, sailing and keeping lookout, handed over the steering wheel and the responsibility of sailing the boat safely to his watch-mate for the next hour, the handover was only complete if the log book had been painstakingly updated. Details included local time, position in latitude and longitude, compass course desired, compass course actually steered, wind speed and direction, average boat speed as indicated by the speed log, and other relevant details like depth when near land, any light-house or land details if visible, the number of hand pumpings needed to clear bilge water (thereby indicating the possibility of a leak) and any other relevant occurrence during his watch.

All the instruments which were positioned on the deck for the helmsman to measure parameters like depth, wind-speed, wind direction, and boat's 'heading' (the compass reading of the direction the boat was going or 'making way') were repeated by repeater instruments at eye-level at the Nav Table. It was the nerve-centre of the boat and the rightful place for the skipper, unless the navigator was plotting a fix on the chart. KS spent endless hours at his post, particularly during the dozens of crises at sea that are bound to crop up on a voyage around the world. He was fed the situation report by the crew on watch on the deck, and often gave his instructions after studying all the data available through instruments at the Nav Table.

Right opposite the Nav Table, on the right or starboard side, as one descended into the cabin from the cockpit or deck using the three small steps called the companionway, was the cooking area or galley. It was a highly compact miniature pantry where two foot-operated pedals could push seawater as well as fresh water (from the limited supply of our fresh water tanks) into the taps in the sink. There was a storage box that could hold extremely limited food supplies and a gimballed gas stove with two burners that could clamp the cooking pot in place through the rock and roll. Whether cooking would be possible or not at any particular time was dictated by weather conditions. In heavy seas it is impossible to cook anything even if the mother watch—strapped around the waist to ensure that he doesn't shoot off in various directions like a human projectile—were brave enough to attempt it. Moreover, storms bring on seasickness and wipe out all desire for food. However, many a delicious meal was turned out whenever conditions permitted. Miniature cooking gas bottles and the diesel for the inboard engine were stored in the stern locker (at the back) which had a breather valve to prevent explosive fumes from collecting. The cooking area also had racks for unbreakable plates and mugs and the limited pots and pans to be clamped down, which, along with a few spoons, made up the ensemble. Many an unfortunate 'mother on watch' would bravely hold his post at the galley even while periodically stepping out on deck to throw up. And yet he would be determined to cook up something hot—if only lintel soup or tea for the weary crew on deck.

A basic minimum food and fluid intake is important since dehydration can set in while working a boat on a wind-blown sea, day in and out, over protracted bad weather. This is particularly so if one is seasick and losing precious body fluids due to frequent retching. Shekhar and Bassi were gifted and were almost never seasick. On a particularly stormy day, Tipsy was on mother watch, and must have thrown up considerably more than the food he bravely prepared for the demands of Shekhar, who was on watch, and not the least bit seasick and obviously hungry! Tipsy has my admiration for this till date.

The main living area or the saloon was just ahead of the Nav Table and galley, past the half bulkheads on either side, and up to the next bulkhead six feet further. Bulkheads are the strong partition walls that hold the sides of the boat apart, giving them strength and preventing them from either crushing inwards or moving outwards. They are amongst the strongest structures of a boat. The mast came through the roof of this cabin, which was also the deck, and was stepped on the keel which was directly below the cabin. The cabin or saloon had a seating cum bunk on each side along its full six-feet length, and another bunk each above them—pilot bunks hugging each side of the boat. The latter had to be climbed into from the lower bunks. So, if an off watch was sleeping on the lower bunk, one had to step over him to get into the pilot bunk above.

The area behind the steps or companionway, or entry point for going below decks and into the cabin, was separated by another bulkhead, which has two berths—one each on port and starboard side. These are called the quarter berths for obvious reasons, being in the hind quarters of the boat. The port side quarter berth, right behind his post at the Nav Table, was the skipper's bunk. The two pilot berths in the main cabin belonged to Shekhar and Bharti, while mine was the starboard seating berth. Along all bunks were 'lee-boards', about 9 inches wide, which had to be lifted up while resting so that one did not fall out of the bunk as the boat rolled, pitched, or yawed heavily in bad weather. Someone once remarked, rather thoughtlessly, that these 'lee-boards' made the bunks look like coffins! Not a very considerate remark I thought! They sure prevented the crew from falling off—but in a particularly violent thump during a storm, Bharti's entire bunk, lee-board and all, came crashing down on top of me. Luckily, both of us escaped with only bruises.

The space below the starboard and port bunks held fresh water tanks of 25 gallons on either side, each isolated from all others to prevent cross contamination. The space behind the seating bunks and below the pilot bunks had lockers for the crew's personal gear: three lockers on each side measuring approximately 2 feet by 1½ feet by 1 foot. That was the limit of our personal space. Compulsory personal gear included thermals, woollen socks, jerseys, a few pairs of shorts, T-shirts, toothbrush, etc., leaving little space for much else like personal photographs, diaries, books, etc. An emergency waterproof bag with bare essentials chosen out of these items was kept in each locker, ready at hand to be grabbed quickly in case of an 'abandon-ship' call. So, when a well-meaning Indian family in Guyana told us that Guyanese gold was cheap and asked if we would like to take some with us, we had to decline without hurting their feelings by saying that we would much rather carry some more fresh water than gold!

In the forward of the main cabin, as the boat narrowed rapidly was the mini sea toilet on the port side. It had a miniature basin that was difficult to spit into while brushing at sea without everything spilling out. The sea toilet was operated by two pumps: one led sea water into the toilet pan through a sea valve, and the other pumped the contents into the sea. There was no concept of bio-digestion, or the stricter norms for such discharge by boats when in harbour, in those days.

Opposite the toilet, on the starboard side was a hanging locker about 2 feet wide, 4 feet high and 2½ feet deep. It held our storm suits, sailing boots, sailing harnesses, life jackets, and a set each of going-ashore navy blue trousers and blazer which were seawater-proof and completely washable.

The very narrow, pointed, forward-most part where both sides as well as the floor of the boat met to form the bow had two folding bunks with storage lockers below them. This held the five fore-sails of different sizes for different wind strengths: from the biggest genoas to the smallest storm sail, a spare main sail, a storm tri-sail, a spinnaker, a stowed spare anchor. The main anchor was also stowed here when not lashed down on the foredeck, and all the ropes used in handling sails. These ropes are called, sheets', because they are used to continuously adjust or 'trim' the sails, to pull them in or 'sheet them in' using the seafarers parlance. This is the wettest part on the inside of the boat. Outside it, the open cockpit and the above-deck area are obviously far wetter. All sail changes are done by opening the watertight toughened-glass hatch leading into this fore-peak area, from the fore-deck above. During a sail-change, the sail bag with the fresh sail is passed up through the hatch and the wet sail just dropped down is bagged and lowered into this hold from a wild and wet deck above, where the crew operates in wet suits, tethered to the boat by harnesses and life-lines which prevent them from being washed off the boat as waves break continuously over it.

Tucked in just below the companionway was the Volvo Penta inboard diesel engine. Although its laminated wood cover was sound-proofed as well as could be, when it was running, the area below decks was overwhelmed by its loud diesel staccato. It was really quite difficult to live with except that there was nowhere to get off and go to from an uncomfortable boat at sea.

The engine was run for between fifteen to thirty minutes daily to charge the batteries which powered all instruments and lighting on the boat. The lights inside the cabin were used sparingly as we lived by the mantra 'daylight is all the light we need'. So much so, that for years afterwards, I would get about the house comfortably doing normal chores even in the dark hours after sunset without turning on the lights.

Small boats normally have tillers—the long stick-like handle attached to operate the rudder, and turn the boat. *Trishna* was originally designed and fitted with a tiller. Its previous owners replaced the tiller with a steering wheel, which made the boat far easier to handle through long and strenuous hours at sea. The steering wheel gave many a land-lubber the impression that the boat was engine driven. The steering wheel merely operates the rudder through a train of lever arms. The boat will only turn if it has any forward movement—called 'way'—imparted to it by its 'motor', i.e. the sails, when acted upon by the wind. No wind or no sail, no way or forward movement. So, turning the wheel when the boat has no way won't turn a boat any more than steering a stationary car will turn a car.

Boat Handling and Routine Aboard *Trishna*

Two more crew were added after a stringent process of crew selection, and we had the innovative Rakesh Bassi—who specialised in finding solutions where none existed, and Navin Ahuja—our youngest and most dashing bachelor on board. Thus we now had a complement of ten crew.

Trishna was manned all along by a crew of six. While KS, Shekhar, Bharti, and I remained on board from start to finish, AP and Bassi started out from Mumbai, and were each successively replaced by Navin and Tipsy, and they in turn were later replaced by Bhatta and Mathur who sailed back to Mumbai with us. A 'watch' consisted of two crewmen. There was the starboard watch and the port watch (the names are random sailing terms, given purely for the love of sailing and in keeping with sail ship tradition). The starboard watch had me as watch leader and my watch-mate was Chandrahas Bharti, both for the sail from Southampton to Mumbai, as well as all the way subsequently around the world—as I say, from Mumbai to Mumbai. So, for many years later, it could be said we had spent more time together in close proximity (barely a few feet apart) than we had spent with anyone else, including our wives! The port watch had AP as the watch leader, and Sanjeev Shekhar as his watch mate on the sail from UK to India. Since AP decided to sail only part of the voyage around the world, subsequently one member of the port watch was always under replacement from one of the six replacement team members.

A watch of two was to man the boat for four hours before being replaced by the other watch for the next four. And so it went: four hours 'on' and four hours 'off' day in and day out round the clock, across days, months, and oceans, without a break in sequence, to keep the boat alive and sailing in its element.

During the four hour watch, one crew member was at the steering for an hour, sailing the compass course by reading off the 'binnacle' or steering post compass, while the other maintained constant and sharp vigil, taking sextant sites if needed, or compass bearings while navigating near land, and was at hand for sail changes, and to 'sheet in', and trim sails as the constantly changing wind direction and speed made necessary. They switched positions each hour. The one getting off had to go down the companionway into the cabin, and fill in the boat's log book as well as operate the hand pump below the floor in the area called the 'bilges'. This is the lowest part of the boat from within, and it is necessary to 'bilge out' the collection of sea water that inevitably finds its way into the boat.

The four hours off were the time for anything and everything needed to live—like going to the toilet, eating, sleeping. It was also the time to look into any work that needed to be done in the particular area of responsibility allotted to each one of us. Shekhar was in charge of food and medicines; Bharti had to maintain sails and all rigging, while my role was the maintenance and repair of the boat, including electrical and electronics. As the crew was replaced, each member was allotted a role depending on his proficiency and the needs of the boat. AP doubled up as navigator to KS; Bassi was in charge of all port formalities and paper work; Mathur had qualified himself in HAM radio operation; Tipsy's role was that of overall manager of the whole voyage all along; and Navin and Bhatta chipped in with general boat repair and maintenance, apart from being part of the watch during their stint on board. When ashore, each replacement crew member was part of the ground support and organization cell inevitably needed to back up such a voyage.

I think keeping this watch system sacrosanct and strictly punctual had a lot to do with keeping us sailing safely from watch to watch and day to day all the way around the world. Once each one of us understood the system and drilled ourselves into it, the basic safe sailing of the boat was assured. Leisure would follow during off hours only, and during calm sailing days, when books, star-gazing, cooking, chatting, or simply gazing at the beyond were the general activities. Many a calm night was punctuated by gentle arguments on whether 'that' star was Lupus or was it the other one 'over there', and what the correct pronunciation of the star's name was. We all became amateur astronomers. A reasonable knowledge of stars could easily give us a rough positioning of the boat on the globe, merely by observing them and without recourse to any form of navigation. Luckily, the satellite navigation (satnav) was working well, which greatly reduced the need to do cumbersome sextant-based astro-navigation. However, we kept our skills honed since all instruments were powered by battery and could easily fail due to technical snags or storm damage.

Apart from the two watches and the skipper, the sixth man was on 'clean-ship' and cooking duties for the day. Rotational mother-watch duties provided a break from the repetitive four-on and four-off cycle. It was not uncommon to hear the call: 'Oye, who is the mother of the day?' I think knowing we would only get to eat what we cooked ourselves, made us turn out some reasonable food whenever it was possible to cook. At other times, we would make do with tinned fruit, etc. One of the ways to save fresh water was to add part fresh water and part sea water in the cooking pot, depending upon how much salt the cooking needed.

Using sea water for bathing was really only to cool off during runs in really hot and blistering weather, since it always left a residual thin layer of salt which, being hygroscopic (moisture absorbent), left us feeling sticky and uncomfortable till the time we shed it all off, as it alternately mingled and dried with perspiration. Though some of us warned him, Tipsy, driven to despair by his long tresses in the oppressive heat, proceeded to wash them with bathing soap. However, sea water and normal soap don't go well together, particularly so when it comes to washing ones hair. The experiment left a sticky mess in its wake where each strand of hair was caked with what seemed a milder form of chewing gum. Poor fellow had to comb and air his hair endlessly to work it all out! It took quite a while and he understandably never repeated the mistake.

Asha Speaks

The pair of Royal Bengal Tigers, cured by the best taxidermists in India and with their official registration tags round their necks, had been shot by my gun-wielding landlord father during days when hunting was a 'royal' sport. Shoots often had government sanction, particularly when jungles were to be cleared for agriculture, or a rogue man-eater needed to be put down. The whole house had such 'trophies' and many more were dumped in big trunks. Ours was a landlord family and, being from the warrior-cum-ruling class of Rajputs, such things were a matter of pride.

Another suitor and his mother were to come and 'see' me with a marriage proposal. This one was a doctor in a far off land. Though my mother understood my predicament on such occasions, to my father it was all quite normal and routine—that there could be any misgivings in my mind over such archaic methods and traditions was beyond him.

Only the other day, a lanky, dark, skinny young army officer—sunburnt, since he was crazy enough to have ridden 3000 km from Pune to Punjab and back on his motorcycle , which was modified to run on a diesel engine, along with his golden spaniel dog—was coerced and convinced by my father into coming on a similar mission: to propose matrimony. His moustaches, extending to his cheeks and meeting his sideburns, did not really add to his 'charm'.

Anyway, how did it all matter? I loved my work—I had a teaching job in a girl's college and was pursuing research for my doctoral degree. And, if my application for the prestigious Commonwealth Scholarship was considered favourably, I would soon be in the UK to do what I liked best—study and research. My sister and her husband were both scholars in their own right. I had similar leanings.

Father said the sun-fried Captain was a 'meritorious' candidate for me. What could be meritorious about an Army career, I wondered. But there was something about him, something which I could not get completely out of my mind. He was different in an odd kind of way.

My brother, Kaushalendra was more than a brother: he was a trusted friend. And he promised to find out more about this Captain whose name had begun to figure in many rounds in our household conversation. After meeting with him in Pune, my brother also said, 'He is okay. I liked him. He is meritorious.'

Again, that same baffling word! So there *was* something to him.

We got married, Ashok and I, without really having met properly. It was in a remote village in the heartland of India, in Madhya Pradesh.

A few days after we got married, during the train journey from my home to Pune, where he was stationed at the College of Military Engineering, he spoke a lot. Much of the conversation was about some project he had in mind. He told me about wanting to make this crazy trip to sail around the world, which he said he had been working towards since 1978. It was a bizarre conversation to have taken place between newlywed strangers. I thought we should be getting to know each other more intimately. But he did not seem the type to care much about such mundane things.

I immediately thought: 'He is trying to show off and impress me'.

As time went by, I realized that he was indeed deeply involved in planning this venture. He had tremendous confidence. They had already sailed from Bandar Abbas in Iran to Mumbai in a small Sea Bird class boat barely 18 feet long.

There was something definitely different about him.

The prestigious Commonwealth scholarship for me to pursue research work in the UK came through. I went away to London within eight months of this strange marriage. During these eight months I also carried on with my job in Gwalior, which meant we had actually lived together for less than two months! But I told myself, it didn't matter! I had a life ahead of me in London. Who knew what would come next? Why worry now? Opportunity seemed to be beckoning—I had to go and grab it!

Researching fungal toxins with the Medical Research Council in Carshalton Beaches, my year in the UK went by like a dream. Ashok had three months of enhanced leave from the Army, and we spent it driving around Europe in a small car on a shoestring budget. It was an unforgettable trip—a dream run. It was rough while it lasted though. My time in UK ended rather abruptly with my return to Pune. There I was, expecting our first baby within the next two months!

So much for life beckoning!

Our daughter, Akshi was born a breech baby through a Caesarean section. Over the years, as she grew, I could see how much of her crazy father she had in her.

There was no stopping AK (as Ashok was popularly called). When he wasn't sailing dinghies for some national or international regatta, he was windsurfing. And during the monsoon, when boats do not venture out in Mumbai, he would go hang-gliding in the hills around Pune. It seemed safe enough. I had watched him up in the air—a small eagle-like figure, soaring for a long time before coming down as the sun set.

One day, AK went hang-gliding. I did not go with him that day.

'He should have been back by now. The sun set a long time ago,' I thought to myself.

Suddenly, there was a knock at the door. I removed Akshi from my breast, covering myself as I went to see who it was. I did not allow myself any thoughts of apprehension. I was so sure it would be AK returning. So why worry?

As I answered the door bell the officer with whom he had gone hang-gliding that afternoon, stood in front of me. He had a peculiar look on his face. He was trying too hard to keep up a smile and his usual cheer, but there was definitely something he was not entirely able to hide.

'AK has had a minor accident—nothing to worry about! He is in the Command Hospital and is being attended to. So, there is really nothing to worry about at all,' he said.

But that look still wouldn't go. There was something more. Oh God—what was it? How bad was it?

'This is the Army, and I am far away from my home. I can't show too much anxiety. I can only hope he is as well as can be. Oh God, I hope all is well,' I told myself.

The Commandant, General Sachdeva, sent his official car. And, an hour later, I knew how bad it was. Yes, he was alive. But all four limbs were immobilized, and his jaw was stitched up.

Yes, he was alive.

Kaushalendra left his medical studies and rushed to be with me.

୨୦ ଓ

The nightmarish days passed, one painful hour at a time; the doctor's opinions and various complications of his condition kept emerging as his basic medical parameters stabilized. The uncertainty of it all was gut-wrenching. Kaushalendra began maintaining long periods of silence. All was definitely not well. The toes of AK's left foot began going bluish-black. AP (Ajay *Jeeja* to AK), his sister's husband, a medical specialist and neurologist in the army, had rushed to Pune from Allahabad where he was posted. For some reason, he had brought along a scrabble set. Later he told me he was testing AK for toxicity based on how well he could play the game: had the poison spread too much? Could he be saved?

On 13 March 1983, he reassured me. 'You need to go back now. You have been here all day. Akshi also needs you. I'm going to be here with AK,' he said.

But again, there was that mask. Why was he not looking me in the eye? Was all under control? What was wrong? How could I ever tell? After all, outwardly, it was just another day drawing to a close. There really was nothing to indicate that this was the Devil's own day.

And, before I got to the hospital next morning, my lanky, dark, crazy AK had lost his left leg from just above the knee. Yes, thanks to AP, he was alive. Any delay in detection of the toxicity could have cost his life. The emergency operation had been done after midnight, after I was sent back home.

God bless AP.

We had a good idea who to blame. Some professionals also spoke about clear-cut documentary proof in his medical records. But do blame and retribution really solve anything? There is really no blame to be apportioned in life. Both the good as well as the dark parts of life have to be lived—no matter what.

After days of introspection, AK said, 'We don't show this much concern for so many others who meet similar misfortune. Isn't it a bit selfish to try to sort out people, or the system, only when something happens to *us*?'

He had always held the belief that life was worth living and enjoying for its pleasant moments, of which he firmly believed there had been, and would always be, plenty. One only had to look out for them!

And so, we moved on.

Loss of Limb

The College of Military Engineering—the CME as it is popularly called in Pune—is reputed to offer one of the coolest tenures to those privileged to be posted there. It basically offers a very organized and balanced lifestyle, with set working hours, time set aside for outdoors, and an equal measure of time for social interaction and the family.

The bright sunflower yellow bird, with a 40-feet-something wingspan, was an intimidating creature, and she was ready to fly. At every puff of breeze, she flexed, now creating a lift, then again a stall as the continual wind force and angles changed and worked on the acutely designed aerofoil wings—not unlike a brute flexing its muscles and raring to go.

With my harness strapped to the kingpost, I balanced the huge wings, alternating between lifting forces and the weight of the high performance hang-glider.

'Ready?'

'Yes! OK.'

As the helper holding the nose wires to steady the kite let go and darted aside, I began my power run for take-off.

Babu and Mangal were there, as also Alok Bajpai and Joshi, in our hang-gliding ensemble that bright sunny afternoon.

Hang-gliding is fascinating for the flyer and the non-flyer alike. Just the other day I had been soaring in a ridge-lift air band for over an hour as Asha and some friends watched. I am sure I must have looked like a tiny bird three or four hundred feet above the ground where I was soaring with a surprised eagle for company.

I was under transfer to my regiment somewhere in India's forward posts in the North. But there was still this one high-performance kite that I had not flown.

'Not many days are left for my move, so let's do it today,' I had thought to myself.

My 73 kilos were lifted effortlessly by the powerful kite in the oncoming 12-knot evening breeze. The rushing wind sang a garbled rustling song through the noise holes of the blue helmet—and that was all I could hear. Adrenaline pumping, all senses on the ready, I got into prone position at the earliest after take-off.

'Must bank the kite to the right, to make a left turn; got to stay in the on-coming lift band created by the breeze coming up to the ridge and rising as the two meet' I told myself.

But why was the kite not coming out of the steep banking? Why was everything so suddenly silent, and in soundless slow motion? The kite—now facing the ridge face it had just left—continued in a seemingly silent and slow-motion face-off. The alloy spars crumbled as my body hit the rock face—silent, slow, and benumbed as if in an unreal world, with complete loss of physical feeling.

What was happening?

There was this bumpy cross-country ride, lying prone in the back of the big army ammo truck with all these guys around me.

'I'm okay, yaar, just crashed! ... will be okay.

'Darkness all around, so it must be night,' I remember thinking as I came round after what seemed like bouts of blacking out now and then. I think I was lying in a stretcher on the floor of a hospital.

An authoritative voice, perhaps the night emergency duty doctor, said, 'Don't try to take the clothes off. Just cut it all away.' And a pair of scissors cut away the denim jacket and jeans I was wearing.

The vagueness, the feeling of being somehow remote from reality and the soundlessness would not go away.

Then followed an emergency operation at night, to put a steel rod through the left femur. Both my legs were immobilized, as also the arms, due to various fractures. The left arm seemed to have been given more attention. My jaw was wired up and shut; my mouth was caked with a mix of drying blood and saliva.

Asha was there, outwardly serene as always. Not a wince, not a single sign of distress, her pride too much to allow any display of personal emotion. But her eyes could not hide the inner turmoil.

Why was everyone saying 'things will be okay' repeatedly?

Of course they would be okay. Things always become okay!

Or do they?

Asha's brother, Kaushalendra was studying to be an orthopaedic surgeon. He had rushed in from Indore.

'Move your toes...move them...to increase the blood flow...to allow the collateral capillaries to take over. Move your toes...move them...'

And I did, for unending dark hours in the Intensive Care Ward of the hospital. Almost every day someone new came in to occupy the bed next to me, or the one further up. Almost every day someone left—and not always alive; day in and day out.

Kaushalendra did not know how to tell his younger sister that all was not well with my left leg. The toes were turning bluish-black. Medically, Kaushalendra was finding it difficult to influence the specialist doctor in charge. A smart paratrooper, in fact, more of a smart paratrooper (taking and returning smart salutes) than a good doctor committed to his patient, the doctor was hardly open to inputs.

'Do you have these latest gadgets—like the Doppler machine—in your 'civil' hospital, young man? I am sure not. So, don't worry, let us do our job. AK is a young fit soldier. So what if blood is not reaching the dorsal artery of the foot? New collateral capillaries will develop! At most there will be the loss of a toe or so! No need to worry at all. We know our job.'

But an inch and a half long rupture in the femoral artery is not likely to be sorted out by rapidly forming collateral capillaries, no matter how magically Mother Nature tries to blow life into a limb doomed by a smart-saluting doctor.

And certainly not in time to save the oxygen starved cells from decaying, dying and rotting.

Kaushalendra handed over his vigilance duties to AP, my sister Usha's neurologist husband, who still carries the reputation of being an even finer human being than the very fine super specialist that he is.

Tubes through the nose fed me watery sweet milk and soups.

But why was the tube being put in again?

At this time of night?

It was attached to a pump which took out all the liquid feed given an hour ago.

'Sign here,' I was told. And I thought to myself, 'How does it matter what the paper says, when my life itself is in the hands of the doctor? He alone knows best. Concentrate on making the signature look respectable...you are a young, proud Army man.'

Asha had been by my side till an hour earlier, and AP made me play scrabble—moving my pieces as well as his since both my hands were immobilized by fractures. He then asked Asha to leave.

'I am here, so you can go. Akshi also needs you.'

It was then that I began to sense that something was not normal. Why did AP wheel in the mobile X-ray machine himself? Why were they shifting me to a stretcher? Where was I going? At this time of night?

Outside the Operation Theatre, (Colonel) Dr. Chahal—amongst the most loved and respected of surgeons—was in his operating gown with his team. Someone was wrapping a white bandage from toe to knee on my left leg.

'Remove it from here (toe) to here (knee),' I could hear Dr. Chahal saying.

The panic came on quickly: 'But, Dr. Chahal, sir...'

Where was he? Where had he disappeared? And where was AP?

'AP? AP!' I shouted as best I could through the wired up jaws.

Ah...there he was!

'All will be well...he is the best doctor and an even better human being...bless him!' I thought, reassuring myself.

'AP, what are they saying?' I asked.

But he wouldn't even face me! Why was he behind my head where I couldn't see his face? It was dark as it is, and the veranda was low-lit. 'AP, take me somewhere else... anywhere...but not here!'

'You don't have days, you only have hours,' he said.

A moment's silence.

So this was it!

Let's get it over with.

⁂

Gas gangrene is the fastest spreading form of gangrene. They say that if it is suspected, one must leave one's unfinished cup of tea and rush to tackle it first, before it snuffs out life if it ingresses into the vital organs. So this is why doctors call the limbs 'appendages'—they are dispensable, because life can carry on without them.

Or can it?

The most caring and competent nurses are put in charge of cases which most need critical nursing care to recover. Such patients are monitored often on an hourly basis, if not put under constant observation. So it was that, every morning, while the hospital still had me on the DIL (Dangerously Ill List), I would awaken to a soft whisper and gentle tapping, 'Wake up, Mr Singh, wake up!' A soothing sponge to calm and clean my ravaged body would follow. And, just as I would slip into a lulled state of bliss in competent and caring hands, there would come the inevitable needle—the 50 ml Vitamin B Complex!—jabbing where it hurt the most. And I would be jolted rudely into my broken and painful reality.

During my days in the intensive care ward, I came to see, most intimately, the intensely demanding and emotionally exhausting lives of the nursing staff. My most indelible memories are those of these incredible women providing life giving care, backbreaking hour after hour, to patients with whom they had to empathize without emoting. To care for a fellow human being, particularly one who is sick and vulnerable, with kindness, competence, professionalism and detachment, and to do this for a ceaseless traffic of patients year in and year out is a feat that only one who is truly inspired and blessed can achieve. I am fortunate to have been blessed by their touch—gentle hands that nursed me from the brink, to live and love life again.

The sheer intensity and richness of the human experience has been such as to make me reiterate to myself that I would never trade these days, hard as they have been, for a seemingly softer option if given a chance to choose again.

With my left leg removed above the knee, I had the rest of my life to rediscover its challenges.

Here began my lifelong association with Dr Sushil Jain and the Artificial Limb Centre. The good people there work long and hard to enable scores of amputees and people with disabilities to lead more functional lives with prosthetic limbs, callipers and other such. But as they say, 'Ultimately, you've got to do it yourself! No one else can live your life for you!'

'So let's get down to it!' I told myself.

One night they shifted a new patient into the neighbouring bed in the Officer's ward, where I was now recuperating.

As I woke up, I saw a familiar face, though it was upside down as the fellow hung in a yogic position practising a headstand. It was Him, my dear course-mate who had never learnt to run till he joined the NDA!

'What are you doing here, yaar?' I asked in surprise.

He told me how he had narrowly escaped a sniper's bullet in Sri Lanka. The bullet had grazed his knuckles, taking away some of the bone, narrowly missing his head, while he had been speaking into the army walky-talky, holding it to his head during action. That seemed really close. God does seem to be watching over us.

During the day, he had a visitor, and it was none other than Miss Pretty Face from the Academy! They had got married a month earlier. I was really glad for them.

So that explained the look in their eyes way back in our fifth term in the Academy, as they sat demurely at a respectable distance, supposedly only talking!

Out of hospital, and back in my Army quarters, the same old haunting thought: what about the sail around the world? The mind would rove over all possible situations about life on a small sail boat at sea. How would I, on one leg, tackle the wet and slippery deck, jumping around riding waves at sea? Taking a shower in the bathroom one day, the wet tiled floor became the wet deck, and I just had to find out. I jumped out of the shower, onto the wet tiles, to find out how my one sound leg would balance me out on a wet boat! After all, jumping on one leg onto a wet deck was, well, exactly that...jumping on one leg on a wet deck. The predictable happened. I came crashing down. The amputated stump was instinctively directed straight down, as if the missing leg was still in place to land me in the fall. I landed, all 73 kilos of me, down on the end of my amputated stump in one agonizing crash! Fortunately, the freshly healed femur bone in the stump held. The pain in the bone subsided in a few days. The quest of how to manage on a wet and slippery deck, remained!

CHAPTER 8

TRISHNA IN MUMBAI: THE STORY CONTINUES

With the safe passage of *Trishna* from Southampton to Mumbai, there was a felicitation function organized a few days after we reached. Asha was in Gwalior, expecting our second child. I telephoned her on 6 February 1985 to ask after her health and to also suggest that since it was to be a Caesarean section, the operation could perhaps be postponed by a day or two so I could attend the function before proceeding to Gwalior to be by her side.

Her soft, yet somewhat cold and faraway reply was, 'Don't come…I'll manage by myself.' I realized then, how lonely she was and how selfish I had been. We had missed much in the five years of our marriage.

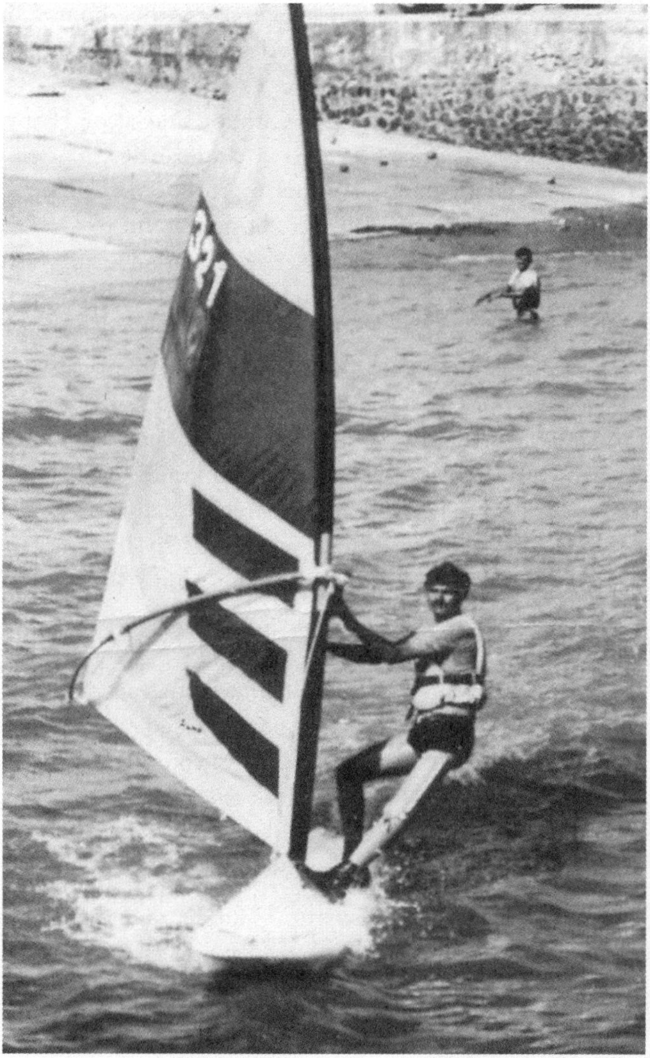
321

'Is yachting going to consume yet another home?' I wondered. So far one had only read about such things, and it had always appeared someone else's problem.

I caught the next flight out to Gwalior. Our second baby girl came on 9 February 1985, two and a half kilograms of joy, after giving herself and her mother some trouble. I had my reward; Asha and I were both grateful to God. I quipped to my sister-in-law: 'See, I'm a good manager... there to start the show, and then back for the results.'

Soon it was time to begin preparations to sail around the world. But did we really want to? Now that we were on the threshold, each of us had to do some serious soul searching. Having by now sailed over 8,000 nautical miles, often in heavy weather, I knew that I could, with luck, circumnavigate the world. But did I really want to?

Soma Pillai clearly didn't. He decided to drop out in favour of continuing his dinghy racing. And AP said that because of family commitments he would sail only part of the way.

General Parikshit Puri, the Engineer-in-Chief, and our Patron, had a word with each of us. He asked me, 'Having now sailed from the UK to Bombay, do you think you can sail around the world? Do you want to?' Not many would have asked a one-legged person the same questions! I admired him for the faith he reposed in me.

> Long separations from the children and personal estrangement from one's spouse can play havoc with one's emotions, impacting clear thinking and judgement. Bonding with the family was top priority. The General

> insisted that we (all of us) go on a month's leave. Our answers would then be more considered and sure. Thus debriefed, we headed home on leave.

I fought my internal battles and talked over the matter with Asha. I had started this, and I had to see it through. If I didn't, it would haunt me all my life—a ghost impossible to exorcise.

        ❦ ❦

Asha: 'Can he still sail around the world and follow his calling, despite the amputation that has rendered him heavily incapacitated?

Does he still really want to? He is face to face with the decision of a lifetime.

If he backs off now, he will grow old never knowing if he could have done it! He will forever be haunted by his unfulfilled dream...that-which-perhaps-could-have-been.

He has made his choice. I hope and pray it is the right one.'

        ❦ ❦

Bharti, married only a few months earlier, also decided to sail all the way.

So, the four of us—KS, Bharti, Shekhar and I formed the permanent crew. Six others, Tipsy, AP, Rakesh Bassi, Surendra Mathur, Navin Ahuja and Animesh Bhattacharya were to sail roughly a third of the way each so that, at any point in time, *Trishna* would be manned by six.

We now applied ourselves to preparing *Trishna* for the sail. 28 September 1985 was selected as our probable date of departure after detailed passage planning, which included the study of weather patterns across the various oceans of the world.

Preparing a boat for a voyage around the world is as much a challenge as the voyage itself! The old army saying 'The more you sweat in peace, the less you bleed in war' holds true even in this context. The more you sweat on shore, the safer and happier you will be in a small boat at the mercy of vast oceans once you are out there.

Every instrument of *Trishna* was tested and overhauled: these included electrical and electronic instruments, winches, toilets, steering column, the auxiliary engine with its alternator, the sea cocks and the bilge pumps. Additional water tanks were installed. The hull was dried out and scraped down; additional coats of epoxy resin were applied, and were topped off with anti-fouling paint. A new 100-watt, long range, high frequency radio set given by Bharat Electronics, Bangalore, was also installed. This increased our communication range to about five thousand nautical miles. Everyone at the Naval Dockyard Bombay, where all this was done, was very helpful.

Even so—perhaps due to the frustration and pressure of work—I made the following diary entry.

> Mostly things here are done the exact way they are not supposed to be done, but that seems to be a national heritage. We are all doing it and blaming others.

The plumbing and electrical wiring diagrams of the boat were made, to be referred to for troubleshooting and repairs at sea. Typical checklists included everything conceivable, such as the contents of the life raft, contents of the tool locker, contents of the navigation equipment table, and a list of charts needed for the voyage. Some were to be replenished at pre-selected ports since it was not possible to carry the heavy load of all charts, coastal pilots, list of lighthouses, and radio beacons and so on. There was also the list of all emergency repair kits (like the sail repair kit), the medical and first-aid kit (at sea it is normally a medical kit and not merely a first aid kit since it is assumed that no second or third aid will come in time), the fibre glass repair kit, the marine toilet repair kit, pop riveting and swaging tools to carry out emergency rigging of alloy spars (like mast, boom, or rudder, etc.), the auxiliary engine spares list, the winches spares and parts list, the electrical and plumbing spares list, and the list of all courtesy national flags of ports we intended to visit. Alphabetical and numeric nautical flags were to be used in case the only remaining communication link was semaphore or flag-communication.

Thus, the lists were really endless. Other items included spare cells, matches, spares for fog light and water-proof torches, for the gas burners and its gas leads, film rolls, the signalling flare gun (a Very-light pistol), adequate flares, spare cordage, steel wire, steel strips, a bolt cutter to cut loose the mast and steel rigging in case of dismasting, etc., the depth sounder and mast-head light spares. There was also a list of contents of the tool box.

A careful and exhaustive list was made of tinned and dry foods, and an elaborate stowage plan was put in place for all boat and food stores, such that priority boat and man survival items could be grabbed quickly even in a dark upturned ship in a heavy sea, while non-critical stores could find their place when needed by way of deliberate retrieval. All stowage is done in a way that nothing can come loose and get thrown around as the boat is tossed about in heavy seas.

Apart from getting the boat ready, I had to get my specially fabricated limb fitted and tried out.

Twenty-four hours in a day just did not seem enough to do all this. We would be tired and edgy by the time we reached our rooms. Our families had been living in cramped quarters and the children were missing school.

> Tired and spent by the day's work, Asha and I would often go down to the sea-front at the Naval Command Mess in Colaba and just sit there for a while, staring out at the sea, in its various moods, always different with the varying moon phases. There seemed a kind of communication between us, without words, as we both simply stared at the sea. Something came through, something tangible enough to keep us going there every evening that we could manage.

Diary entry (undated):

On the shores of the mighty oceans, as I cock head to wind, nose to sea, eye to weather, ear to the deeply powerful rumble of the Sea God, powerful waves impregnated by the winds carry a message all the way across the mighty ocean, before breaking along the small stretch of shore my humble human eyes can fathom. While you beside me, my love, feel the nip in the sea breeze, the discomfort and the cold, and coax me to go indoors and turn in to the comfort of a warm bed instead of standing and aimlessly staring beyond the horizon, my senses perceive the calling, the lure, the mystery, the exciting secrets that the darkness of the mighty, unfathomable ocean holds as it breathes. I stand enraptured, hoping for some silence from the noisy world of man around so I may submit all senses at my disposal, to see beyond the seeable into the perceivable, the imaginable. The ocean lulls me into subservience; it calls for all I have, and I, in enraptured daze, follow its pull. The lure holds the scent of an innocent yet enticing voyage of self discovery of immensely intoxicating and euphoric proportions. The moment is enticing and fulfilling at once.

While you feel the cold and discomfort of the rain and wind on a trek, a climb, or a sail, I feel the thrill of the after-storm. An opportunity to be one with Mother Nature—learning, growing, experiencing, endeavouring, innovating at times to stay alive. A chance to put all my skills and abilities to work; a possibility that my very

> being may be put to test; a gamble of my power to reason, to test myself, to surmount my own abilities. In the endeavour lies a secret test and at the end of it, the high of having overcome myself, of having moved to a state of euphoria. While on one hand one is a person who cannot understand why one should face discomfort in extreme weather when one could be comfortably ensconced in the safety of a protected home; and on the other, a person who smells an opportunity offered by Mother Nature to be one with her—the euphoria, the excitement, and the impending high of possible triumph—not over Nature, of course, but over your own limitations; for a bigger folly in perception is difficult to imagine than one who would endeavour conquest over Nature rather than his own self.

Before we knew it, the long break we thought we would have in India was over.

Diary entry (undated):

Around this time, I began having regular dreams in which, in different situations, I would be required to hasten along or break into a run chasing something and, after a considerable consumption of mental energies, would begin to fly. I suppose these dreams were caused by the conflict between my urge to move on faster and my actual physical inability to do so. These dreams always sapped me of a lot of energy, and I woke up in emotional confusion. The anxiety of trying to get things done faster on the boat probably precipitated these bouts.

To speed matters up, while the rest of the crew took a refresher course in nautical subjects at the Naval Academy in Cochin, I stayed behind to make sure that the work on *Trishna* did not slacken. There was lots to be done, then checked and double-checked.

28 September 1985 was not too far away.

Asha Speaks—The Sailing

When he'd chattered nonstop about sailing around the world on our maiden train journey together to the military station at Pune, AK hadn't been trying to impress his new wife. He had been actually conditioning me for the inevitable. Though, as things transpired, it was only four and a half years later, and after his left leg had been amputated that he was actually ready to go.

He had never wavered from his goal in the interim, never a single thought for a single moment. Yes, for the months it had taken him to get back on his feet, he had put it away in some small locker inside him. But the thought of giving it up? Never.

After the stay at the hospital in Pune, we moved to Gwalior. AK began his re-assimilation into society and daily living as he knew best. The first step was dealing with his new limb, and walking. He had already refused the walking stick they offered him at the Artificial Limb Centre at Pune. After the first agonizing step or two—barely a three or four inch shuffle each—he rid himself of all apprehensions and sense of foreboding. In his view, walking consisted of only two steps—a left and a right—and he had already taken them both. All he needed to do was to repeat and perfect them. When told that he could fall down, his reply was that such fears were well founded only for a before-the-amputation scenario. Having lost a leg, foolish is the man who is afraid of a mere fall!

There were times when he wore the lifeless limb the whole day only to see how long was long enough. Once he even slept overnight with it on. He always said doctors did not know best since they were not amputees! He ramped up his walking daily—beginning with a few steps, then climbing stairs, then stepping over small potholes or drains, and then doing manageable distances. I think this happened more quickly than I had imagined. Perhaps it was all because earlier one evening, just after fitting on the new limb, he realized after stepping out of our home to walk me to the nearby Officer's Cinema Hall that he would not be able to complete the walk. He quietly turned back. It seemed clear to him that merely living an ordinary human's everyday life was the immediate challenge!

The Royal Enfield motorcycle, which had been our mode of family transport, was not safe to be driven by an above-knee amputee. He tried though, giving up only after taking me out on a short spin one night, with no traffic on the road to negotiate through. That was typically him. He had to try everything himself before giving up on anything he wished to do. And so, seeing a teenager on a moped by the roadside, AK asked to borrow it for a spin. Though unsure if the machine would come back to him one piece, the poor boy did not have the heart to refuse, and soon we had our new family transport! We could not afford a car then.

I remember the look of incredulity on the face of Ashok Mahadevan, then editor-in-chief of the *Reader's Digest*, India, when AK proudly said, 'Now I too can get up in the morning, go to the toilet, and be ready in uniform...all within ten minutes!' AK had tackled and solved another of his basic functional inabilities. This probably sounds absurd to the casual listener. But these were the building blocks he had to master. He was getting back.

Level with others now, he was ready to start again, tackling life as he knew best.

❧ ❦

Harry's advice that they should buy a boat instead of building one in India was a sound one.

By the time the plan to sail around the world matured, they already had their sailing boat: *Trishna of India*. They sailed it from Southampton to Mumbai. The voyage was not without its tough days. The senior powers-that-be in the Army were now convinced that they had a viable team on their hands—a team that had clearly demonstrated that they stood as good a chance as any to succeed.

The great day of 28 September 1985 stared at me. I had to prepare myself to see them off for a long, long trip around the world. AK's morale was very high, even after losing his leg.

Though I smiled all the time, my heart was sinking in the deep sea!

I was seriously worried, wondering how much AK would be able to do with his one leg. How would he climb and walk on a highly unstable boat? He had re-learnt to walk with his artificial leg barely a few months before the first phase of the cruise—buying the boat and sailing it back from UK to India—which had started in July 1984. Lots and lots of un-answered questions were in my mind. But, at the same time, I felt that it was not fair to stop him from doing what he really wanted to do. He was so emotionally attached to the idea. I decided that I would be with him, and give him my love and support to realize it successfully.

On 28 September 1985, families and friends of the crew, senior officers from the Army and Navy, looked on as the six departing crew members made their final preparations to leave Mumbai on their trip around the globe. They seemed all charged up at the prospect of the never-ending work ahead of them. But each time one of them looked up to meet the eyes of his loved one, there was a clear exchange of emotions: of hope, of aspirations and, above all, of love and longing, and a promise—a faraway promise to be back, a reassurance that all would be well.

As AK clutched our young Aditi, barely seven months old, and held on to the tiny fingers of Akshi, now almost four, numerous conflicting thoughts and emotions made their way in and out of my confused mind.

All I could do was simply look on, and pray, 'Please God look after them. Give them safe passage...give them what they have been working on for these past seven years. They have earned at least this much...a prayer from all present for their safe return.'

For the next few hours there was continuous activity and

unending bustle, and finally, *Trishna* slipped her mooring lines and drifted away—first slowly, but as the sails were hoisted, she began gathering way. The distance between us increased; *Trishna* slowly grew smaller and smaller, as we continued waving.

All I could do was pray and pray again, and hope as deeply as one can ever hope, for their safe return.

I don't know if man created God for his emotional needs, or God created man. Nor do I know if God needs man or not. But I sure clung on to my God, with all the faith I had. 'Please God—get them safely back, however long it takes.'

Trishna had long since disappeared, but we continued to peered into the sea for it. Maybe it was *that* speck? Or was that just a darker cloud among others? Or an approaching fishing boat coming over the horizon? Finally, when nothing at all would pass for the boat, we all turned back, trying to make courteous small talk to keep our emotions at bay.

After seeing them off, two years of uncertainty, tensions, and dangerous moments (for the boat) were ahead of me. With a heavy heart and a feeling of deep helplessness, I returned to Gwalior with my two little daughters.

I put up a big world map, a calendar, and an idol of my God in my room. They helped me to pray, to count the days, and mark the distance all through this greatest trial of my life, and to face it all privately.

I faced several days of depression, agitation and worry, and getting over these feelings was sometimes considerably difficult. Mixed feelings of anxiety, joy and loneliness were there to stay. Sometimes I felt great; at other times,

I was plunged into depression. There were days when I felt extreme self-pity. I had to make a lot of effort to get past these feelings.

Akshi also missed him a lot, and I found it difficult to explain and convince her about each and everything. The younger one was too young to understand anything. She did not know what 'Papa' meant. Any coloured photograph of a man was 'Papa' to her. Any phonecall meant 'Papa' was calling.

I decided to keep myself extremely busy—even overworked—to get over these unpleasant feelings. Thus, I was glad for my teaching job at the KRG College, Gwalior, which has been with me for the past nine years. I also immersed myself into a lot of embroidery, knitting and all kinds of handicrafts. And there was also my role as a mother, taking care of my two daughters. All this kept me busy, and helped me keep bad and depressing feelings at bay.

The successive days and months brought home the truth that they were finally gone. The only ongoing thought was that, with each passing day and each passing moment, they were covering precious lengths of their long journey of fifty thousand kilometres. Often, the prospect left me too confused as I tried to go along with the flow, day after long day.

Then the telephone calls began coming in. The first one was after 27 days and came from Mauritius. The next call was a long time coming, and the wait and anxiety were heavy to bear. But I knew they needed to make it around the Cape of Good Hope to the middle of the South Atlantic Ocean, nonstop to St. Helena. Only much later did we learn of what they had gone through while rounding the Cape: that the boat had been presumed lost since communication had broken down during a horrendous storm. On November 1985, I got a telegram from Tipsy, which said: 'no radio communication from or with *Trishna* for the last seven days'. But by then, the boat was thankfully well out of the storm. Blissfully unaware till the crisis was past, I kept up a parallel voyage around the world, clinging gratefully to each word on their progress, and praying.

AK wrote or called whenever he could. In many ways, his letters were a source of strength and hope, but they also created anxiety and depression.

AK's letter:

> The two photos of Akshi are nice—she must be growing up each day! We must keep strong feelings of love, goodness and happiness—nothing else matters. I am losing precious moments of our time together with the children. It will be over 4 ½ years of separation in our 7 year marriage by the time we are back—this jars the mind, leaving the senses benumbed and feelings confused. Can't help feeling it's not good—it's somehow damaging the delicacy of feelings (sic), making me callous and at times irate. The accident, and the intensity and pace of work are bound to have far reaching effects—we must be careful about these. Firstly, we must try to understand these effects. Then we must see what best we can do so that the least of these harmful effects are felt. I am particularly worried about Akshi. You and me (sic) must see how best to overcome all this.

> ...the biggest safety equipment with me is your love.
> God is with us, we must be careful and see that what we
> do is within the limits of the achievable.

Many times, the only news I would get would be through relatives and friends in Delhi. They would make 'local' calls to the controlling office in Delhi and get updates whenever possible, and then call me STD (subscriber trunk dial—often only done at a PCO) to tell me: 'they have left Mauritius...', etc.

Faith in God was anchored in more deeply than ever.

It was all we had.

And, I had my job—and the girls.

❦

Regiment

There was another telephone call that came in off and on, every thirty days or so, from AK's Regiment: 'Is there anything we can do ma'am? Are you all right ma'am?'

The Indian Army always had us 'civilians' in awe of them through our younger days. Words like 'Battalion' and 'Regiment' overwhelmed us...little did I know how closely I would come to engage with it all.

After our marriage, AK would talk of his Regiment, the 57 Engineer Regiment, with pride. It seemed to be a living breathing entity. There'd be a faraway look in his eyes when he spoke of it, always with deep respect, and a sense of belonging, as if it was sacrosanct—its sanctity not negotiable at any cost. He could speak for hours, over days, about the great time he had had during his first posting as a commissioned 2nd Lieutenant to the Regiment, in the forward Himalayan areas of Sikkim. Of how every day brought a challenge, a danger often to life and limb, and their numerous novel experiences. Most stories had adventure beyond the normal but he and his friends seemed to take it all in their stride. This was true even when they partook in a gruelling 'khud race' in high altitude areas, each man weighed down by more than twenty kilos in weapon, ammunitions, equipment and food, over the 110 kilometres circuit, ranging from 9,000 feet above mean sea level, slithering and goat-hopping down to 3,000 feet, before reverting uphill to climb through passes, over spurs, circumventing abysses, streams and gorges, to climb up to 14,500 feet, and then descending back to 9,000. It was a race in which the *Paltan's* (Regiment's) *izzat* (honour) was all that mattered. During a khud race a soldier could cough blood and collapse dead before any assistance could reach him. The miniscule and insignificant man plodding up and down the ethereal peaks—most revered as incarnations of the Gods—tested human endurance to its limits even as he experienced the sheer exalted grandeur of it. The advantage of the slight insanity that sometimes accompanies youthful vibrancy and energy, has made him as much part of the lofty heights and the very mountain air.

I was not to get to know the haloed 57 Engineer Regiment till after AK's amputation, and his return from his voyage around the world. He volunteered—in fact insisted against the advice of his superiors—to be posted back to the Regiment. Being an above-knee amputee, he had had to sign a bond indemnifying the army against anything that may happen to him upon joining his Regiment which was then operating in the rugged and insurgency affected areas of Nagaland. He was warned that the areas were not for 'disables'.

I soon learnt that for soldiers and officers alike, the Regimental bond was magical. Together, they were men transformed. The brotherhood was at first difficult to comprehend. After all, what was it that held them together? That they would never let each other down even at the cost of the family or their own self?!?! Why? For a wife, it could be often inexplicable and exasperating. What was it really?

All I can say is that I have, over time, changed sides and become as much a part of the Regiment as them. It has begun to mean almost as much to me, as it does to them. And yet it remains a phenomenon easier experienced and understood, than explained logically.

Occasionally, one would hear the terms, 'civilian', 'businessman', 'politician', spoken in a derogatory manner ('bloody civilian' and so on). Hadn't I too, once, been a 'bloody civilian'? Was it not a negative side of their regimentation?

Those days of youthful zest and consequent extreme expressions are over. I believe in the individual and collective value system offered by the great way of life that is the Army. And yet, the civilian and the military can be equally exasperated and uncomprehending of each other's value systems—these 'bloody' Army guys!

PART II

SAILING AROUND THE WORLD

CHAPTER 9

MUMBAI TO MAURITIUS

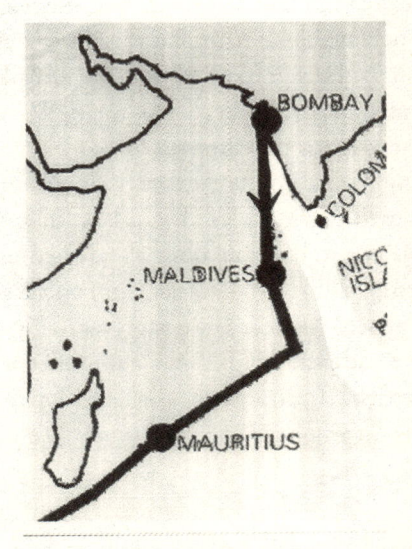

Sailing out of Mumbai: The Voyage Begins

The last few days were a blur. Apart from the usual cocktail parties and farewell dinners, we were introduced to the President, the Prime Minister, and several other dignitaries on a brief visit to Delhi.

Once back in Mumbai, last minute checks were carried out, over and over again. A video recording system was fixed. After the persistent efforts to tune our high frequency radio failed, Bharti, in charge of communication and signalling, suggested to the manufacturer's engineer that he be hoisted up the 50-foot high mast to locate the problem. The mere suggestion worked wonders, and the engineer, un-hoisted, soon had the radio tuned very quickly indeed!

Shekhar was busy counting out long lists of carefully selected, sealed and labelled foods and medicine. He was also to be our medicine-man in addition to being mother superior. He had made out lists of common ailments, and dosages of suitable drugs for each of them. We were hoping he would not get the two lists mixed up!

All along, a steady stream of visitors kept pouring on board, each leaving a kind word or thought behind. Admiral MP Awati brought along a sealed envelope.

'I want to give this to you,' he said, 'but only if you promise to open it at sea.' Mystified, we accepted, only to discover later that he had gifted us his vice-admiral's epaulettes as a good luck charm! The note enclosed read: 'I may not be able to sail with you around the world but my tabs will.'

❧ ☙

28 September dawned on Mumbai as any other late monsoon day: pleasant temperatures, with showers and

winds expected later in the day. *Trishna* had been dressed up with all her colourful flags flying, and had been brought alongside the jetty. After a farewell speech by General Vaidya, the Army Chief, we said our goodbyes to our near and dear ones. In India, it is not customary to kiss in public, so each of us met our dear ones with some reserve, all saying the same thing: 'Good bye and good luck until we meet again!' I too bid farewell to my mom and dad, sister and brother, and their families, and Asha, and our two daughters. Why did the same questions come to mind again and again? When will I see them again? Will I ever? But the questions were kept well tucked away, below layers of reassuring padding created by a firm confidence in *Trishna*, in ourselves, and in hope.

ം ം

Since no good Indian ever begins any venture without an elaborate invocation of the Gods, a *pooja* was our last activity before we slipped the lines, and *Trishna* moved away from the jetty, amidst cheering and waving from the large crowd. A few boats followed us, and the waving crowd slowly receded from view.

A large overcrowded motor launch with our families aboard came so close to bid us farewell that it almost rammed into us! What an un-glorious end that would have been! Soon the waving hands and cheering faces faded from view, as we headed west by south-west out of the harbour, past the protective waters of the tall and majestic Prong Reef lighthouse, and into the open sea. Within an hour, Mumbai, barely 5 miles away, was enveloped in noon smog, and land was out of sight.

But we were not alone yet. A large and colourful butterfly, lone and fragile, was to be our companion for ten more miles before it finally fluttered off.

We had planned to first stop by Mauritius, before the long nonstop passage of over 4,200 miles (about 8,000 kilometres) past the Cape of Good Hope to the St. Helena Island. Thence we would sail across the Atlantic towards the Caribbean, and the Panama Canal. The Pacific was to be crossed with halts on some of the Ocean's small islands. Then we were to sail to New Zealand and Australia, across the Timor Sea, passing Indonesia on our way to the Malacca Straits, the Bay of Bengal, Colombo, and back to Mumbai.

In a few days, we settled down to the four-hours-on, four-hours-off, routine. On the second day, there was a minor emergency as all electrical instruments suddenly went blank. A quick check revealed that the culprit was a specially fabricated switch for the long range radio, and this was soon set right. The radio itself was working well, and we spoke daily to Mumbai and Pune.

The southwest monsoons were receding after giving India plentiful rains, and the north-easterlies were beginning to move in. During the day, there were the gentle south-westerlies; but before dusk, the sky would darken, and a good thunder storm with a 45-knot wind would begin. Though such squalls lasted less than an hour, they resulted in huge seas which kept us uncomfortable throughout the night.

One of these turbulent squalls shook loose the VHF radio antenna fixed atop the mast. Shekhar, being the lightest of us all, was the unanimous choice for going aloft the next day to fix it. Every small oscillation of the boat is magnified out of proportion when you are at the top of a 50-foot mast at sea, and the swinging up there may well be through 15 to 20 feet. However, Shekhar managed to get the job done without getting seasick or disoriented.

Diary entry:

6 September 1985

> Squalls and rain off and on. SW monsoons are still here, receding. Favourable currents, good progress. Some of Asha's muthree (salty cookies) and cake are still left for all. Should reach Male (Maldives) tonight. Will stand off for the night, entering only in daylight; there are treacherous coral reefs.

The combined glow of the two neighbouring Maldivian islands, Male and Hulule, was sighted after dusk on 6 October. We approached them, but stood off from the entrance to the narrow passage between the two in deference to the dangerous coral reefs. It was to prove a wise decision, since even at daybreak next day we found navigation tricky. At one time during the night, we were sailing straight towards the coral reef. Seeing the phosphorescence of breaking waves on the reef dead ahead, we realized our folly just in time and tacked away hurriedly, avoiding disaster so early into the voyage. Next day, we anchored off Male in the channel separating Male from Hulule. The channel is rife with strong currents, and a jagged reef-ridden coastline and anchorage, necessitating constant vigil while riding anchor.

The only other small craft anchored under these conditions was a German yacht of comparable size, possibly slightly bigger. The crew, as it turned out during our stay, were a typically bronzed blonde German couple. With no beaches around, and certainly no beach life as the westerners know it, one wondered what the yacht could be doing, riding anchor in the tide and reef ridden channel. We later sailed out while they stayed on, not venturing ashore or communicating with us. For those listening, there may be a connection with what subsequently followed years later at Male.

Our main aim at Male was to get fresh water. Our requirement of 40 gallons cost us almost 40 dollars. Bassi and Shekhar made for quite a sight as they heaved our supply in plastic drums loaded on a hand cart, the only available local utility for the purpose.

Next morning, we heaved at the anchor chain in preparation for setting sail. But it refused to budge. Only after we had used the engine to override the anchor and force it, did the line come free. At the other end, we found only a part of our once new, now broken, anchor which had obviously snagged in the coral bed. So, minus our main anchor, *Trishna* set sail south-eastwards towards Mauritius, about 2,000 miles away.

As we sailed into the horse latitudes with their uncertain and confused winds, our progress slowed. Hot, sunny, sweaty days, and warm, sweaty, still nights were the rule as we sailed the last hundred miles to the equator, and listlessly crossed it on 12 October.

Diary entry:

> 18 October 1985 10.00 hours
> 71deg 45min E, 9deg 10min S
>
> Nine days out of Male, and over 10 days still left to go for Port Louis (Mauritius).

The elusive south easterlies set in at last, and soon *Trishna* was trotting along at 5 knots. Progress was to be rapid and fairly comfortable from here, except for the last few days' run into Port Louis.

Diary entry:

> 24 October 1985
>
> ...the trade winds have become fairly steady, though at times they are rather strong and more like tirade winds! We have averaged 160 miles a day these past four days. We are to sight Mauritius later in the day.

The sail from Maldives had been an eventful one. A minor household calamity occurred on our fourth day at sea as the jar of cooking oil came loose in a squall, and its contents spilled all over the wet and heaving floor, making it even more slippery. Despite being wet and seasick, we cleaned out the mess, working below decks on all fours, our noses to the smelly and sickening bilges.

Our method of conserving fresh food also led to problems. In an effort to make sure that we consume the food most likely to spoil first, mother superior Shekhar insisted one day that we have bread for breakfast, bread and salad for lunch, and bread with vegetables for dinner. The next day, he would claim that only fresh oranges were good for health and that, therefore, we should each consume half a dozen a day!

One evening, before dusk, a small tired bird alighted on *Trishna*. It was ill and permitted us to wrap its fragile body in a cloth, and place it inside a bucket for the windy night. A large flock of our birdie's fellow creatures followed us the whole moonless night through, chirping agitatedly in response to an occasional feeble chirp from their friend in the bucket. Despite poor visibility and strong adverse winds, the drama continued till the early hours of daybreak, when the flock dropped away. The next day our ill birdie died, and we consigned it to the deep blue sea.

The lower part of my artificial leg is a hollowed out piece of willow. Every time a wave swamped the cockpit this hollow would fill up with seawater. On being relieved by the port watch, as I would sit with the limb outstretched horizontally, this cold sea water would then shoot up the tunnel formed by the sleeve of the trouser leg wetting me to the core. It was miserable, especially on cold, moonless nights. On the 18 October, the tenth day out of port, seeing some fair weather, I decided to clean my stump as well as the limb-socket, using antiseptic lotion and cotton. It felt much better, less itchy and smelly.

We reached Mauritius on 25 October after midnight. *Trishna* sailed into Port Louis, and was riding anchor by 2.30 am on the 26th. The customs official, who came aboard later to clear us for entry into port, appeared wary, and kept asking all kinds of questions.

We finally realized why when he blurted out at one

point: 'You see, in my fifteen years, you are the first sail boat with an all-Indian crew'.

Cleared of entry paperwork, *Trishna* tied up alongside a Mauritian tug boat called *Apsara*.

Mauritius was peaceful and idyllic; and we got a lot of rest. We had sailed almost a month out of Mumbai, and got things ready for the next and longest stretch of our voyage to St. Helena in the mid-Atlantic.

There was much to be done. Boat and crew were to be readied for the long passage of over 7,500 kilometres to St. Helena. This could be a 45-day nonstop passage, or longer, across half the Indian Ocean plus nearly half the Atlantic Ocean. *Trishna*'s water tanks, including the additional tanks we latched on, could carry only 150 American gallons of freshwater, on which we could sail for up to 60 days with severe rationing. Some sails needed repairs; all equipment and systems needed looking over. There was also a persisting mystery: the engine oil level in the auxiliary engine, which we used daily for charging the boat's batteries, was reducing, and needed topping up much too often, though the engine itself seemed to be running well. Was the sump cracked? Or was it a leaky bearing? It was to stay a mystery for a few months more.

For the moment, we simply carried an additional can of engine oil. Water tanks installed at Mumbai had rubber hose connectors which gave off a disagreeable taste and smell. These were changed for plastic connections. Some urgently needed spares for my artificial limb had arrived from Colonel Sushil Jain of the Army's Artificial Limb Centre at Pune—and the bionic appendage was soon swinging merrily again without a creak.

The sad news of the death of Major Jai Bahuguna and two of his mates during their Everest attempt reached us there. Jai had been, and will always remain, a dear friend, and I felt deep personal loss as did scores of people all over the country, at the tragic end of the gentle Jai and his friends. It was a stark reminder that God's will and the belligerence of Nature are to be accepted with humility.

CHAPTER 10

MAURITIUS TO ST. HELENA ISLAND

30 October 1985 – 10 December 1985

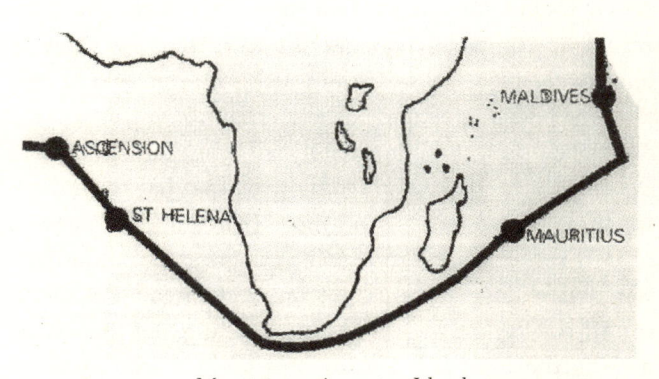

Mauritius to Ascension Island

Trishna sailed out from Mauritius on 30 October. The passage to St. Helena was to be the roughest in our voyage.

We had decided, for political reasons, not to call at any South African port. This was a kind of protest against the then prevalent policies of apartheid in that country.

The first few days brought uncertain light winds, with routine boat activity. Life on board was rather busy even during relatively calm sailing. There is always something to be done to keep a 15-year old boat seaworthy. Also, the watch system ensured that we were almost always short of rest, since God had not made man to sleep in three stretches of three hours each, four hours apart. Even in moderate weather, the crew on watch was fully occupied: now changing the large sail for a smaller one, now rigging out a boom or bringing it down, constantly trimming (adjusting) the sail, steering the boat, and being vigilant against any potential danger. In rough weather, keeping watch took a lot out of each man and, often, the crew would be completely exhausted and seasick. As soon as our watch was over, we would dive into our rolling and jumping bunks, at times without even bothering to remove our wet clothes, and immediately fall into a kind of stupor. When we were shaken up again three hours later to resume watch, it would feel like no more than three minutes of rest! This routine was to become the grind day and night, watch after dogged watch, for months on end. Although the off-watch time was four hours, handing over the watch, making the log book entries, and looking into areas of individual responsibility on board ensured that the actual time available between watches was much less. There was always something that needed attention or make-and-mend. After that, and setting aside some personal time for the washroom and updating one's diary (when the weather permitted), we were left with barely three or three and half hours a day at best to catch up on rest.

As we sailed further south, gale force winds began to build up. In one such gale, I lost my woollen *topi*. Although it fit rather snugly, a gust simply plucked it off. In another, I almost lost my limb. I suppose, being partly of willow, it would have floated, and with it, probably so would I if I were to be washed overboard—but it would be with my head down and limb up! Not a very happy thought for me because I had not figured out what I would do in such an eventuality.

Six men had been out at sea in a small confined space, day and night, through good weather and bad—with all its anxiety and action—for several months. This did not include our sail from the UK to Mumbai. For the older crew, this would make it nearly a year of being in closer proximity to each other for a far longer duration than with any other humans, including the wives!

And it was bound to tell sooner or later.

In the initial days of sailing from the UK, I would remove my artificial limb only every third or fourth day. Later, as we settled into our daily routine, and both the watch crew settled down to regular boat handling in all conditions of sea, it became convenient for me to remove it every time I was off watch. It was also a hygiene requirement, and keeping it on three to four days continuously was beginning to chaffe and blister the stump. It could eventually make me incapable of standing on watch—a situation totally unacceptable at sea. After removing it, I would let the limb lie on the floor boards next to my bunk, as I rested. Any crew movement inside the boat—going to the bows to pass a sail up through the fore hatch for a sail change, or even to the loo—necessitated stepping over my prone artificial limb. It had become a routine procedure.

One wet and uncomfortable night, with the boat pitching about a bit, one of the guys on watch was trying to get past my bunk's lee board, hands grabbing holds as he moved, which was the done thing. Lying semi-asleep with my weather ear open, I heard a murmur of protest: '*Yeh saala* limb *bhi na*!' ('This bloody limb!')'.

The moment passed, but my mind found a solution— after all, there is always one! During my next off-watch, four hours later, I stowed the offending appendage in standing position along the mast by using some shock cord from the spares box. The matter was resolved for all our future days at sea.

The use of cabin lights was restricted to minimum since they were directly connected to the batteries being charged by the running of the engine, and hence to the fuel we had to carry. In this, as in all other matters, we had a strict code of do and don'ts. These soon became habits which were to outlast our voyage. Some of them still bring forth laughs or rebukes at home, depending on the degree of irritation caused by my chronic, almost obsessive habit of getting things done to perfection. At sea this eye for detail may have been a life-saver; but years later, back at home, my nitpicking threatens to disrupt life in a very different way!

Being trained to live with privations is the one thing

Army training and our way of life built into us. This was also the reason why we weathered out the inevitable tribulations together rather well, right till the end of our voyage.

> There were moments of tribulation on board as was bound to be. Knowing that we only had each other, come what may, in the wide blue world, day and night after day and night, through good weather and bad, I think, helped the social dynamics on board. Inevitability is in itself a solution. Even so, there were areas of friction, most certainly more during long windless days of inactivity than during the really rough ones. Rough times bring a sense of urgency that binds, since mutual reliance is the only way out of such situations.
>
> Many of us may have introspected on why, now and then, we'd go through a 'rough patch' with one or the other of the team. As for me, I reasoned that probably due to my condition, which necessarily slowed down my physical reactions, I had developed a mechanism to get over the inevitable 'time lag' by thinking a few steps ahead all the time—I had to; the others did not. Consequently, I felt flustered if any of the others did not think ahead too, not realizing they had quicker reaction-ability on their side.

On the fifth night out of port, as we were passing south of Madagascar, a furious storm picked up before sundown, and lashed us all through the dark furious night before abating the next day. South-easterly winds of over 35 to 45 knots brought steep seas over 30 to 35 feet high. Freak seas and the pitch dark moonless night made us lose our sense of direction while steering, and the boat gybed involuntarily several times at night, as the helmsmen got disoriented.[1] Luckily no damage was done to the boat or the rig and sails since the mainsail was heavily reefed[2] and we had on the smallest jib as the fores'l thus taking power out of the sails. The wind also made it quite cold, which often gave rise to feelings quite akin to hallucinations.

Letter to Asha[3]:

> 7 November 1985
> About 28 deg S, 42 deg E
>
> Just passed clear of south of Madagascar. Had 2–3 rough days from 2nd till yesterday morning—gale force winds over 40 knots at times, seas about 30 to 40 feet. I lost my blue 'AK' topee! I can't find that coloured family photo I had. Please send me another.

AP and Shekhar relieved Bharti and me at midnight, and Shekhar was on the steering wheel of the jostling and thumping boat through the storm. Both were secured to the boat by strong life-lines. The four of us who were off duty were below deck, and the cabin was shut tight against the storm by securing the weatherboards of the companionway

---

[1] A gybe is when with wind from astern, sail and boom swing violently over to the opposite side, often smashing against the standing rigging as wind orientation relative to boat direction changes.

[2] Mainsail reefed implies it is reduced in sail area by rolling it around the boom using a winch.

[3] Whenever conditions permitted, I would write to Asha, continuing the same letter during subsequent days at sea, till we reached a port and I could mail it.

as a standard drill, locking the duty watch outside. Massive waves from astern (behind) threatened to engulf us. Rare 'rogue' waves broke over the boat, totally submerging it in water and froth now and then. The enormous sea hissed and tossed *Trishna* as the wind whistled an ominous high-pitched tune through the rig. A freak giant wave caught the port side quarter of the boat, and lifted it bodily up and up till *Trishna* was at a 60 degree angle of heel, and diving nose first into the huge chasm of the trough ahead. The overtaking wave engulfed the crew, and breaking on top of the boat, almost completely submerged us. A lifebuoy clipped to the guardrails came loose, releasing itself by its buoyancy as the seas submerged it, and floated away even as Shekhar, surfacing from under the salty deluge, fought to keep the boat on a downwind course, and himself from being swept overboard. Then, as *Trishna* lifted her bows and came upright, another huge wave hit her, rolling her sharply the other way, and almost submerging the guard-rails.

Before the boat steadied completely, AP shouted: 'Ship dead ahead, coming towards us!'

We now faced a dilemma. We obviously had to get out of the ship's path, and had only storm sails up, which gave limited speed and steerage; on the other hand, we had to recover the lifebuoy—we had carried only two. But, turning back for the lifebuoy, which, with its flashing locater beacon, was fast disappearing astern in the deep troughs, would put us dangerously in the path of the oncoming ship. So we had to let the ship pass us by before bringing the boat under control by tripping the jib, reefing the main further, and hoisting the storm jib and turning back upwind to search for the buoy. It was now more than an hour since we had lost it, and the buoy must have been at least five miles astern. For more than four hours we searched for it before abandoning the futile exercise, and turning back again on course for the Cape.

The long range radio antenna wire had been carried away, and only the stand-by was left. It was over twenty-four hours before the mountainous seas abated, and calmer conditions returned. There was very feeble communication with Marve, near Mumbai (India), to whom we managed to pass our position.

By now, we had no green vegetables left, and were running out of bread. The crew was being choosy about food. No one liked noodles or preserved foods. Some were terribly fond of sweets, while others detested them. Often we would prefer to have only a boiled egg, or an apple, or just a glass of water (with electrolyte powder in it) instead of a meal, particularly when terribly seasick. It was cause for worry—a terribly seasick crew, throwing up and retching bile, would not be able to retain even a spoon of fluid. Dehydration had to be avoided at all costs. Radio communication was sometimes erratic, on some days, we couldn't radio home our position. We didn't know it then, but soon we were to be out of radio range with home for nearly ten months, regaining radio contact only on our way back to Mumbai from northern Australia.

One day, a school of squid, around sixty to eighty of them, suddenly darted out of the water across our path. Some landed on the side deck and lay there, injured, squirting a black liquid. We put them back into the sea, although there didn't appear much chance of their surviving.

The southernmost tip of South Africa is called the Cape of Good Hope. It was originally named Cape of Storms by the Portuguese explorer Bartholomew Dias who discovered it and was the first European explorer to sail around it in 1488. Much later, King John II of Portugal renamed it the Cape of Good Hope, so that fresher sea apprentices approaching the Cape would not be overwhelmed by the thought of impending storms, and also because crossing it while sailing eastwards was cause for optimism given that one was approaching India and the East.

The passage to the Cape of Good Hope brought stormy weather off and on. One day, storm winds reached a furious 50 knots (95 km per hour). As the weather worsened, we quickly reduced sails even as the boat bucked and jumped like a drunken horse. Another four or five days of this bad weather and we would be past the Cape, we reckoned. Several times the boat heeled (tilted) so much that we thought that she wouldn't come upright. But each time, she did. The storm lasted thirty-six hours, after which the barometer climbed five points, and within hours winds were down to a comfortable 15 knots. Soon, even the sun peeped out of the dark stormy sky. It felt good. We were about 400 nautical miles from the dreaded Cape. The weather was good and sunny; we were being helped along by the strong Agulhas currents. On 15 November, we covered 170 nautical miles in 24 hours.

We approached and passed the needle-like rock formations of Cape Agulhas at dawn on the 18th. There were no winds. Only the 5-knot-strong Agulhas current kept us moving. We now passed the southernmost tip of Africa. The last two days had been windless, with a dense fog that brought along its own gloom. With visibility even during the day down to barely a few metres, we had sailed alert for the noise or sight of ships, or breakers—the first sign of shallow reefs—our life jackets and fog horn at the ready. Sailing in busy shipping waters in dense fog is probably the

Ploughing through rough seas off the Cape of Good Hope.

most nerve racking-experience in a small boat at sea.

Skipper had ordered strict rationing of freshwater. Two of the four water tanks were empty. We were about halfway to St. Helena. Brushing teeth and rinsing our mouths were restricted to alternate days. While the first cooking gas cylinder lasted twenty-eight days, the second lasted only five. Obviously, it had leaked. So we had to conserve cooking gas too.

Diary entry:

> 17 November 1985
> 34deg 03min S, 21deg 50min E
> 91 NM East of Cape Agulhus.

Standing at the point of approaching the formidable Cape of Good Hope! The southernmost point of Africa is Cape Agulhaus. We should hopefully be past it by 18th midday. The Cape of Good Hope is further west. May take 3 or 4 days more to be out of the bad (sic) area. 12 to 18 days after that we expect to reach St. Helena Islands. Can see two ships going westwards towards the Cape with us. 91 NM ahead lies Cape Agulhaus, and about 60 or 80 NM further west lies Cape Town. We are almost past the Cape! The Gods have been kind—easy sailing so far—with strong favourable Agulhaus currents, up to 5 knots at times! Reading books, writing letters or diaries, music on the radio—South African radio—some English and a little Hindi also on the radio. Time zone is GMT minus 1 hour.

We had barely sailed 20 joyous miles past Agulhas Point, imagining that the worst was over, when huge seas began building up. The bright sunny sky suddenly became dark, stormy and overcast. Even as we hastily reduced sail, Cape Town Radio's storm warning for the area came up on the air:

'Attention all ships! This is Cape Town Radio, Cape Town Radio! Winds expected 50 to 60 knots easterlies, gusting to 65.'

Our instruments were already reading 55 knots. Allowing for boat speed downwind, this meant that there was already a 63 knot storm (about 115 kilometres per hour) blowing. It was to be the severest storm of our voyage. With all sails down, and only the bare hull and standing rig exposed to the wind, *Trishna* was tumbling along at over 10 knots, through colossal seas well over 55 feet high. At times, the rolling wave crest would break just astern, and several hundred tons of cold frothing sea would threaten to submerge us. For sailing downwind, extreme caution and concentration was needed while steering to avoid the boat's natural tendency to broach, or turn sharply upwind. For if she did, she would certainly roll over on her side, with the huge seas catching her broadside.

There was also a certain grandeur to the storm. The awesome display of Nature's power can inspire both fear and exhilaration when one is, in addition to witnessing it, actually a part of it. Huge chasms of wave troughs 50 feet deep would appear ahead of the bows as we surfed the crest of a wave in a screaming, jostling ride, and down we'd plunge. But instead of going straight to the bottom of the sea, *Trishna* would emerge majestically again with the next oncoming wave. When waves broke, frothing and hissing, *Trishna* would be engulfed in foam. It was as if we were sailing through a furious sea of soap bubbles. The only recourse was to keep the boat sailing with thirteen reefs in the mains'l, and no jib (foresail) at all, dead downwind. The slightest deviation from dead downwind steerage, and the boat would be tossed around by the next wave, with a serious fear of broaching and all possibilities of the guardrails or even mast dipping into the waters as the boat heeled hard, or even a capsize.

We lost our remaining solitary lifebuoy, our man-overboard-locator dan-buoy, as well as our remaining stand-by radio antenna in the storm that night. Thankfully, the winds abated the next morning.

I managed to take some photographs after the peak fury of the storm was past, though the camera itself was ruined afterwards due to the several overwashes of salt water. Lifelines clipped, I had been able to reach the pulpit at the fore of the slippery deck on all fours, and back again—without getting washed overboard!

It took a while of the after-storm sailing time to let the storm and its severity wear off our minds before the sombre mood gave way to some semblance of a normal relaxed frame of mind. The better part of the day passed in a mood of contemplation of the sheer power we had been part of as mere specks buffeted by the fury of Mother Nature. Unspoken thankfulness for having survived through was writ on every face as eye contact was avoided for some contemplative reason—maybe of a feeling too new to be immediately deciphered. Such was the general mood, when, AP mumbled, 'Something to tell our grandchildren about!'

Diary entry:

> 22 November, 1530 hours
> 29deg 08min S, 10deg 50min E

Terrible storm on 18th just as we had thought we have peacefully crossed the Cape by passing Cape Agulhaus. Between Cape Agulhaus and the appropriately named Bay of Storms, very close to Cape Town, winds began rising. Storm warning on Cape Town Radio followed soon after. Storm raged all through the day and night, and into the next day. Winds at 55 knots, gusting to over 60; seas 40 to 50 feet high. South-easterlies—so with us quite in direction—helping us charge ahead at great speed even with almost no sail at all. The boat is really good, and handles it very well.

Lots of seals around a place called Seal Island, between Agulhaus and Cape Town. Also saw a huge whale, fortunately not too close. And an albatross—largest bird (?) with a wingspan of about 6 feet. Wish these sightings had not been on a grey, ominous, stormy day—they would have made pretty sights.

Trishna had now said her stormy goodbye to the Indian Ocean.

The sail across the Atlantic up to St. Helena, and then to the Caribbean, was really quite calm. Having given us a taste of their might, the Gods now gave us weeks of safe, pleasant sailing.

We hoped it would last.

There was an abundance of exquisite sea life en route: seals, turtles, snakes, various fish and birds, schools of dolphin, and even the occasional whale. Scores of flying fish would dart out of the water in unison, and glide a few hundred metres before plopping back into the sea. Any that fell on deck made delicious eating. A huge albatross circled *Trishna*, gliding gracefully. It looked almost like a mechanical glider as it passed overhead without once flapping its wings.

As we climbed the globe northwards, once more towards the equator, at first the winds were southerly, later swinging with natural precision to the south east as we entered the trade wind belt. Cool nights brought heavy condensation, and an occasional drizzle. One such morning, there were two huge complete and unbroken rainbows to be seen. The strong Benguela currents were helping us onwards with a strength equalled only by the Agulhaus currents earlier.

Diary entry:

30 November, 2320 hours

> Out of radio contact with Marve (India) since the 18th storm. Past 24 hours winds died down to nothing. Flat calm—like a glassy lake. Crawling ahead very slowly. Now 31 days since Mauritius and land; eager to see some ground, some port. Fresh foods long since finished, also eggs, etc. There is some water but not much—must use it carefully.

Bassi was the only smoker among us. And he had rationed his consumption so that his stock would last till St. Helena. It was always a treat to see him light a cigarette on deck, especially when the weather was bad. Whatever the weather, he almost always managed to light up, somehow shielding the flame for that split second. It had been thirty days since we left Mauritius. Our water tanks were empty, and only three plastic cans of 20 litres each remained. *Trishna* sailed once more through the equatorial belt, with hot, humid days of uncertain winds, or at times no winds at all. On such days, the sea was a sheet of glass from horizon to horizon.

Since nature cannot be hurried along, we could only wait patiently for the winds to pick up. Would we miss the tiny island, and drift aimlessly into the Atlantic without food or water? On 1 December, we finally began to get some steady though meagre winds after almost twenty-four exasperating hours of calm. As we sailed along at 2 knots, a whale spouting water appeared barely 150 metres off our port bow. It moved straight towards us, its huge black hump above the water. Everyone rushed on deck, lifejackets in hand, and waited with bated breath for *Trishna* to cross clear of its path. We tried to start the auxiliary engine in an effort to motor to a safer distance, but just then, as if preordained, the engine developed a snag, and no amount of cranking would start it. Luckily, we crossed barely 30 to 40 metres ahead of the 40-feet long sea monster. Sensing our presence, the creature executed a fascinating laborious dive. First the hump rose 10 feet. Then the huge back surfaced, and with a wriggling movement, the whale began its submarine-like dive. The forked tail, 8 to 10 feet across, rose and propelled it downwards with a powerful slow-motion flipper action, leaving behind a huge turquoise turbulence.

The past few days had been days of relaxed sailing—

of reading, star-gazing, or simply looking out into the emptiness that is an ocean, from horizon to horizon. For me, it was a good time to fill up a few pages in my diary.

Diary entry (undated):

> In ocean cruising, 'hope' is a continuous game between the Gods of Nature and the sailor. It now seems as if the Gods are presently on our side. Winds in the open oceans are the least predictable; and a yacht has no facility for weather forecasts. The human mind reaches out with hope. It is a complex mixture of feelings, ranging from trying to force your will upon Nature, hoping it will work(!) to imploring the Gods to keep the boat going in the conditions at hand, and again to pray, 'please God, give us good seas and fair winds'.
>
> Hope in itself nurtures a host of mixed reactions, ranging from hard-nosed strategizing to extreme emotions, conjectures, apprehensions, a deep sense of gratitude, joy and elation, a deep sense of being—and hope again! Hope always dominating the rest.
>
> Sailing the high seas is so much a matter of feelings. If you look at it this way, one gets to understand the kind of people who take to cruising the oceans. It is beyond the technique of moving boats—which by itself is not too difficult. It is actually a matter of passion.
>
> Man is indeed a fragile creature, existing within narrow natural limitations of temperature, air quality, water, food, humidity, noise levels, etc. Even feelings can end his life! It is amazing how scant regard we have for, or how little we associate ourselves with Nature and its moods. In our everyday existence of socializing, eating, sleeping—we take Nature for granted. In hot weather we

get into a cool place; in a storm we stay indoors; in rain we take shelter. Seldom are we one with Nature. Thoughts of it take up our attention only in passing. We are actually arrogant with Nature, the very creator and preserver of life! Once in a while, Nature rears its head—and millions perish. Even so, we treat it with disregard: relief work, shelters, renovate, and rebuild—and then we carry on as before on our narrow rutted tracks.

How often are we one with Nature? In the rain? In the howling winds that uproot trees in their path? How long do we endure them without shelter—five minutes? Fifty minutes? Half a day? A few days? Not being certain if we will be around at the other end of the storm—that is truely knowing and being with Nature. If we develop a deep respect for the creative, preserving and destructive forces of Nature, then things fall into perspective. Without understanding Nature, we cannot understand life.

This is in large measure what sailing the oceans is all about: being one with life and Nature. A mixture of different states of mind in the diverse moods of time and the seas creates a spectrum of feelings: from the hyper-buoyant to the depressive. All along, Mother Nature gives us an opportunity to feel that she is close to us—with us. When the boat surges ahead at breakneck speed over surf and chop, accelerating over waves to a high at its top speed, all are one: boat, man, Nature. As one gets the boat to hold top speed on the crest of the giant wave, simply graceful, majestic, buoyant in body and spirit, for that fraction of time one feels one is not alone at the helm; that a hand other than one's own is working with you, through you. You join the forces of Nature—and experience a feeling of pure joy, of pure being, of pure oneness. These moments add to the overall love and joy of being in a small sailing boat in a big, empty (?) ocean, its uncertainties being but the spice to the main course.

The awe at the whale sighting had not yet worn off when we first perceived the dim outline of St. Helena ahead.

Thirty-three days after sailing from Mauritius, *Trishna* was riding at anchor in Jamestown bay. From there, we telephoned Tipsy in Delhi. Since we had been out of radio contact ever since the storm, everyone at home was more than anxious. Some had even given up hope. Tipsy had asked ships in the area, including the Royal Mail Ship (RMS) *St. Helena*, which makes a round trip from the UK every fifteen days, to look out for us. The radio station too had been asked to listen for our SOS signals. So everyone was really relieved when KS's call went through.

It was good to be on land after such a long and stormy passage; to see land, other human beings, and ordinary things like roads and red-roofed houses once again. We strutted through the town's 150-metre-long Main Street. Everyone also ran up and down the 699 steps of the Jacob's Ladder on Ladder Hill, overlooking the bay. Not having climbed so many steps at a stretch since the amputation, I was apprehensive about being able to do it in one go. But I managed it, even though it took me an hour. To use a variety of muscles instead of straining only one set, I climbed one step at a time for a while, then switched to two, and then back again to one. It was sweet indeed to reach the top having found my land-legs again!

St. Helena is a one horse town. Solomon and Sons, the

company that filled our empty cooking gas bottles, owned the petrol pump, workshop, machine spares store, shipping agency and the hotel as well.

Ascension and Tristan Da Cunha Islands are also under the Governor here. The Governor, Derrick Baker, wanted to know what we would do if pirates attacked us. This was a real problem for small boats at sea in those days. We said that pirates were not likely to trouble us since, given how weather-beaten we were by then, we probably looked fiercer than they did! He seemed convinced by the answer. Baker took us around his official residence, the Plantation House, where we also met Jonathan, a 200-year old tortoise.

The RMS' *St. Helena* sailed in the next day, but unfortunately there was no mail for anyone except me. I felt I should share my letter with everyone.

One of the RMS crew, seeing *Trishna* at anchor, asked us casually what her nationality was. When he heard that she was Indian, and had a crew of six for the small boat she was, he was taken aback and said: 'Six? What are they doing? Migrating?'

☙ ❧

Letter to Asha:

> 5 December 1985, midnight, St. Helena
>
> Reached on 2nd early in the morning. Staying by turns on alternate days at Hotel Consulate on Main Street—to be able to sleep on a bed! Small island with a population of five thousand only. Jamestown, the capital, has only

fifteen hundred people.

Booked a call to you yesterday as well as today—no luck. Will try again tomorrow. About your coming to Jamaica or Panama, if you have the money then come on your own—it will be worth the expenditure. Do not hesitate at all.

Letter to Asha:

9 December 1985, 12.30 a.m.
Consulate Hotel, St. Helena Islands, South Atlantic

Today is our turn to sleep on the beds! AP and I have just come back from the house of the only Indian here, Dr APS Grewal. Good being at home—any home. Saw some Hindi movie cassettes; refreshing change.

The people are nice and kind. They are completely cut off from the rest of the world. All young—boys and girls—are constantly looking for a chance to leave the island at any cost. They want an escape from the island which is their home! A two-way ship passage to the UK is 1200 pounds. A one-way air ticket is about 350 pounds!

Finished seeing the island in five hours, including an hour for lunch! The Governor lives in Plantation House, where he had called us for drinks. The house has a tortoise over 200 years old! Then there is the Briars, where Napoleon Bonaparte lived for six weeks as a prisoner, till the Longwood house was ready, and he moved there.

Apart from these, sight-seeing involves looking at hills and valleys and, of course, the sea.

It is 1.15 a.m. now (10 December), and I have to get up early to get the boat ready to sail out at about noon. The passage to Ascension Island may take six to ten days.

NDA II

The slow march past the Quarter Deck signified the successful culmination of three years of very hard training. We had all perceptibly changed, although the fact that this change was possibly the biggest and most meaningful one in our lives was not yet discernible to us just then. We just were not at the age to see it that way. For us, three years of meaningless madness had come to an end as we successfully passed out from the Academy. The meaning and richness of those invaluable years took its own time to grow upon us. And now, decades later, we know we will never forget those years, nor will we trade them for anything in the world.

The Naval Cadets went to their Naval Academy; the Air Force Cadets to their Air Force Academy; and we, the Army Cadets, went to Dehradun to join the Indian Military Academy (IMA) for our final year before becoming Commissioned Officers.

It will not be wrong to say that the one year at IMA was not much more than yet another year of seemingly meaningless madness that had begun when I was just eleven, and my father had dropped me off at RIMC.

Of course, he had aspirations for me. Every Indian parent has. A major one was fulfilled as I passed out of the portals of the Chetwode Building in IMA, on 23 December 1973, when we were pipped with one star each on our shoulders at the stroke of midnight and with the symbolic switching off of lights signifying the passage from one time zone to another in our young lives, and I became Second Lieutenant A.K. Singh. I was commissioned into the Bengal Sappers—which was what I had opted for and was proud to join.

The excitement of it all was exhilarating. 'What did you get, *yaar*? Infantry? Mechanised? Armoured Corps? Artillery?' But the surprise of surprises was that *he* had, quite unobtrusively, requested and been assigned to the toughest of the tough branches of the Indian Army—the Indian Para-Commandos. I secretly marvelled at and admired the steely determination that now clearly shone through this funny boy who had joined the NDA aged sixteen, and was in grave danger of hurting his tendons for life since he had never ever run in his life up until then! He was a well-coordinated power-pack of a lean, wiry, tall body now. But the serene humility was still there.

And what a handsome man he had grown into!

CHAPTER 11

BIG OCEAN, TINY BOAT: ST. HELENA TO BALBOA AND SAILING INTO THE PACIFIC OCEAN
10 December 1985–5 April 1986

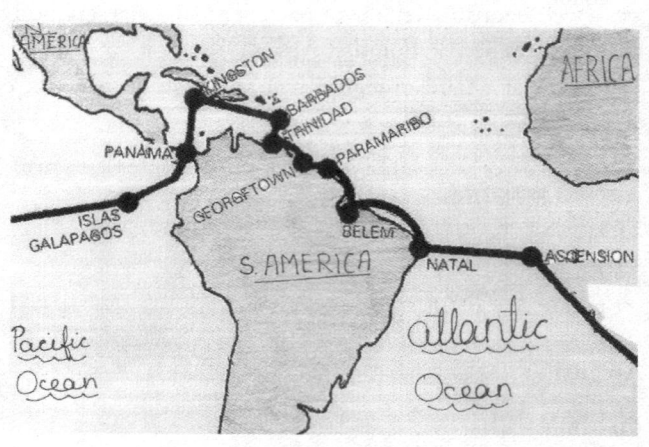

Across the Atlantic, into the Pacific

The 700 nautical mile sail from St. Helena to the tiny Ascension Island was uneventful. Reading was a popular pastime during this leg, and AP would be routinely found engrossed in books of the fat and philosophical variety. New novels and periodicals picked up at Mauritius were consumed voraciously. Our appetite for food, however, dwindled. I did my various isometric exercises every day.

Letter to Asha:

>12 December 1985, Thursday, noon
>About 11deg 23 min S, 10deg 22 min W
>about 310NM from Ascension Isles

Calm seas, following trade winds from the SE. Making good speed. It is difficult to pass time on the boat. Various muscles used normally on land, for walking, etc., are becoming weaker due to lack of exercise under the conditions. At St. Helena, I tried to walk as much as I could. Will do the same at Ascension. The few books and magazines on board have all been read—we change some and pick up others at the ports.

Letter to Asha (continuing):

>14 December 1985, Saturday, 1430 hours
>About 50 NM from Ascension Isles.

Ascension Island can now be seen about 50 miles on our port bow.

Ascension Island

On one especially dark moonless night, globules of luminescent green and phosphorescence of all shapes and sizes kept appearing and disappearing around us, as if operated by a random strobe switch. It was eerie, but very beautiful.

We sighted Ascension Island's tall conical Green Mountain one clear evening when still 50 miles away. It hadn't been easy to get an OK from the British foreign office for us to call into the island for water supplies. We got their consent just before we sailed from St. Helena. We had permission only to walk along the water front, and just during daylight hours. There was no response to our radio calls as we approached the 'super-secret' island. Finally, some lights, many of them red, appeared—presumably aircraft warning lights atop radio masts. Soon, a big inflatable boat with a powerful motor emerged from the dark.

It had two men in it, one of whom simply said: 'Follow me'.

'Are you from port control?' we asked.

After a pause came the laconic reply: 'Whenever yachts come here, we take them in'.

We followed them to Georgetown which is more of an anchorage than a port.

Two oil tanker ships were anchored there, and we were to tie to a line that one of them passed to us.

'In the morning, you will be taken inshore to the small boat anchorage,' one of the men said, as his boat sped off in the dark towards the other ship.

At daybreak, a look at the island told us that it was indeed all we had suspected. Dish antennae and several tall radio masts sprouted all over, like weeds. A very small hamlet and plenty of rock completed the picture. Green

Mountain, now in a cloudy haze, was the only little bit of greenery we could see.

There were plenty of black fish in the water. We were told not to swim if we had any open wounds, because if these 15-centimetre-long fish—cousins of the piranha—smell blood, they attack by the hundreds. Black fish are not good to eat. At dawn, after Bharti had tried in vain for hours to catch one, Bassi figured out a way. He put a crust of bread in a bucket, lowered it into the sea, and then pulled it out with two black fish! Having fulfilled the challenge posed in catching them, we returned them to the sea. Such was the boredom of standing idle on board on a clear tropical morning, and not being able to land to explore the small intriguing island we had sailed so many miles to reach.

Letter to Asha (continuing):

17 December, 1530 hours
Tied Astern the Tanker Ship *Maersk Ascension of London*

Reached here on night of Saturday/Sunday (14th/15th), and have had about a two-day stop here. It is a small island, 8 miles by 6 miles, with zero ethnic population, and about 800–900 people living here, mostly from BBC, Cable & Wireless and NASA, etc. After about 10 to 12 days' sailing, we should be across the Atlantic, reaching Natal, Brazil.

The boredom of being tethered to a ship in the waters of a new island whose shores were so close at hand, after having crossed hundreds of miles of ocean, was excruciating. But, dependent on the 'mother ship', and advised as we were by our hosts not to go ashore without invitation, we had little choice but to wait. The tedium was broken by an invitation to board the ship to which we were tied: the *Maersk Ascension*. On board the ship we met our mystery man from the previous night, Chief Officer David Thompson, who turned out to be a humorous and cheerful chap. The master of the ship, A Cattel, was a model of sea-faring courtesies, and offered to help in every way. Later, before we sailed on, he graciously gifted essential requirements of water, fresh vegetables, eggs, bread, tinned stuff, fresh fish, and diesel from his ship's supplies as a gesture of seamanship and friendliness. In any case, there was no place on the island where these could be purchased from.

We were finally given permission to land on the island, with the proviso that we return before nightfall. The resident doctor on Ascension, Dr Subhash Suktanker, drove us around the island, and topped up his warm hospitality with a sumptuous lunch prepared by his wife. Geopolitically speaking, Ascension Island is unique. It is British territory, mostly used by the BBC and the Americans with NASA and Cable & Wireless. There is no local population and the settlers from Britain and the US are literally the masters of all they behold and survey. Theirs is the only power and water supply on the island. The island's terrain of soft volcanic ash is like the moonscape, with nearly no water or vegetation. There are lava floes, craters, and stony outcrops, much like our landscape in Leh. The volcanic stones of porous composition are interesting—large rocks can be surprisingly weightless. Like gleeful children we took turns at being photographed in the classic 'Hanuman pose': with a huge 'rock' lifted easily in one hand! They say the moon buggy underwent trials here before the US sent it to the moon!

The Senior British Naval Officer, Lieutenant Commander Nigel Walsh, gifted us a cache of books and novels from his library, before he and Dr Subhash waved us goodbye as we hoisted sail in a fresh wind, and set course for Brazil the next day.

Trishna was now in the equatorial belt. Temperatures began to rise beyond comfortable limits. It was hot and stuffy, and we sweated all the time. On deck, however, one was better off with a little breeze, especially in the small shady areas provided by the sails. We rigged up a protective awning in the cockpit for the watch on duty.

These were calm and gentle sailing days, with the trade winds pushing us steadily on towards Brazil, about 1,250 miles away. The skies were clear, with an occasional blob of cloud.

Letter to Asha:

> 24 December, Tuesday, 0830 ship's time
> 370 NM from Natal

Today is Akshi's birthday—four years have gone by! I don't even know what Aditi looks like! By 1987, by the time I'm back...? God knows! At times I wonder, I'm becoming immune to feelings. You will have to thaw me out when this is over.

Of course the mind comes back to the present and there are cheerful things around. The most cheerful being that we are moving fast and covering a lot of distance—

> about 120 NM a day—and should be in Natal by the 27th where I will post this letter.
>
> I dry-cleaned myself today and changed my underclothes, shorts and T-shirt, and then prayed for Akshi, that she should have a rich and fulfilling life, full of confidence and contentment. She almost appeared before my eyes. Incidents long gone keep coming back—remember when she said, 'What is telling lies, Momma?' Anyway, I can only compensate for lost time when this madness is over. I wish I had not been so strong headed, then I would have stayed home instead of 'proving' a silly point by sailing for over a year. Thankfully God is with us!

It is always wise, as well as comfortable, to work on the boat and equipment during calm sailing. The mystery of the rapidly reducing engine oil had been partly solved when an investigation revealed that it had been leaking, and collecting below the engine in the bilges. Over three buckets of offensive and smelly oil-and-seawater mix had to be removed. Was it simply a loose drain plug or something more serious like a cracked engine body? No amount of careful inspection yielded an answer.

Brazil

The lights of Brazil appeared after dusk on 27 December as we closed on to Natal on the north eastern shoulder of the subcontinent, guided by the powerful Natal lighthouse. But it was only after daybreak that we approached the extremely restricted entrance through the outer reefs or 'recifes'. The yacht anchorage is at the yacht club, a little way up the river Potengi, named after a local Red Indian tribe.

Trishna narrowly missed disaster while entering the narrow channel at the river mouth. It became alarmingly clear as we approached, that the southern half of the channel had a dangerous reef over which tell-tale surf was breaking. By the time we realized this we were almost on top of it. With a fresh following wind and strong currents piling us on the reefs, it was a situation that could have easily turned nasty. Sails were tripped instantly and the engine started in a hurry, and we motored up-river safely past danger. Soon, we were anchored off the floating pier of the yacht club. It was a good feeling to have crossed 3,750 miles of the Atlantic in about thirty days.

To make sure we got all we needed, some well-wishers had hired a shipping agent for us. Now a big ship definitely needs an agent to help with paperwork, victualing and repairs. But it is a different matter for a small yacht. We had handled all formalities on our own so far. A similar situation earlier at Port Said had caused us to part with a lot of money, which could have been avoided. Mr Hugo, the agent at Natal, was going to charge us US$500 for getting our immigration formalities done. It was certainly a lot of money for something we could handle ourselves. Skipper KS tried to explain to the gesticulating agent that we really did not need his services; but he clearly didn't understand.

Instead, a round of soft drinks appeared, and Hugo managed to say in broken English: 'Everything will be done on Monday'.

But when the determined KS finally got his message across, Hugo was furious. He insisted on being paid US$150 as holding charges. We thought we got off lightly!

The Brazilian Navy looked after us in Natal. We had proper rooms and beds to sleep in, and meals to eat in their mess. Also, Mr Shankaran Kutty, a genial professor in oceanography and one of the few Indians in the area, kindly called us over for a meal. The good professor had cooked the meal himself, since he had lost his wife some time ago.

As we ate, his washing machine choked and coughed over our salty and grimy clothes!

The New Year dawned for us here, and there was a lot of wishing each other 'Felice-de-nov' before we sailed on. But we had not seen the last of colourful Brazil yet, as we rounded the Cabo De Sao Roque Cape, and headed west in a spirited breeze.

Diary entry:

4 January 1986, Saturday

Sailing along the North Coast of Brazil, past Fortaleza.
Hope to reach Belem, at the mouth of the Amazon River, in 4 or 6 days.

The ex-Chief of the Indian Air Force, Air Chief Marshal (Retd) Dilbagh Singh, was then the Indian Ambassador to Brazil. Due to his efforts, and of the gracious Brazilians, we had a comfortable stay, both at Natal as well as at the next port of Belem up the Rio Para, one of the tributaries of the great Amazon River.

Brazil is a country with the largest conceivable mixture of races—Portuguese, Dutch, Spanish, Italian, German, Japanese (the largest Japanese population outside Japan is in Brazil), African, Chinese, etc. Many locals admit that the culture that has emerged from this potpourri is more liberal-western than even the American way of life. The country seems to be on a perpetual holiday, with soccer, volleyball, discos and dancing as nearly full-time occupations for many. Inflation was 200 per cent! So, in the time we sailed from Natal to Belem, the cost of postage to India had doubled! Confused about the number of zeroes marked on the prices of every item, we finally reckoned that 1,000 cruzeiros were the equivalent of one Indian rupee!

The actual shoreline meandered considerably. Since we kept a steady course, we were at times, anything up to 50 miles offshore. The sea changed now and again from a deep blue to a shallow-water-green, and then back to blue again. An occasional school of dolphins kept us company. A flying fish or two, picked up from the deck in the morning, was a daily addition to our breakfast.

The 20-mile-wide Rio Para is only a part of the 200 mile wide great Amazonian delta. Our sail up to the Rio Para had been good, but winds began gusting by the time we entered the river, and soon a full thunderstorm began raging. It was tricky sailing in the unknown currents of a tidal river in spate during the monsoon. Visibility was poor. There were also numerous shallows and sand bars. We had to be extremely alert. My stump chose to begin hurting at this time, and standing at the steering wheel became an ordeal.

That was not the end of my problems. One day, as I was catching some rest after being relieved by the port watch, Bharti, who was sleeping above me, came crashing down, bunk and all, on my head. The catches holding his bunk had worked loose. Fortunately, no one was hurt. Soon, bunk re-installed, both of us were sound asleep.

Belem

Belem is a big city, about 70 nautical miles upstream on the Amazon River, on Rio Para. It is fraught with tricky sailing conditions: sand bars, strong currents, and dangerous floating logs. Locals even warned us about crocodiles in the river from the dense jungles on both banks, all the way up from the 35 mile wide mouth of the Rio Para.

Sailing and boat handling at sea had become second nature to us by now. So routine were our drills that crises like storms and deluges did not evoke a second thought; we responded by reflex. We now handled with practised calm all our little episodes, like the one when we nearly climbed atop an unmarked reef while entering Natal, or a week later, when we groped our way blindly in a storm up the Amazon River, with its numerous sand-bars, navigating through a thick haze which cut off all visual landmarks and beacons. We steered *Trishna* in the stormy and tidal river through the dark night, with deadly floating logs and other debris as well as crocodiles for company. We dealt with equanimity the more routine troubles on board, with something or the other needing attention all the time.

Fortunately, even in the poor visibility, we located a lighthouse as well as a wreck (to remind us of the urgency of accurate navigation), and sailed the 70 miles up the river, often having to pick our way between massive floating logs.

Trishna tied up at the naval anchorage of Belem at 5.30 am on 9 January 1986.

We took on some water, tools and spares at Belem. During a routine test, one of the two 90 Ampere batteries was found to be weak, and had to be replaced. We could not set right the long-range radio though. It was virtually impossible to work without a mosquito repellent, and every afternoon, around 2 pm, it would rain heavily, as if brought on by a hidden alarm clock.

Some naval officers invited us for a drink at the bar that evening, and Brazilians and Indians chatted away using gestures, mime, back-slapping, and every form of expression imaginable. I don't know if we understood a word of what the other said, but a strong sense of camaraderie certainly prevailed, enhanced no doubt by the copious flow of drinks.

High water was just past noon on 13 January, so we hoisted anchor at 2.30 p.m., and sailed past the township and down the river.

Leaving Belem

The winds were against us even on our way out, and a storm had picked up. We were moving rather fast in the muddy waters, and there was a real danger of hitting floating logs at high speed. The jib sail was lowered to reduce speed. Along with shoals and shifting sand banks, unlit fishing boats presented an additional hazard. Some had the annoying habit of turning their lights on only when fairly close. A few did not even do that, and we narrowly missed colliding with one. There were ships about too. And we had thought that crocodiles and mosquitoes would be our only problems when sailing up and down Rio Para!

It took us a full day's sailing to clear the mouth of the river, and another two days to cross the amazing Amazon delta going from east to west. Sometime during the evening of 14 January, while still traversing the delta, we crossed the Equator, and were back into the northern hemisphere. This time, we enacted the traditional ritual of holding King Neptune's Court, although we had already crossed the Equator once. We were to cross it twice more before sighting Mumbai and home.[1] It was good fun, with the king awarding silly punishments. For instance, one could be asked to run around the deck with an upturned bucket on one's head! The ceremony had obviously been thought up as a way to dispel gloom among a ship's crew during the hot and normally listless equator crossing. It certainly presented some lively distraction on board the *Trishna*, except that the sail was far from sluggish.

---

[1] King Neptune's Court: Sailors sailing in ships before the mast, in the days of the great discoverers, resorted to this ceremony as a pleasurable pastime while crossing the Equator, to boost morales during hot, humid and dull days of slow and tardy sailing. The ceremony of 'Crossing the Line' is now an initiation rite in the navies, merchant navies and on board sail training ships that commemorates a sailor's first crossing of the Equator. It is also a test for seasoned sailors to ensure their new shipmates are capable of handling long rough times at sea. Sailors who have already crossed the Equator are nicknamed (Trusty/Honourable) **Shellbacks** and 'Sons of Neptune'; those who haven't are called (Slimy) **Pollywogs**.

The strong Guyana current was helping us along at a good 5 knots. Also, monsoon winds built up to gales, and frequently to storm force, and it was very uncomfortable sailing upwind. On the 16th, the winds increased to 30 knots, and on the following morning, to 40. The jib sail was pulled down, and the main, tired of the incessant flogging, finally gave way and tore. But skipper and Bharti, despite being terribly seasick, mended and hoisted the sail again. The bad weather persisted for over two days. Eyes, lips and beards were caked with salt, and all of us had a constant, revolting, stale taste of salt in our mouths and nauseatingly all the way down our gullets, to be felt each time we swallowed spittle. Even the insides of our nostrils and ears were caked with dried salt! It was a wretched and revolting feeling. The only consolation was that we covered over 150 miles that day!

Suriname

So strong were these west-bound currents that they threatened to sweep us right past the mouth of the Suriname River which we were to enter for our next port of call, at Paramaribu. The continental shelf here is so silted over by the tropical river that it is barely 15 feet deep even at places almost 10 miles offshore.

The next morning, the port authorities asked on the radio: 'Any military man on board?'

On being told that we were indeed 'six Indian Army officers', they asked us to wait out at sea. There followed a thirty-minute conversation in Dutch, and we heard '*Trishna*' and 'military police' repeated several times. Just when we were beginning to picture ourselves in a military prison somewhere in the rainforest, a pilot launch appeared, and we were asked to follow it into port. On reaching New Harbour, the military police came on board, with weapons and all.

They were courteous enough to say: 'We have to check. It is only routine!'

Diary entry:

> 19 January 1986, Sunday
>
> We are motoring into the Suriname River—to Paramaribu. Suriname was a Dutch colony mostly, though it changed hands between the Dutch and the English a couple of times, finally gaining independence in 1975, and later coming under military rule and becoming a dictatorship. There are many Indians, and we were pleasantly surprised to know that Hindi is a popular language, even being taught in many schools!
>
> Now reaching Paramaribu on the 6th day after leaving Belem. Hope to stop here for 2 days. We are almost one-fourth of the way around the world.
>
> Found my family photograph! Dearer because I had missed it.

After changing masters several times, this rainforest colony of Suriname is said to have been returned to the Dutch by the British in exchange for New York. The former chide the latter to this day that they had managed to keep Suriname longer than the British kept New York!

Over 38 per cent of Suriname's 35,000 people are of Indian origin, and speak Hindustani. Talky-Talky, a kind of

Pidgin English, is most popular. About half the population lives in the capital city of Paramaribu as the rest of the country is mainly virgin forests.

That night we slept ashore in the back room of a Hindu temple. We also saved a small fortune by sending our mail to India in the Indian Embassy's diplomatic bag. Replenishing water and food supplies, which now included some truly exquisite tropical fruits which we merely had to gather from the forests, *Trishna* sailed back down the now familiar Suriname River and into the sea, before setting a westward course.

As per our plan, we were to enter the Pacific Ocean only after March. Having made a fast passage so far, we were not rushed for time. In order to rest the crew and keep the boat in good condition, we decided to sail easy for the remaining passage up to Panama.

Guyana

Georgetown, Guyana, was where we were hoping to pick up all our mail that had accumulated since we'd missed it at Mauritius, St. Helena, as well as in Ascension.

It was only a few days' sail to the Demerara river delta and Guyana. A pilot launch which had been sent out from Georgetown to guide us in, mistook a large cargo ship for *Trishna*. The captain probably thought that with six army officers, *Trishna* had to be at least a small ship, with many subordinate working hands too, steward and all! He was quite surprised to see little *Trishna* no bigger than the fishing boats sailing about, and roughly the size of a ship's lifeboat. A patrol boat guided us in and we tied up alongside one of their patrol boats.

Guyana in Amerindian means 'land of many rivers'.

Our Guyana halt enabled us to rectify several mechanical and electrical defects. The Guyanese Defence Forces (GDF) kindly put at our disposal their maritime workshop facilities. The sailing lights, leaking toilets and a broken companionway catch were fixed here.

Diary entry:

26 January 1986

> Been working at the boat nonstop 7.30 a.m. to 7 p.m. for the past 4 days. Very satisfying and rewarding. Lots done.

The mast head light, the marine toilet, the centre table and a couple of other things that needed attention, were fixed. Several other preventive maintenance tasks and checks were carried out. The mystery of the leaking engine oil was finally solved too—but not before the engine was removed, hoisted, cranked, and revved up while suspended in mid-air thereby affording all round inspection. It was then that I noticed the oil, warm and less viscous now, beginning to trickle out of the loose inspection cover plate. The faulty cover was tightened, and the engine was re-installed with relief.

I was halfway through my work one morning, when a beaming face appeared in the companionway.

'Namaste, I'm Pushparaj, Indian cyclist on world tour.' I liked him immediately. Tall, wiry and light on his feet, he had a dark, handsome face, and sported a trimmed moustache and a glowing set of white teeth. He chatted as I worked. He even helped hoist me atop the mast to fix the sailing lights.

That evening, we were invited to the GDF boxing championship. It is the only fight I have seen with a woman as one of the judges. I was tempted to ask if she boxed too (in those days women didn't).

'One has to be a bit crazy to do this sort of a thing,' said the Chief of the military regime, Major General Norman I McLean, referring to our sailing venture.

The tall and athletic General, with a forceful, bespectacled face, and short cropped hair, had a ready sense of humour. Introducing his staff officer, he said: 'Colonel Dell had gone to Trinidad as one of the members of an international tribunal to try members of an abortive coup on one of the islands. Some of the members of the tribunal learnt so much about coups, they went back to their countries and conducted their own successful ones later...ha ha ha!' The Colonel fidgeted with a far away look in his eyes. Quite a game this!

The General carried on oblivious to the Colonel's discomfort: 'I went to a conference of the dictatorial heads of states of the West Indies recently. I found that one of us had promoted himself to Major General from a Brigadier. So I came back and promoted myself too to a Major General...ha ha ha!

The GDF kindly flew us deep into Guyana in one of the small Cessna aircraft. We saw the famous Kaiteur Falls, reputed to be the highest waterfalls in the world at 741 feet. The country was dense forest and more dense forest, now and again broken by a silver ribbon of a river. The river banks had small patches of human habitation, generally people panning the river for gold, diamonds and other precious stones. They used modern machines to pan the rivers and river beds. There were small airstrips since small aircraft were their only means of connecting with the outside world.

Trinidad

With following winds and currents, we approached Trinidad rapidly, and made for the Galleons' Passage between Venezuela and Trinidad. We entered the protected Gulf of Paria through the Boca Grande. The tall, handsome figure of Navin Ahuja—who at 21 years was the youngest member of the *Trishna* team and was to replace Bassi— could be discerned on the jetty as we approached and tied up at Port of Spain at 10 p.m. on 29 January 1986. We were to have our first crew change there.

Diary entry:

29 January 1986

> Bassi is geared up mentally for the change. His mind is already far away, back home. We will miss this hyperactive lively member of our close-knit team. No farewell is usually pleasing. It must be a good feeling going back home though.

Navin had brought lots of mail, which was eagerly distributed and set upon. Everyone wanted to know everything about back home, and Navin was the centre of attention for quite a while.

The West Indies are synonymous with cricket, mellow golden rum, and rhythmic music, especially Steel Bands and Calypso. There was a calypso called 'The Ship is Sinking'.

But, it had to do with the sinking Trinidadian economy! The one I liked most was: 'Everybody Happy – Everybody Glad/Here in Trinidad!'

Barbados

We then sailed north from Trinidad for Barbados. The passage was against strong currents and weather, and the newly inducted Navin was quite seasick. For the first few days, we made almost no headway, tacking against the strong currents between Grenada and the north coast of Trinidad, till it appeared that we were condemned to do this forever—like the proverbial genie climbing a greased pole. Then, we finally broke the deadlock in heavy seas, and found the northbound currents for Barbados. Just seeing the glow of the island made us feel warm.

By daybreak next day, we were safely in port and everyone turned in for some rest, except Navin who, excited at the end of his first passage, was busy writing lots of letters home.

After minor boat work and some sail repairs, we took on water, and were ready to leave.

Diary entry (undated):

> Up early today. It is an overwhelming prospect to have to write about 20 letters in an hour, then wash out the storm suit and the oiled-woollen jersey, and catch some rest too before sailing.

KS spoke to India after calling up Barbados Radio, and got the exciting news of the birth of a daughter. He later named her Trishna.

Jamaica

We sailed north-by-northwest in heavy seas, to pass between the islands of St. Lucia and Martinique to enter the protected and calmer Caribbean waters. We then set a westward course for Jamaica. The going became good once more, with following winds and currents. We sailed past the Dominican Republic and, after seven days out of port, sighted the prominent Blue Mountains of Jamaica. A number of wrecks along the eastern passage to Port Royal served as a reminder of the fate of careless navigators, as we sailed past the Norman Manley airport on the starboard side, into the sheltered waters of the Port, and tied up alongside the coast guard jetty. We later moved to an anchorage close by.

Since *Trishna* was moored safely, all of us were able to stay ashore for our two-day halt. We split up into three pairs. AP and I stayed with my wife's brother, Kaushalendra, and his wife, Nidhi, both doctors employed there. As we were being driven to their house, the car went over a pothole and both its left wheel rims got bent and both tyres were punctured beyond repair.

Quite an introduction to Jamaica of the eighties!

Our departure from Port Royal too had an element of drama. *Trishna* was ready to sail by mid-day on 21 February 1986. As friends and well-wishers waved a farewell from the shore, we began to heave anchor. But pull as we might and wave as they may, the anchor refused to be weighed. No amount of tugging or revving up of the engine to override the anchor worked; it just refused to budge. The people ashore, tiring from all the waving and smiling, seemed to be saying: 'Aren't you going?' And all of a sudden the anchor came free, still attached to another rusted anchor with which it had become entangled on the sea bed. The rusted culprit was quickly knocked off, and our hosts smiled and waved with renewed gusto on seeing us move off at last.

The short run to Panama was covered in five days. Although the winds were very light for the first few hours, they soon picked up, and were constantly on the port beam or quarter, except for the last day, which was a downwind sail. We set a southerly or, at times, even a south-by-south easterly course, to cater to a prevailing westward drift.

The Panama Canal

As we approached the Panama Canal, shipping traffic increased. We sighted the high point of Manzanillo which lies to the east of the port city of Cristobal before noon on 25 February while still 30 miles away, and reached the narrow channel to the Cristobal harbour the same night. We entered the sheltered waters along with another ship, so close to it that we were in constant danger of colliding.

Groping through the mire of flashing red, green and yellow lights, with a backdrop of neon and other bright lights from ships and shore installations, *Trishna* had a narrow escape from being run over by a ship charging down upon us from astern at full speed. It appeared to be heading for the Canal, and had apparently not seen us. Of course, we were probably at fault too. In the maze of lights, we did not know where we were! Getting hurriedly out of the ship's way, we called Cristobal Radio for directions, and were soon at the anchorage for yachts by 10.30 p.m.

Meanwhile, we had been raised on the radio by Phantom himself! 'Now we have really reached the rainforests,' we thought.

We called him back: 'Phantom, this is yacht *Trishna*'. Our caller turned out to be less exotic than we had thought; it was CB Fenton and Company, the local shipping agents, who wanted to know if we needed any assistance with immigration and other formalities!

Finally, some restful sleep, the kind a sailor can only get when he is carefree in the safety of a port after a long sea passage. By now we knew exactly why reaching a port has so much romance attached to it.

In the morning, immigration, health and boat measurement formalities were completed quickly and efficiently, unlike the slipshod Egyptian Suez Canal and its '*baksheesh*'.

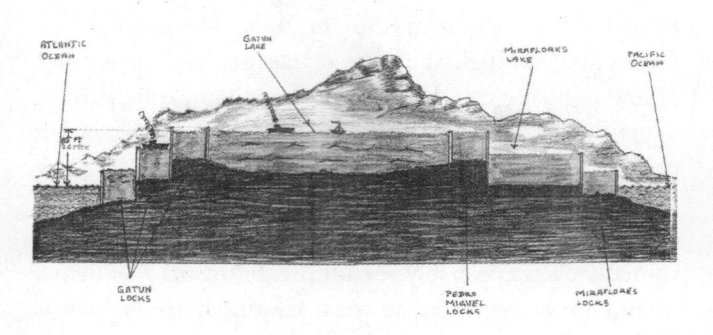

The Panama Canal

The Panama Canal connects the Atlantic and Pacific oceans and lies between North America and South America. The canal extends from the Caribbean region in the mid-Atlantic Ocean to the Gulf of Panama in the south Pacific Ocean. Before its construction, ships went from one ocean to the other around Cape Horn at the southernmost tip of South America. Cristobal on the Caribbean sea and Balboa on the Pacific Ocean are ports on either end of the canal. From the Atlantic Ocean vessels approach the three stage Gatun locks which lift ships up 85 feet (26 metres) by a system of lock gates, and ease them into the fresh-water Gatun Lakes. The lakes are the source of gravity-fed water through valves and culverts, to the locks chambers, raising their water level, thus raising the ship in the lock chamber. Water is in turn gravity-fed from the higher to lower locks, and finally drained into the oceans. After sailing to the Pacific-end of the Gatun Lakes, we reach the single stage Pedro Miguel Locks. Gravity drains the water to the lower lock, the ship is lowered here by 31 feet (9.5 metres) and we enter the Miraflores Lake. At the far end of the Miraflores Lake are the two stage Miraflores locks, which similarly lower the ships by 54 feet (16.5 metres) bringing them at the level of the Pacific Ocean. The canal is about 50 nautical miles long and is negotiated by ships under their own propulsion. Electric locomotives moving on geared tracks on either side wall of the locks guide the ships in and out of the lock gates.

The canal itself is truly a wonder of human perseverance. Its chequered history reads like a suspense novel. Built at the cost of over twenty thousand human lives and untold millions of dollars, it infuses every Indian who traverses it with an overwhelming sense of pride since a large number of those who constructed the canal, many of whom lost their lives in the process, as much to malaria as to blasting and accidents, were Indians. We paid our respects to them as *Trishna* entered the first of the three Gatun Locks, tied up alongside a tug which was also negotiating the Canal, and was raised to the next Gatun Lock. Three such locks and *Trishna* had been raised 85 feet (26 metres) above the mean Atlantic sea level. An atmosphere of efficient management prevailed. The big ships motored along from one lock to the other guided by eight electric 'mule' locomotives each, two each on port and starboard side at the bows, and an equal number at the stern, running along the walls of the locks on geared rails.

Entering a lock to be raised by 85 feet at the Atlantic end of the Panama Canal, later to be lowered into the Pacific Ocean.

Soon we were 85 feet above sea level and steaming down the Gatun Lake—the largest man-made lake in the world. We found ourselves weaving in and out of pretty wooded islands protected by the World Wildlife Fund. No one was allowed to step ashore, our pilot cautioned. Taking a pilot on board is mandatory while negotiating the Panama Canal. It was about 50 miles of motoring through the well-marked passages in the lake before the descent into the Pacific. The motoring itself was to take over twelve hours, the complete transition taking the better part of twenty-four hours.

After a routine change of pilot, and a two-hour wait to allow for down traffic, we began the descent through the Pedro Miguel Locks, and the two Miraflores locks. Finally, *Trishna* was back at sea level—this time in the Pacific Ocean. In another thirty minutes, we passed beneath the gigantic Bridge of the Americas that connects North and South America, and anchored at the Balboa Yacht Club. We were about halfway around the world, having covered over 13,000 miles in just over five months.

The system of crew change ensured that every few months, there was a new face on board. For the four of us sailing all the way around the world, a crew change was an event to look forward to. The new man always lifted our spirits, and removed the staleness which tended to set in during voyage.

We had been eagerly waiting for Tipsy who was replacing AP, and he didn't disappoint us. He brought lots of personal mail and many packets of homemade sweets. He had also brought a set of spare joints for my artificial limb, sent by Colonel Sushil Jain of Pune. These were to prove really useful later. At 45, Tipsy was the oldest member of the crew. There was never a time through good weather or bad that Tipsy did not come forward for a task, however big or small. Gifted with an unending stock of anecdotes, songs and jokes, he delighted the rest of us no end.

AP, who was leaving us, had been an exceptionally useful member of the team. A reputed international dinghy sailor, he is also an intellectual. For me, as for the others, he had been a dear and sensitive friend, and I was to miss him sorely.

My diary entry from that day reads: 'Said a simple bye to AP. He has been a buddy'.

Trishna had sailed over 20,000 miles now, and it was essential to dry out the percolating sea water from the fibre glass hull by shoring her up and out of the water for around a month. Water can percolate into the fibreglass hull by the osmotic process, and if not dried out of the over fifteen-year old hull, could slowly begin to break down the cell structure of the material by a chemical process, finally destroying it and reducing it to powder. Thankfully the chemical process is a slow one taking several years. But structural weakening continues with sea water trapped in the cells of the fibreglass. Since we did not have much time, we decided to shore her up for three weeks instead of a month, and to use this time to carry out a thorough overhaul of all fittings and instruments. We reckoned that having sailed almost half way across the world, with rested bodies and minds and an overhauled boat, we would be able to complete the second half of our voyage successfully. In many ways a half-way mark can be a threshold of sorts.

Trishna was hoisted out with help from the US naval base. A quick inspection showed the hull and the spars to be sound. The various jobs were sorted in the following days. Sails were spread out, washed, dried, inspected, repaired and stowed. So it went with sheets and cordage, rigging, fittings, water tanks, food bins, toilet, engine, electrics, radio, navigation equipment and safety gear. Our families also chose this halfway point to visit us. Shekhar's father flew in from Varanasi. Asha teamed up with Bharti's wife Manju, and they flew in together. There were happy reunions. It did a lot of good to our tired minds, and eased our tensions. A few days together, then back they went.

Trishna was fumigated and anti-fouled before being lowered back into the sea. The long-range high frequency (HF) radio, out of action since the storm at the Cape of Good Hope, was also fixed.

The time had come to move on. After all, half the globe still remained to be sailed, and on 5 April 1986, we sailed out of Balboa and into the Pacific Ocean.

CHAPTER 12

THE MIGHTIEST OCEAN ON EARTH—THE PACIFIC

The Sail to Auckland

In the hope that it would be gentle towards seafarers, Ferdinand Magellan, the Portuguese explorer who led the first expedition ever to circumnavigate the earth, had named the vast body of water he saw before him 'Mer Pacifique'. He probably never suspected that it was the largest and mightiest ocean on earth. And as we set sail into the Pacific, we hoped fervently that Magellan's wish for the ocean would come true for us. *Trishna* sailed out of the Gulf of Panama on 5 April 1986, heading for the Galapagos Archipelago just under a thousand miles away.

The retired Chief of the Indian Navy, the legendary Admiral 'Ronnie' (RL) Pereira wrote in his letter to me, dated 18 March 1986:

The sea is a great mistress; she is really a magnificent lady of great stature, but as I have found out, you must treat her with enormous respect; for she is inclined, if you do not do so, to suddenly smack you with a back hander—if ever you get too familiar with her—which can be quite disastrous.

I was once caught in a cyclone while running between Maldives and Port Blair—a very small bit of ocean to you, but it taught me so much of life. I realized so vividly what a despicable and inconsequential human being I was—and indeed all of us were. It made me realize the enormity, and ultimately the kindness and goodness of God, who was merely giving us a lesson, and putting us back in the correct slot, with a small reminder that there is something much bigger, wiser and better than us human beings, and that we owe everything to a greater being above us.

You must now be crossing the Pacific, and that must be your greatest hurdle, for that ocean can be imperious and very unrelenting. It is quite an uncharitable bit of water, but I am quite sure the whole world will be watching you and praying for you, and you *must* come through...

...about Asha): Probably she will, as will all other wives who may be so involved, circumnavigate the world ten times, while you only do it once! A serviceman's wife is really the greatest one could wish for.

For the first four days and nights, we inched ahead on windless, glassy seas. With the slightest sign of a breeze, the large and extremely light 'drifter' sail, made especially for light winds, would be hoisted. But the ghost-like passing whiff would soon die down, and *Trishna* would settle down to the rhythmic flogging of the rig and sails as she rocked with the omnipresent gentle swell. The drifter would be pulled down so as not to damage it. The main sail was kept aloft to reduce the rhythmic and irritable rocking, which causes damage to rig and sail by beating it about.

We noticed a peculiar phenomenon on two successive nights. A rustling noise—much like breeze blowing through dry leaves—would approach the boat from astern. Then the rippling sea would overtake us *without* the expected breeze coming with it, and then everything would be still again. This would happen every few hours, lasting for about half an hour each time.

Letter to Asha:

9 April 1986
9 p.m., ship's time
About 2 deg 30 min N, 80 deg 30 min W
Approx 580 NM from Galapagos Islands

We sailed out of the US Naval base, Panama to the Balboa Yacht Club, where the gracious Mrs SJ Singh, wife of our Ambassador, embassy staff, families, and other prominent Indians had gathered to wish us goodbye. SJ Singh is away to Nicaragua. We had earlier taken on water, food, etc. and set sail at about 1400 hrs on 5 April, into the open Pacific Ocean.

We headed south—sailing a 180° course—for three days. Winds were very light, and in the past two days, we have moved only about 50 miles. These areas—5 degrees North to 5 degrees South of the Equator—are called 'doldrums', because when the earliest adventurers and seafarers sailed out in search of the 'Indies'—meaning India—for its riches, they often got stuck here in depressing conditions with no winds.

But *Trishna* is a modern boat, and moves even with very light breeze. Also, we have food and water for now!

Today, the winds came up, and we are moving well. We hope to be in the Galapagos group of islands in six to ten days.

Galapagos Islands are known for the Charles Darwin Institute and the Research Station on Santa Cruz Island, which studies the extremely varied wildlife on the islands, not seen anywhere else. They say that, after a thirty or thirty-two-day visit to the islands, Charles Darwin propounded his now famous Theory of Evolution.

At last, a steady breeze sprang up on the fifth day, and we got going again. It began to get a little cooler as we moved south, and crossed the Equator for the third time on 14 of April 1986.

Diary entry (undated):

The stump is badly chaffed, so I stood on watch without the limb.

Puerto Ayora

After obtaining the mandatory permission from San Cristobal Island, we reached the principal island of Santa Cruz on 17 April, where the all-in-all of the Puerto Ayora, Lieutenant Deodoro Ruales of the Ecuadorian navy, welcomed us. Service traditions the world over are similar, and we are thankful for the small courtesies received. Mrs Ruales and their two small children were amicable conversationalists, despite the language barrier.

'Thank God I have boys! Girls are good only for sailors!' she managed in heavily accented English. We were halfway around the world, and yet the social problems appeared to be the same!

Diary entry:

18 April 1986
Santa Cruz Island, Galapagos group,
'Bahia Academy' (Academy Bay)

Calls home are routed through Guayaquil, Ecuador, to India. Ecuador is the parent country of these Islands, and derives its name from 'Equator', which is Ecuador in Spanish.

Tipsy got hold of a motor launch on charter (hire), for 30,000 sucres per day, including meals! (10 sucres = one rupee). So we are touring the Islands of Galapagos in style!

The flora and fauna here are not found anywhere else in the world. Protected by law, no one is allowed to do anything to upset or scare the animals. The first impact of seeing so many sea lions at close quarters frisking fearlessly about the beaches in total disregard of our proximity was enchanting. Here is one place on earth where animals are not persecuted by man, and are totally without fear of him.

Galapagos Islands are a natural preserve, and have been declared 'Protected Islands' by the Ecuadorian government as well as UNESCO. Being washed by various ocean currents, they have an ecology which is unique in the world. The climate is pleasant all year round, although they are virtually on the Equator. The Islands were discovered by de Berlanga, a Spanish Bishop of Panama, when his ship is said to have drifted westwards while he was sailing to Peru, without any wind for several days. Because of heavy mist and fog, as well as strong currents, it was difficult for seafarers to successfully navigate to the islands. This resulted in the building up of mythical stories, and for a long time these islands were called mysterious or bewitched islands.

Whalers and pirates alike hunted the giant Galapagos tortoises indiscriminately for food, since they were a source of fresh meat needed on a long voyage. These tortoises are often four to five feet in diameter. Even sea turtles and fur seals were likewise mercilessly hunted, many of the species becoming extinct in the process. Some are now on protected islands where no one is allowed to go.

Charles Darwin visited here on his ship, the *HMS Beagle*. His five weeks' study of the flora and fauna as well as the geology here, impressed him greatly. He found differences in the same species of animals and birds that had evolved through centuries, but on different islands. For example, he noticed that on the greener islands, turtles had short legs and necks; on the scruffy, less green islands, turtles had longer legs and necks needed to reach out higher for food. He later went on to propound the now famous 'Theory of the Evolution of Species'.

Two days flew past as we explored these enchanting islands. It was really marvellous to be among exquisite and rare animals and birds totally unafraid of man.

No one here had seen a Sikh with a turban before, and Tipsy was soon nicknamed Ali Baba. One man actually asked him if he was a magician! After two days, preparations began for our 3,000-mile voyage to the Marquesas Islands. Carlos, the driver of a pick-up van kindly loaned to us by Lieutenant Ruales, drove us down to fetch water from a stream. We nicknamed him Monte Carlos for his daredevil approach to driving—much like a Monte Carlo rally driver!

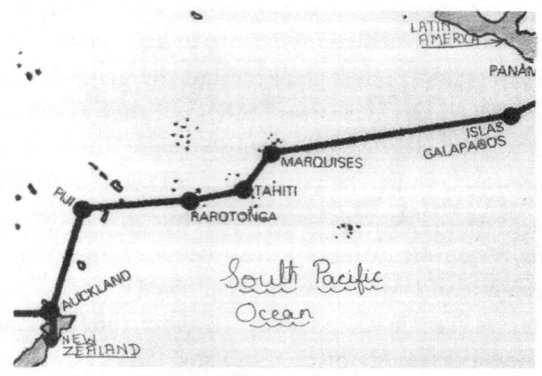

Galapagos Islands to Auckland

Bidding farewell to Ruales and Carlos, we sailed out of Puerto Ayora on 23 April 1986, and settled on a west-by-southwest course for French Polynesia.

This 3,000-mile sail went quickly. As we went further south, our progress became faster. Good south-easterly winds helped by the strong south equatorial currents, often flowing at two knots, made our passage very fast indeed.

Although it was getting cooler at night, the days were still clammy below decks, and my limb was almost always hot. Pools of sweat collected in the bowl-like lower portion of the socket. I had to clean it out regularly. Also, the steel joints had rusted through, being ordinary steel and not stainless steel which is unaffected by corrosive action of sea water; this was a constant source of worry.

We covered 140 miles each on the first two days. On 25 April 1986, *Trishna* actually completed 50 per cent of its circumnavigation; we were exactly halfway around the globe from Mumbai. From this point on we were headed back home, and not away from it.

Our route was so predictable on this leg that skipper began to suffer from insomnia. So he took on one watch-keeping shift every afternoon. This gave one of us an additional four hours off every day.

To pass time, everyone began reading books and the Indian periodicals we had picked up earlier. *India Today* was very popular, though we jestfully called it 'India Yesterday'. We also constantly listened to radio news, since we had by now begun to catch All India Radio. It was good to feel connected with what was happening back home.

A bucket full of seawater thrown over oneself was the best way to keep reasonably clean and cool. We could not use soap since it does not lather with seawater, instead it creates a gummy, sticky mess.

Diary entry:

8 May1986
6 deg S, 123 deg W

Sailing fast and peaceful! About halfway across the mighty Pacific Ocean.

Nuku Hiva is about 750 NM ahead. Heard a full news item of AIR on radio today. Also pushed the ship's time back by an hour. We are now nine and a half hours ahead of IST—well into our second half of the globe now!

I am on mother watch. Made *upma* for lunch, *aloo-mutter* with mushrooms, and rice for dinner; tinned fruit with condensed milk after dinner. For breakfast, we had oatmeal cereal, boiled eggs, and a glass of juice—I think the eggs are going bad, they are now fifteen or sixteen days old.

It is hot. Cotton light shorts—synthetics are very uncomfortable. Stump is blistered. May take a week to heal. Not interfering with my boat work or safety, so nothing to worry about. Sailing is peaceful, boat not heeling more than 5 degrees or so, so it is good this has happened now!

Sometimes a fatalistic weakness comes on, only making me go into self-pity—very dangerous for mental health. Must remain dynamic in thought. Somehow must finish the voyage successfully. In many ways, this voyage is a pilgrimage—teaching me a lot of things about myself, and about reason—and life. Some questions get answers, then many more questions appear. What craziness is this? Why am I doing this? But then it passes, and a sense of purpose returns. After all it is not too long now—six or seven months.

A brief thunderstorm once in a while would give us a freshwater shower on the deck, and allow us to collect rainwater to augment our stock of drinking water. Of course, we had to be ever vigilant. One cannot ever fully relax at sea.

Landfall for a small yacht at sea is a very special and very personal occasion—especially after a long 3,000 mile passage. One gets charged with a mixture of emotions and feelings as one approaches land. At the wheel, one tends to stare out towards the direction of land, hoping to be the first to sight it.

Taiohae Bay

After the twenty-day sail, our second-longest and one of the fastest (averaging over 150 nautical miles a day), we sighted the island of Valuka. We made it into Nuku Hiva, 54 miles further west, just after dusk on 13 May. It was 8 p.m., and the small town was asleep. Soon, so were we, after dropping anchor in the picturesque Taiohae Bay.

In the morning, we got a clear view of the glorious harbour, with high green hills in a semi-circular arch in the background. The bay was created after part of a volcanic crater collapsed and was filled up with sea water. There was a jetty (for ferries), and some fishing boats and motor launches were anchored in the bay. There was a solitary waterfront road, and a few red-roof huts along it. First, a good bath, then a hot lunch ashore, followed by more restful sleep.

The Maori culture was to be with us from here all the way up to New Zealand. Everywhere—in public buildings, houses, shops—there were statues in wood and stone of the Maori God Tiki. We were welcomed at the local school in the traditional fashion: crowns of Tiare Tahiti, the local flower, were placed on our heads. The people were so friendly that it was hard to believe they had been cannibals till not so long ago. The carved beheading stones and axes served as reminders.

The now defunct Taiohae Bay Yacht Club is next to Morris' Chandlery. Monsieur Morris was probably as old as the yacht club itself. He is a kindly, wrinkled, toothless soul with his glasses hanging around his neck by a string. His stories of the time when he was a gunner in the Allied air force during the World War II were as soulful as the gentle Taiohae Bay breeze and the lapping of the waves across the road from his store. The islands are, quite literally, the lands of plenty, with all types of tropical fruit strewn about all over the green island's countryside—there for the picking.

There is such abundance that no one has to work hard to make a living. But since modern attractions like alcohol, autos, motorbikes, music, electronic gadgets are now readily available, young men have begun to get ensnared in the material world.

For our onward voyage, we simply went into the woods and picked our requirement of guavas, bananas, lemons, pamplemousse (grapefruit), etc.

After motoring past the other boats at anchorage and waving our goodbyes, *Trishna* sailed out of Taiohae Bay as the sun began to fall behind the hills on 17 May. A course was set to pass north of the Tuomoto group of islands before approaching Tahiti from the north.

Good progress was made on the first two days, after which we got well and truly becalmed. The sea was a glassy expanse, and we covered barely 120 miles a day, and that was mostly due to the prevailing westerly drifts.

The windless conditions were to last for almost six days. The mirror-like seas reflected the sun's rays straight into our eyes. It was hot and sticky all the time. Sleep now consisted of tossing and turning in narrow, hot, and sweaty bunks. Tropical fruits and fresh lime were consumed in large quantities. The boat rocked incessantly in the swell, causing the rig to knock about with an irritable rhythmic orchestration as ropes, blocks, and sails knocked about with mast and boom. The exhaust pipe of the engine perished, so smoke leaked into the cabin when the engine was run every day for charging the batteries. During this time, all of us had to come up on the deck or risk choking on the vile exhaust while suffering the racket kicked up by the diesel engine.

Fishing was seriously attempted out of sheer boredom, and after many luckless hours, regretfully given up. Stargazing became a popular pastime on night watch, and Shekhar would insist that the smudge he had spotted was Hailey's comet.

'Want a bet?' he said, his voice full of challenge.

But, of course, there was no way to confirm.

The skipper deviated from his normal policy, and allowed us no less than three 'happy hours' during which we each had a few drops of the French wine kindly gifted to us by Monsieur Jean Jean, the French Administrator of the Marquesas Islands, when he along with his gracious lady, had come aboard to pay us a visit.

I had blistered my stump badly, but since I was able to attend to my duties *without* the limb during this peaceful passage-making, the blisters got a chance to heal.

Frustrated by the lack of progress, we motored for five hours on the 26th. It dispelled part of the frustration by making us feel we were moving, however little, though in reality we exhausted some of our limited stock of diesel and added merely 15 or 20 miles to our progress, And then, the spell broke; the winds sprang up accompanied by a thundershower, and we were tearing ahead towards Tahiti at a fast seven knots under the clear blue skies, and in deep blue seas.

Papeete

It was still blowing the next morning. We knew we should be only 30 miles from Papeete, but we could not see the beautiful island. We approached Tahiti in gales of over 35 knots under a dense cloud cover, with visibility less than two miles. It finally cleared when we were barely five miles away. Papeete Radio answered us on our VHF radio, and a launch came out to meet us. A French naval officer boarded us, and took us to a berth at the naval jetty. Soon, a higher ranking officer came along to greet us, and introductions and good wishes were exchanged in a mixture of English, French and gesticulation —diplomacy was being practiced by simple soldiers.

The beautiful island is surrounded by a natural coral barrier reef, with clear blue water between the reef and the island. Fishing vessels were all around: these included the traditional dug-out boats called pirogues, with their outriggers connected by bent cane, moving fast and straight under power with modern outboard motors, as well as the fast, sleek, motorboat-type fishing launches. Pleasant, healthy, tanned Tahitians manned the boats.

Although a few Pacific islands remain untouched today, most are nothing but commercial tourist resorts, right off the drawing boards of some firm in America or Europe.

Their innocent, heavenly aura vanished long ago, along with their wealth of flora and fauna.

But as far as we were concerned, we were relieved that all modern engineering facilities existed in Papeete since *Trishna* needed a lot of fixing.

The alternator and the toilet pumps needed mending; the galley sink pipe had broken; foot pumps for water to the galley sink had broken; and there were several other repair and maintenance jobs. The French Navy's workshop offered us all the help. They even gave us rooms to stay in their officers' quarters.

The limb I was using had helped me sail over two-thirds of the way around the world so far. The corrosive action of the acidic saline sea had been slowly eating away at the metallic knee joint for almost two years—right through the sail training in UK, the sail to India, and now from Mumbai all the way up to mid-Pacific Ocean. Tired of carrying its burden, having performed a job it was not designed for, the Old Faithful broke into two clean pieces one day. I momentarily panicked as it buckled under me unexpectedly. But on inspection, sheer relief flooded me as the damage could be fixed by welding and then riveting the old joint in place. I had to fight back the panic of 'what if it can't be fixed?' Cross the bridge when you come to it; better still, avoid visualizing bridges until you get to them!

'It will probably hold,' I thought.

The French Naval workshop refused at first. 'You should go to the hospital,' they said. 'This is a specialist's job.' But on my persistence, they agreed to help.

Carrying the Old Faithful to the French Naval workshop in Tahiti.

Diary entry:

> 2 June 1987, Tahiti, French Polynesia

On the 30th, my poor artificial limb, after so much of hard work, finally broke. I guess it is not designed for this kind of use. I have been on my faithful crutches for the past two days, and am going to repair it today.

> Yesterday we went to an island called Moorea to see the typical Tahitian 'Tamure' dance, and also drove round the island.

The Tahitian phrase *'ai ta peyapeya'* caught everyone's imagination, and began to be commonly used. It is their equivalent of 'no problem'.

So, with the limb joint now welded and fitted, *Trishna* sailed from Tahiti. We decided to visit nearby Bora Bora to see an island known to be less touristy then.

Bora Bora

Bora Bora was relatively untouched by the modern world. Our two-day halt there enriched our lives immeasurably as the Tahitian family of Philippe and Carmine Estall literally adopted us, and wouldn't leave our side for a moment. Philippe's sister, Turia Densat and her family, also joined in playing family to Indian sailors so far from home. Most of them could not speak much English, and we knew no Maori or French, yet we managed to converse. Philippe had an infectious laugh—his face wrinkled all over with creases of humour as he laughed about anything and everything. It was clearly the face of a man who laughed a lot! Thanks to our new friends, we did not miss India much for a while, and felt at home.

Soon it was time to leave. The Estalls and Densats came to see us off, along with their one year old, Jim. Then an hour long ceremony of saying farewell began. Kim and Turia had brought more bunches of bananas, coconuts and pineapple to add to Philippe's presents. Many locals said they had never in their lives seen such a send-off to a yacht. Young Marjorie Densat garlanded us with shell necklaces, and we cast off with heavy hearts. Our hosts were so genuinely affectionate that indescribable feelings of nostalgia and wistful sadness overwhelmed me. Indeed, I was so moved that I thought if another Captain Bligh[1] were to sail to

---

[1] In 1787, *HMS Bounty* left England for Tahiti in the South Pacific to collect breadfruit saplings to transport to the West Indies where it was to serve as food for slaves on the sugar plantations. Breadfruit was cheap to produce and grew throughout the year. After a ten-month journey, *Bounty* arrived in Tahiti and remained there for more than five months. According to accounts, the sailors were attracted to the 'idyllic' life and sexual opportunities afforded on the Pacific island of Tahiti, revelling in the comfortable climate, lush surroundings, and the famous hospitality of the Tahitians. Fletcher Christian, the aristocratic first mate, fell in love with a Tahitian woman named Mauatua. Three weeks into the return journey from Tahiti to the West Indies, Christian and his fellow mutineers seized the ship. Bligh and eighteen of his loyal supporters were set adrift in a small 23 feet (7 metre) long open boat in the middle of the Pacific, apparently handed the equivalent of a death sentence. The mutineers then variously settled on Tahiti and Pitcairn Island, the latter being probably the remotest place on earth, and not yet accurately charted. In an extraordinary feat of seamanship, Bligh navigated the open boat on a forty-seven-day, over-3,600 nautical miles voyage to Timor in the then Dutch East Indies, without a compass, navigation equipment or charts. He returned to England, reported the mutiny to the Admiralty in 1790, more than two years later, and soon sailed back to Tahiti, from where he successfully transported breadfruit trees to the West Indies. The British government dispatched *HMS Pandora* to capture the mutineers. Sixteen were arrested within two weeks. On her way back, *Pandora* was wrecked on the Great Barrier Reef with the loss of thirty-five lives which included four mutineers. The ten surviving prisoners were eventually repatriated

these islands again, he too would be abandoned by his crew in the face of so much hospitality. The simplicity, openness, sensitivity and self-confidence of the people there is really quite a heady cocktail.

We had missed two mail bags, at Tahiti as well as at Bora Bora.

As she passed the outer ring of reefs, and sailed through the extremely narrow entrance, *Trishna* drew further and further away from this dream world at a good six knots.

These Pacific Islands and their people are really beautiful. They seemed to be the closest to Paradise on earth.

Soon, we changed to a smaller head sail as strong head winds threatened to make us seasick. Tipsy was on the unenviable mother watch. He bravely fulfilled Shekhar's demand of a hot lunch before throwing up, and being thoroughly seasick himself. No one felt like eating much for some time.

That afternoon, while at the wheel, I saw a wave crest breaking just ahead, with a black log-like object falling

---

to England and tried in a naval court; three were hanged, four acquitted, and three pardoned. A British ship searched for Christian and the others but did not find them. In 1808, over twenty years after the mutiny, an American whaling vessel was drawn to Pitcairn by smoke from a cooking fire and discovered a community of children and women led by John Adams, the sole survivor of the original nine mutineers. According to Adams, after settling on Pitcairn the colonists had stripped and burned the *Bounty*. Internal strife and sickness had led to the death of Fletcher and all the men but Adams. It was decided to leave the settlement in peace. The mutiny has been commemorated in books and films, the most famous being *Mutiny on the Bounty*.

with it. I bore away sharply and shouted 'whales!' even as another huge whale jumped clear out of the water. So close was he that I could clearly see the well-like breathing hole called spiracle in his head. Two days later, I sighted another school of whales, some of them jumping clean out of the water. I barely managed a whisper 'O God!' as one huge creature appeared suspended in the air for a fraction of a second before plunging back, as if in slow motion, into the inky depths, leaving behind a huge circle of turquoise froth.

Tipsy now developed a cough and cold, and a little fever. He took no chances, and consumed tablets of all colours by the handful, simultaneously trying out antibiotics, homeopathy, the housewife's remedy of honey with ginger, as well as saline gargles.

We now discovered a stowaway on board. One bunch of bananas had a cricket in it, and he chirped away merrily every night. As we sailed towards Rarotonga in the Cook Islands, the weather and the sea remained rather bumpy. Gone were the sunny days of the tropics. There was even an occasional depressing drizzle which lasted for hours. The skies were overcast and gloomy most of the day.

Rarotonga

We reached Rarotonga in the Cook Islands, on 13 June 1987. Characteristically the winds died down to nothing during the last two days. Girdling the typical barrier reef are the twin harbours of Avarua and Avatiu, and we motored into the latter.

The port officials there took away our last banana bunch

(import of the plant being banned) and along with it, I presume, our cricket, for we no longer heard his merry serenade.

We splurged on a restaurant dinner at the Tamure Resort, where Tipsy offered to sing for the guests. He belted out a few oldie-goldie numbers à la Elvis Presley. The crowd went mad with delight—most of them had never seen a Sikh before and certainly not one doing a 'Presley'. Even the special Samoan group performing there was thrilled.

Cook Islands consist of about thirteen major and many more smaller islands, which were governed by New Zealand till quite recently. Rarotonga, the biggest island and main port city, is the seat of governance and administration, with a population of eight or nine thousand. There were four or five Indians, six or eight Fijian Indians or Sri Lankans, etc. with whom we could identify ethnically. Some of them were there on a WHO training programme. The people were very homely and hospitable, and a gentle and soothing atmosphere prevailed in the city.

In the Marquesas Islands, the lady mayor of one of the villages presented each of us with a *pareo*, the ethnic outfit commonly worn by the local women. It was basically a printed stretch of cloth, about 2½ metres by 2½ metres, a gift for our ladies back home. How we were to send it to them, or when, was a matter altogether unconsidered amidst their overwhelming goodwill.

A spin around the island is, as the locals say, 'a 45 kilometre drive at 45 kilometres an hour'. The kind Mr Sayyad Quayoom, senior administrator in the Ministry of Health of Fiji, then on a WHO assignment here, drove us around to prove it. There must have been close to twenty churches on our way since there seemed to be one every other kilometre. We were invited to a village church for the Sunday mass. Children sang hymns and read from the Bible. It was peaceful and soothing for us. The speaker, Mr Apanere Shaw who was also the Justice of Peace, reminded everyone that the Polynesians originate from mainland India, and they were hence our cousins.

'We, the braver ones, dared and reached here from India in canoes,' he added.

I couldn't help wonder if our having sailed down there from India the longer way across the globe might suggest to him that we were not entirely unworthy as his cousins!

The next day, many people came to see us off. As I lifted and took on board a 20-litre jar of water from the inflatable boat as a last minute replenishment of supplies before weighing anchor and sailing out, my limb broke again at the same spot. It was already 4.45 in the afternoon. The only workshop nearby would close at 5.30 p.m. A super quick re-welding job was managed with local goodwill and help as I took to my crutches again, temporarily.

We finally cast off, and slowly slipped out into the early night as our patient well-wishers ashore yelled farewells: '*Kia Orana Area Ra*' and '*Kia Manuia*'. Our foghorns blared our goodbyes, and our searchlight flashed a 'thank you' as they receded into the dark, past the cars of friends parked on the shore which began to blink their headlights in a wild, rhythmless disharmony.

Soon the island was lost in the dark and *Trishna* was back on her purposeful journey, alone and one with the sea in the Pacific night.

The good people of Rarotonga, as also earlier of Bora Bora, had loaded the boat with bunches of bananas, coconuts, and cartons of oranges and sweet lime, and we ate well till they lasted.

We headed north for a while before altering course to north by north east for Fiji. As per our original plans, we were not to call there, but its large Indian community was very keen to play host to the *Trishna*. We had made some fast passages and thus had some time to spare, and since it was not much of a detour, we agreed.

At these latitudes, about 20 degrees south, we were in a belt of unsettled weather. Winds were moody. Thunderstorms were frequent. Generally, we had hardly any time to trip the sails before a squall struck. It is a yachtsman's nightmare to get caught in a gale with all canvas up. Days as well as nights were often overcast. The fact that the moon was entering the third quarter made the nights longer and added to the gloom.

It began getting cold too. Storm suits and jerseys began to be worn regularly.

We blew a head sail when a sudden squall caught us with all our canvas up. The intermittent drizzle, occasional flashes of lightening, and claps of thunder—sometimes quite a loud clap!—added to the ominous conditions.

After more than a week of such inclement and nasty conditions, we had a series of clear bright days. But on these days winds dropped to nothing.

Out of frustration, I wrote on 26 June: 'This must surely be our slowest passage yet'.

During battery charging on one calm windless day, the engine had just stuttered to a halt due to an airlock in the diesel line when two whales came to inspect us from as close as 50 metres. All we could do was gape in a helpless, immobile, compelling spell, entirely entranced by the spectacle. Breaking the spell, the skipper ordered life jackets and safety gear on deck—just in case. He and I rushed below to clear the fuel line, and tried to start the engine. But before that could happen, our giant oglers—if whales could laugh then they certainly must have been laughing at our helplessness—had dived and disappeared.

A slight wind came up, and *Trishna* was under way. Two days later, we again sighted four whales about 300 metres away. They stayed with us for over half an hour.

On 25 June 1986, we crossed the International Date Line, thus re-entering the eastern world and losing a day, going instantly into the 26th! But we were still over 10,000 sea miles from Mumbai.

Diary entry:

26 June, 1986
About 300 NM from Fiji

The South Pacific seems to be full of whales. Saw two from Bora Bora to Raratonga in one day, and two more two days later; had to quickly change course to avoid collision. One jumped clean out of the water only 30 metres away!

> It was estimated at 35–40 feet long. Fantastic sight! From Raratonga till now, we have seen groups of two to four whales on three occasions. On the 22nd, two whales circled *Trishna* very close—awesome sight. Thankfully they did not attack or try to be playful. This evening too, saw four whales—the closest being 300–400 metres, and the furthest about half a mile away—they were located by their spouts.

My artificial knee joint, although welded, was still bent quite out of shape. One calm day, Navin and Bharti helped me get it back in shape, with one holding down the inert appendage firmly while two of us worked back the buckled steel joint, using the boats winch for leverage!

Suva, Fiji

Low pressure caught up with us again a few days before we reached Suva. Winds became squally, gusting to over 35 knots. Life on board became uncomfortable, particularly after the calm spell. Bharti's 25th birthday passed on the stormy 1 July. The next day, we approached Suva just after noon. We were thankful for the daylight, since the approach was treacherous, full of hidden reefs in three consecutive rings. We could see a Taiwanese wreck—its luckless captain had probably tried to enter by the most direct apparent route, instead of the safe-marked roundabout passage.

'*Nisa Bula*, welcome to Fiji', read the huge banner, and the Fijian police band struck up a welcome tune as we sailed up alongside the pier to be greeted by Thettalil Sreenivasan, our High Commissioner, and his wife, Mrs

Lekha Sreenivasan, who brought some lovely flowers for the boat. This warmth shown to us by everyone we met in Fiji made our visit there more than worthwhile.

Though Fiji's ethnic Indians are born and brought up there, they still consider themselves Indian rather than Fijian which, of course, causes no end of trouble.

Colonel SL Rabuka, OBE, MSc, AFAIM, Commander Royal Fijian Military Force, hosted us to tea. A year later, he was to dismiss the elected government, clamp military rule, and assume charge of the archipelago. With us, he was amiability incarnate, and his tea was excellent.

Four days later, we sailed out of Walu Bay, peeling away from a waving mass of friendly people. As always, the people seemed to be waving their hearts out till they receded to a blur and, once again, only the deep mysterious sea remained all around till wherever the eye could see.

For the first two days out of Fiji, progress was good. Then the wind died down to nothing for a day. Again it blew for two days—strong and uncomfortable south westerlies—and we sailed head on against 35-feet waves till the 13th. Then, the winds first moderated and steadied, swung south, and then southeast. The barometer was still climbing as we changed to the next bigger sail. This variable weather stayed till the 15th. The skies were generally overcast, giving us gloomy, chilly days and nights.

From the 16th, gales building to storm force lashed us for three days without respite. Winds were 40 knots and more. The seas were big and confused—not regular and long, but short and steep, with wave heights up to 35–40 feet. And all this time, it rained—a cold, grey, depressing drizzle. The short choppy seas and gusting winds increased the thumping and hammering of the hull by walls of sea water and, at noon of 16 July, the main sail parted at the seams with a loud rip. A furious sea smashed the boat hook lashed on top of the boat, and carried it away. We hoisted the spare main sail; but it, too, blew out in the violently gusting stormy winds, aided by the hammering choppy sea. Since the North Island of New Zealand was on our starboard side, and the storm would wreck us on the lee shore unless we made headway against the wind—or upwind—we hoisted the storm tri-sail, now seriously sensing the possibility of getting shipwrecked if we did not crawl upwind, thereby allowing the storm to drift us helplessly downwind, and eventually on to the rocks.

In the rough seas, all of us were flung about the boat—the toilet door catch broke when Shekhar slammed against it.

KS and Bharti took turns at mending one of the torn sails. It was tough work, having to put each stitch on the thick sail cloth, threading the needle through the earlier thread holes one by one in the dark, gloomy, buckling storm. They were also repeatedly seasick since any task on choppy seas that demands intense hand-eye coordination greatly increases nausea. But their persistence paid off, and the main sail was hoisted again, heavily reefed, on the 18th. Thankfully the stitches sustained, and *Trishna* held her own in the battle to remain upwind away from a lee-shore threatening a possible ignominious shipwreck. The storm abated only later that evening, after which *Trishna* was back again on a purposeful course under sail.

The weather cleared as we sailed past the various outlying

islands that stand guard to the east and north of Auckland. It was like sailing in heaven, weaving a path between the indescribably beautiful islands on that bright sunny winter morning. Over the radio we heard that a New Zealand yacht had lost her mast in the storm we had recently encountered, and had to be abandoned by her crew to save themselves. Luckily, a passing ship had rescued her crew. Thanking our stars that we'd weathered the storm without such extreme problems, we felt relaxed and cheerful.

So complacent were we that we almost got run over by a container ship in the dead of night. Coming up to relieve the port watch, we saw to our horror, a black steel monster barely a few hundred metres away, bearing down straight at us at full speed. The bright pin points of its red and green-port and starboard-sailing lights contrasted sharply with its dark form. Both the lights equally spaced out on each side of the dark hull form at night was a sure indication of us being directly in the ship's path. We were inching forward pathetically slowly, right across the huge ship's bows. It was already too late for us to take any avoiding action, and all we could now do was to hope that she would miss over-running us by some stroke of sheer providence. On came the ship, its engines pounding, its bow wave visible in the dark night as water piled up on its speeding bows. All we could do was shine our tiny searchlight desperately in the direction of the ship's bridge where the officer on watch should be, to attract his attention, and hope the Gods had not yet deserted us. Our luck held. Suddenly, the ship gave a hard starboard rudder, and veered sharply to the right, still turning in a huge curving path as it thundered past us barely metres away.

Someone on board had seen us just in time!

Badly shaken, we sailed towards the outer Auckland harbour in a chastened and sombre mood. Conversation died down to nothing, as each one turned inwards to thank the Lord for this providential escape from certain death. Having sailed over three quarters of the home, it would indeed have been an unfortunate and inglorious end.

New Zealand

Admiral OS Dawson, the former Indian Naval Chief, and presently our High Commissioner in New Zealand, was there on the jetty to welcome *Trishna* into port. We spied the beaming and waving Bhatta too on the jetty, as we landed after our fourteen-day sail. He was to replace Navin there.

We had sailed across the Pacific, and Ronnie's letter was waiting for me.

Extract from Ronnie's letter:

7 July 1986

> I should reckon that all of you will be able, or indeed, would have wrung out more seawater from your underwear than 99 per cent of the maritime community would have sailed over.

The athletic Bhatta, with his loud and frequent laughs and backslaps, was a welcome addition on board. Earlier, two persons were needed to heave anchor; now Bhatta alone was enough. He was also a good cook, though perhaps too partial to cooking fish. But then, he was from Kolkata where *machher-jhol-bhat* (fish curry with rice) is staple diet.

Unfortunately, the replacement limb Bhatta had brought with him for me did not fit, and created sores and blisters on my stump. So the battered one I was using, now welded and repaired several times, was repaired some more at Auckland and pressed into service yet again, much against the advice of the kind prosthetist who, upon seeing the battered and much repaired limb insisted, 'it has far outlived its life, you need a new one'. But limbs were expensive abroad, and I was not sure if I could afford one.

Trishna urgently needed new sails, having blown out both the main sails and a head sail, and Dave Giddens, a chubby and cheerful sail maker, came over and took measurements. He delivered good sails in record time.

Tidal variation was over three metres, so we tethered *Trishna* to a jetty, and when the waters receded, she beached herself. We quickly hosed down the underwater portion, and inspected it. Thankfully, she seemed in good shape.

I spent an afternoon with handicapped children at the Takapuna Grammar School at the neighbouring Wilson Home for crippled children. Unaware that there were several terminal cases amongst us, I was all optimism and gung ho about plugging on in life with gusto, and looking forward towards better days ahead. The stark realization of my faux pas dawned on me when someone mentioned the terminal cases *after* I had left the facility. I was left deeply distraught and embarrassed by the revelation. There is such little understanding of the ground realities that such children tackle all over the world and we do so little to alleviate their pain. I prayed to God for forgiveness for my entirely unintended but nevertheless colossal insensitivity.

With Naomi James, the solo circumnavigator, at the launch of the Kiwi Magic in Auckland.

The New Zealanders were launching their yachts, *Kiwi Magic* (also called the *KZ 7*) and the *Plastic Fantastic*, their challenger for the America's Cup race. The solo circumnavigator, Naomi James, was to launch the famous boat. Someone thought of inviting us too, and I took the opportunity to meet the enchanting yachtswoman in person. The thirty minutes or so spent with her left a lasting impression on my mind. If it was difficult to visualize her tall and stately figure fighting a horrendous storm alone at sea, the determination in her delicate yet firm face and steady blue eyes made it easier to understand the force in her. Yet, even she could not help breaking down with emotion as she knocked the champagne bottle on the bows of the *KZ 7* saying, 'May God bless her, and all who sail in her'. Just then, the band struck up the popular tune, 'Sailing Away'—first in Maori, and then in English.

Vani Rao flew in from India, and it was nice to see Vani and KS together. They looked so happy.

CHAPTER 13

THE TASMAN SEA AND THE SAIL FROM AUCKLAND TO DARWIN

From Auckland to Darwin

A sapper officer of the New Zealand Army brought the weather forecast for the coming week. The news wasn't good. Severe storms were raging all over the Tasman Sea. One ship, struck by sheet lightning, had been forced back to port in Australia. Part of Sydney had been flooded, and six lives had been lost. The depression was now moving eastwards towards New Zealand. This worried us, but we decided to stick to our schedule nonetheless.

A day later, we had rounded the northern tip of North Island and were heading for Sydney, a thousand nautical miles to our west, when the barometer began falling sharply. The deep cyclonic low pressure was on its way. Soon, it was on top of us, and the familiar storm routine began. Striking sails, changing to smaller sails in head winds of 25 and soon 35 knots, as the seas built up. As compared to the long trans-oceanic seas in an oceanic storm, the seas here were much shorter and far more choppy. They were hence much steeper, and dealt sledge-hammer blows on the fragile hull which seemed at times too severe for the boat to bear, not to mention the brutally weather-beaten and seasick crew handling the extreme cold of the southern latitudes for the first time.

And then, what I dreaded most, happened. My artificial limb snapped as I struggled for balance at the wheel. As the boat heeled over dangerously in the heavy seas, feelings of utter helplessness overwhelmed us. Why did this have to happen now?! As boat and crew battled it out, I crouched, frustrated and despairing, in a cold dark corner. This was the most dangerous condition to be in. Inactivity in severe cold leads to hallucination about deep warmth and comfort and an irresistible urge to lie down and slip into sweet slumber. But nothing could be more treacherous for if one gives in, deep hypothermia can set in, pushing the sailor towards a sweet, warm (cold), and drowsy end. I fought my demoniac desire to drift off aggressively.

This drama spanned two and a half days. The storm intensified to a furious head-on 50 knots, with steep 45-feet seas as we tried to make headway. We were cold, miserable and battered. Skipper had gone without sleep for more than sixty hours, and he looked pale and colourless, with his red, bleary eyes in deep black sockets. Finally, even he was near collapse when we decided to heave the boat to.[1] With everything tied down and secured, the wheel pulled hard over and lashed, *Trishna* was left to ride out the furious storm by herself.

❧ ☙

Our brave *Trishna* was riding out the storm hove-to with the barest of sail cloth up, the storm tri-sail back-winded by an opposed storm jib. This allowed the boat to face the vicious hammering as quietly as was possible, fighting the storm just enough so as to not slide with it on to a possible

---

[1] 'Heave to' means the boat is secured as best possible for riding out the storm, with the storm trysail and heavily reefed mains'l as well as rudder tied and lashed down so that the forces created by the wind and seas oppose each other, directionally steadying the boat as best possible, making no progress, drifting downwind all the time, but hopefully riding out the storm before one can resume control and upwind passage.

New Zealand lee shore. The crew was in storm suits, strapped to the boat with harness ropes, taking turns in pairs at keeping anchor watch, stretched to limits we did not know existed within us. We were striving hard to keep hypothermic terminal sleep at bay.

Boat lives, we live—we knew this savage truth about the southern oceans. Also, what any oceantrotting sea dog will tell you: good boats outlive good men.

As the storm raged I laboriously cut steel pieces from the spares I was carrying. I drilled holes using the hand-drill, and riveted them with a pop-rivet gun to the limb—steel blades and drill bits snapping as the boat thundered along on a wild ride in the storm. It was slow and tedious work, but at last I triumphantly stood on my own two feet.

As I straightened up, however, the rivets got warped, and the limb was again laid to waste, twisted at an odd angle. Oh the despair, the utter helplessness, the feeling of total defeat. But the human mind can really withstand a lot more than we can ever imagine and we emerge stronger each time. Renewed resolve overtook the threatening despondent helplessness and I returned to the basics! The rivets had obviously not been strong enough. This time around, I used stronger nuts and bolts. Meanwhile, the boat jumped and tossed, and drill bits and saw blades kept snapping and breaking. For a while, the nuts and bolts held, enabling me to stand every single watch of mine. But soon they too buckled under the levered strain.

I returned to the task once more through the haze of seasickness, cold and fatigue. This time, I also used ropes to lash the limb in such a way that the more it buckled, the more the correcting tension of the lashing increased. It finally held. I savoured this very meaningful, very personal victory far away from anywhere—I had beaten the Tasman Storm!

On the fifth day the fury abated. A fair amount of damage had been inflicted inside the boat. In addition, the canopy had been punched in by the force of the waves. Thank God, the hull appeared to be structurally sound.

On the first day after the storm, we made good progress towards Sydney, and soon were in radio contact. From our point of view, we couldn't be getting there fast enough. We finally sighted Sydney on 17 of August 1986, having been at sea for over fourteen days. My 32nd birthday had passed in the storms of the Tasman sea.

I still like to think of it as a providential (divine?) watershed in my earthly existence.

Sydney

For me, personally, Sydney meant freedom from the overpowering anxiety about the limb. There was never a better land sighting! A sense of relief took over as I literally limped into port.

Struggling for survival, and not being able to write my dairy for the past several days, I made the following entry as we sighted Sydney. It was a rather quiet and contemplative lot of roughed up sea-farers who sailed in.

Diary entry:

17 August 1986

The human mind is very malleable. Elation and depression are dependent on the mind's disposition, as also on the surrounding circumstances. Hope, all along, is possibly a major player—giving rise to a sense of elation when we perceive the end of the storm at hand, though we may still be in it, being tossed about and terribly seasick! And also, vice versa—giving rise to ominous apprehension at an approaching storm. Moments are fleeting, feelings ever transient. No sooner than a rough stormy day and night is over, hope with clear skies and bright sun peeps through. Gone is the gloom of being in the worst storm ever, along with its accompanying tensions and black apprehensions, its body-breaking and utterly exhausting moments. It is replaced by the sense of riding a new high. The spirit soars: serenity, the exultation of being one with Nature, of being on the crest of a wave. Moments are fleeting and, unless taken note of, get lost in the anonymity of the rich and cumulative experience as a whole.

If one looks back in search of moments of joy and elation, or of depression and being down under, moments that have crested or troughed for their pleasure or pain value, several of them come to mind.

The deep tingling pleasure, the unbound relief and the soaring of the spirit, of everything being just right, the timelessness of the moment experienced on the first sighting of land after weeks of struggling, of tense and wearying days and nights, filled with foreboding and apprehension, and the underlying sense of hope(!), of constantly glancing at the approaching horizon—the first sight of land is indeed a rich and sweet moment. The intensity so depends on the struggle itself. The harder the journey, the sweeter is the moment of its end. This is even more so when the landfall ahead marks, probably, the last of the predictably rough weather on our way home.

Two ships—one struck by sheet lightening—had to turn back to Sydney in the storm that flooded the city with rain, taking six lives. The storm crossed over tiny *Trishna*, struggling in the Tasman Sea, and moved on to New Zealand where storm warnings were issued. We rode out the storm hove-to, for over two and a half days, taking all the sound thrashing the storm belted out—ever vigilant, ever tense, ever wet, cold and weary, going about constantly securing the boat like zombies or ghosts, before the weather broke, and the sledgehammer pounding of the monstrous seas was replaced by a gentler but equally forceful push and thump of the omnipresent Tasman Sea Gales, following one after another, with gaps.

As the difficulty of the endeavour is complemented by the joy at the journey's end, the intensity of happiness and well- being is also complemented by the depth of the anxiety and dismay at its absence. My anxiety was greatest when, in the Tasman storm, my artificial limb (having been repaired at Papeete in the Society Islands by the French Navy, at Rarotonga in the Cook Islands by the Indian friends there, and at Auckland by the Artificial Limb Centre where a broken swivel knee-joint was replaced) broke clean in two during a pitch black stormy night while I was steering ship on watch. My distress could not ever have been greater! All kinds of thoughts flooded in: how would I sail to Sydney with the storm in full force? Action overtook despondency. The moment would brook nothing else.

Cutting out steel reinforcing plates, with help in turns from skipper Rao and the off-watch team, cutting hammering, drilling, fastening, using nuts and bolts, screws, rivets and string, etc., the limb was 'repaired'. But each time, the repair would last only a day or less, and the leverage offered by my body weight at the knee joint would undo it again and again, so that the process of repairing, cutting, binding, riveting and putting it on, and then using, breaking, repairing again, carried on daily for the next four days. All along, *Trishna* was being tossed about like an insignificant speck that we were, with the skipper exhausting himself to the point of collapse working with the watch on deck—and then the next watch on deck—and so on, for the next three or four days and nights, till he collapsed into a fitful two-hour nap. But only after *Trishna* was hove-to. And all along, I ensured that I stood every watch of mine—for this was no time for *Trishna* to be carrying passengers.

Two lulls and two storms later, we sighted land in the late hours of 16 August! The sweetness of the moment lingered with us as we made our way into the harbour, until we got to Sydney. What a relief! Now useless and beyond repair, my limb had, in its dying throes, managed to see me through till landfall. Oh! The relief was great indeed. Intoxicating and exulting moments!

We visualized all the creature comforts: the bath and scrub, the washing and cleaning, after a long passage with all the privations of being in a small craft. Oh, the wide open and steady bed—and clean sheets! Wholesome hot cooked food! And, restful, drugged, full night's sleep! But all of this was outweighed by the expected letters and news from home! The prospect of new lands and strange cultures awaiting us get compressed into those few moments of sheer joy at the end of a long and stormy passage, as one enters the safe, welcoming embrace of a friendly port.

But there was also the other side of the coin. Few things can be more miserable for the seafarer than depression, when the barometer falls, and plunges one's spirits with it. Gloom has to be consciously fought away all along. The sun hiding behind black cloud, makes night out of day, and the night even darker. The pounding and thrashing of the monstrous seas, often 50-feet high or more, in a 45 gusting to 60 knot storm in dull daylight was bad enough. At night, the pounding seemed to increase as attempts to manoeuvre *Trishna* in the dark by foreseeing and trying to ride over the waves, compounded by the loss of direction and orientation at times, were rewarded only by sledge hammer blows to the hull. One could be steering on the compass course, and yet feel one was going round and round, or crabbing to one side, by the action of the waves. And there were no stars in the black canopy of the sky to lend a sense of orientation.

One can barely eat in the rough sea; on top of that, one generally retches out more than what one ate in the first place. Wet, cold, weak and miserable, sometimes on the point of collapse, the knowledge of the seas and seamanship, a sound boat, hope and optimism, and a will to overcome are what finally steer sailors out of storms.

And so the endeavour continued.

Tipsy was to fly home from Sydney, and Surendra Mathur was to join us. We would miss Tipsy's infectious optimism and his incessant cocky chatter and humour. This was to be the final crew change till our return to India.

Sydney also marked the end of roughly three-quarters of our way around the world. After the Tasman Sea, not many areas of predictably stormy weather remained. Instead, the danger from reefs, shoals and shipping were to increase greatly on our passage towards Indonesia and the Malacca Straits, and onwards to the home waters of the Bay of Bengal.

Having approached Sydney late at night, we chose to lie outside the harbour with an anchored ship for company, till daybreak. Next morning, the sail to Rushcutters Bay and the Naval Jetty through the Sunday morning racing yachts, in the company of the yachts of the Australian Naval Sailing Association and the Australian Sappers who were escorting us in, was heavenly. The city unveiled its beauty to us slowly. The sight was all the more surreal because of what we had just passed through. The famous climber of Mt. Everest, Captain Mohan Singh Kohli, had generously made his house in Sydney available to us. It was time for washing, lounging, cleaning up, stretching out, reading and writing letters—that is, catching up in general on all that we had missed. It was a happy time.

Surendra Mathur looked more like a successful business manager than a soldier. Bespectacled and of medium height, he preferred to listen rather than speak, and was good company. He had learnt the essentials of amateur radio network operation and as a HAM (amateur radio) operator, he was to prove useful on board.

At the Appliances and Limb Centre, David Howell, the limb prosthetist, saw my broken limb in its patched up condition, smiled wryly, and confirmed that it would definitely have to be changed. I was only trying to save some money since I was not sure whether our health insurance with Lloyds of London would cover the cost of a new limb! After all, it was only a strap-on appendage, and even without it, my health was good. So was it at all a 'health insurance' issue? I had never bothered to inquire earlier.

'Does it come under health insurance, or automobile insurance?' I wondered bemusedly.

Any new limb takes time to feel comfortable. At first, small alterations have to be made to improve the fitting, depending on how the prosthesis rubs and chafes on the stump. David said he needed several days to finish fashioning a proper limb; but skipper said we could not wait for a few more days. So, after just four days of trial, we sailed, with the hope that I could fix any problem that may arise in case the limb gave trouble.

Letter to Asha:

> 26 August 1986
> The Limb Centre, Sydney

> Predictably, the worst weathers are now mostly over—unless God gives us a tough time. Some (isolated) rough patches are to be expected though.

Trishna left Sydney on a warm and sunny day, to a charming send off by relatives and friends, some accompanying us till the outer harbour in boats. One by one, these fell astern, the last being the Aussie Sapper's yacht, *Gun Runner*. Soon *Trishna* was alone once more, heading out to the familiar sea. A huge male sea lion was sun-bathing in our path, and we frightened him into gracefully diving away. Mathur took some time settling down to the motion of the boat as we sailed into the Tasman Sea again. Australia, with a population equal to Kolkata's, was to intrigue us for over 2,200 sailing miles more.

The first few days out of Sydney were stormy again, and we realized that we had not yet seen the last of the Tasman Sea. The new limb, not yet fitting properly, felt unfamiliar and odd. This upset my sense of balance, and along with the knotty feeling of tensed up stump muscles, it made me queasy. Both Bharti and I, on starboard watch, were seasick simultaneously. We leaned well over the guardrails, and retched out bile with Bharti still holding the wheel.

Once out of the Tasman Sea, the big seas reduced, and so did the opposing currents. Soon, much to our dismay, the winds dropped even further. On 1 September, Australian radio stations announced the first day of spring. At times, we'd move at 4–6 knots, and the currents would push us back by up to 4 knots. One night, we were actually pushed back by eight miles before the winds picked up, and we began making headway to Brisbane.

Letter to Asha:

> 2 September 1986
> 45 NM short of Brisbane

Happy days are here again! Warm sunshine, peaceful sailing, and an hour or two free in the daytime—so here I am writing to you from the sea again. The sun is moving South for the Southern spring followed by summer, as winter moves into the North. Yesterday, Australian radio announced the first day of spring. I have taken a spare pair of stainless steel knee joints, a folding walking stick, and a pair of hydraulic crutches—for my old age! Doesn't the thought of my old age frighten you?

Got a letter from Nobby Clarke—Squadron Leader (Retd.) DH Clarke, ex Royal Air Force. I may be the first physically handicapped person to sail around the world. He is the official Guinness Book recorder for sailing events.

Green Island

We rounded the northern tip of Morten Island, and turned west by south west to negotiate the intricate passage past various islands to the harbour. After a while, there was a relatively free passage past Green Island towards Manley and the Royal Yacht Squadron where we were headed. We were making leisurely passage on the morning of the 4th to pass south of Green Island. The area was charted as 'mud flats', and was probably not navigable in low tides—a fact which we found out about too late. Suddenly, we were jarred by several sickening, thudding jolts as the 6-feet-deep keel hit solid rock again and again. Skipper was on the wheel at the time, and he started the engine to pull *Trishna* out under power even as we all tried to heel the boat to one side to reduce the draught, and hopefully refloat the boat. But the fast ebbing tide was against us. *Trishna* was soon sitting firmly on the shoal, well and truly aground. Immediately, a new danger arose. As the ebbing waters receded further, *Trishna* began to lean over and sit on her side. She could rupture her bilge if she leaned and rested her ten-ton weight on a sharp rock.

A quick under-water investigation revealed that, fortunately, there wasn't any unusual boulder or big rock as she leaned well over. A few hours later, the tide reversed and, to our great relief, re-floated the boat without any apparent damage.

However, all this happened while the Sunday morning fleet sailed by in full view. The local press didn't spare us either. But let's just say, they could have been nastier. After sitting on the shoal for most of the day, by nightfall, we were tied up alongside the jetty at Manley, with over a thousand yachts for company.

The Australians have a yen for making everything larger than life. So, there is the Giant Matilda, the Big Cow, the Big Pineapple, Super Bee—all of these being motels, stores, or processing plants, built to the designated shapes, in awe inspiring gigantic sizes.

Air India's agent, Bob Farrington came along and inquired if we had any problems. The next day, he brought along t-shirts for everyone, with 'We Got Stuck on

Green Island' at the back to keep alive the memory of our inglorious grounding!

Trishna was hoisted aloft at the Royal Queensland Yacht Squadron, and had her underside inspected. Fortunately, no major damage was discovered. Two days of nonstop work on the boat—there is always some work to be done—and *Trishna* was fit to go around the world again!

On 9 September 1986, we sailed from Brisbane, and soon passed the yellow buoy marking the edge of our very own mud bank upon which we had 'rested' *Trishna* on our way in.

The Great Barrier Reef

Three days of sailing in feeble and variable winds took us past the North Reef Lighthouse on the 12th. We began our long and narrow passage between the Great Barrier Reef—the greatest structure ever made by any living being—and the mainland. We changed to a high cut foresail for an easier lookout for approaching ships. Sailing inside the Barrier affords protection from the huge Pacific waves. Also, the protection of a port is at hand all along, in case of a storm. If one has plenty of time, exploring these enchanting coral islands, particularly further north in warm tropical waters, can be an extraordinary experience. On the other hand, the highly restricted channel, with its heavy shipping and literally thousands of unlit islands and reefs, makes navigation a nightmare and a sharp lookout while sailing is essential to avoid ships and reefs alike. We were extremely grateful for our small magic box—the satellite navigation system.

Intricate navigation all along, constantly referring to charts, weaving in and out of dangerous reefs in a passage often just a mile or two wide, takes its toll on the nerves. Complacency can pose a big risk. Anything can happen at any time. Most yachtsmen take over a month to traverse the path we wanted to cover in less than fifteen days.

The night of the 13th gave all of us some anxious moments as we negotiated and passed Penrith Island. As *Trishna* tacked upwind in the narrow passage, a ship appeared to be coming towards us, just as two lights, obviously ships, were about to overtake us from astern, forcing us into a dangerous corner in the reef-infested waters. There are literally hundreds of sharp coral reefs just below the water surface, many unmarked by lights. Being constantly vigilant is the biggest challenge.

We wove in and out of various narrow passages, heading north, with entries in the ship's log reading: 'good progress', 'excellent going', and 'bright sunny day'. Sometimes now, nights became too warm for sleeping bags, and ordinary trousers were good enough. On night watch, though, weather jackets were still worn. In the daytime, it was t-shirts and shorts. *Trishna*, doing a hundred miles a day, sailed past the Whitsundays. The seventy-four islands of the Whitsunday Island group are mostly uninhabited national parks. Less than a dozen have resorts to suit all tastes. Amongst the islands were numerous safe anchorages. *Trishna* and her crew were on a mission and could scarce afford to check out the beautiful islands. We also passed by lighthouses with lovely names like Coppersmith Light and Cape Bowling Green Light, which was sighted early on the 16th. Various ships, and even a submarine, passed close by, under our sharp lookout to ensure that there was no collision in the narrow passage.

We made a brief halt for water and fresh supplies at Cairns, and sailed out on 22 September. The Great Barrier Reef has some of the world's richest coral, fish and shell life. So we went out to the outer reefs for an afternoon of the most amazing snorkelling. The entire reef is a Sea Life Protected Area, and is said to be the biggest structure made in the world by any form of living beings—in this case, the polyps.

Trishna was becalmed the whole day, and the better part of another, before winds came up again on the 23rd. They stayed fresh and favourable all the way up to Cape York, the northern tip of Australia.

Letter to Asha:

21 September 1986, Cairns

I was hoping to hear Aditi's voice too on the phone yesterday—I guess she first wants to find out who or what 'Papa' is before she can say 'Hello Papa'. Have to be prepared for a big psychological impact on the children when I reach: unruly beard and limp. I don't want to give them psychological trauma. I hope to come back a better man than (I was when) I left. Older? Yes. But wiser? You won't believe it if I say—all your troubles are going to be over! Or will they begin again with me back?

After dusk on 24 September, we sailed through an extremely narrow part of the channel. It was less than a mile wide.

Lights from fishing trawlers blinked all round us. We made small talk with one boat on the VHF radio.

'Any fish?'

'Oh, only one big mackerel today!'

Mathur and I were on watch as we saw a ship's lights approaching, and observed it closely as she came through the narrow channel towards us. She approached so as to pass close by on our port side, as is the convention. But, she had left almost no room between her and the coral reef marked on the chart to our starboard side. We waited. Were she to hold her course, she would pass dangerously close to us. With mounting anxiety and disbelief, we watched as she kept coming towards us, refusing to respond on the radio. She was merely a few hundred metres away, and we were bang in her path. Skipper started the auxiliary engine; at the wheel, I threw the lever in high revolutions forward. Even as the boat gathered way, getting closer to the already close reefs, Mathur flashed the searchlight frantically at the bridge of the dark approaching silhouette. The huge hulk responded by a quick alteration of course, just sufficient to avoid us.

We were badly shaken.

Our friend, the fisherman, called us on the radio anxiously in the dark even as the wash of the ship hit us. 'Indian yacht *Trishna*, are you OK?'

The danger had passed and, as the ship receded astern, we resumed the passage up-channel.

Thursday Island

We rounded Cape York, leaving the Coral Sea and entering

the Arafura Sea on 26 September 1986. In the revealing daylight, *Trishna* sailed the last miles to the anchorage off the waterfront on Thursday Island. Tony, a local fishing lad, saved us the effort of rowing ashore in our dinghy in the strong currents by giving us a free ride in his motor launch, and, by 10.30 in the forenoon hours, we were ashore.

The local people made a living by keeping shops or hotels for the touring agents of various companies that import everything from the mainland. Fishing and hunting on the islands, many of them uninhabited, were the traditional occupations. Some pearl diving was still done. A general atmosphere of siesta prevailed. I suppose it is foolish to work when there is no need to.

If you asked anyone on the island, 'What is there for a visitor to see or do here?', the answer is always: 'We have a few pubs'.

'Are pubs more active on weekends?'

'No mate (pronounced *maiit* with the typical Aussie drawl), they are active all days of the week, aye.' This last bit is said in a sing song manner, similar to 'man' or 'men' used as suffixes to sentences in Jamaica. All work stops at 6 p.m., and the pubs were soon full. Loud talking, table thumping, and drunks staggering back home, were a regular sight.

༄ ༄

After the settlers from the western world got tired of massacring the aborigines, they spared no pain to protect and preserve what was left of them. Millions are now spent on their upliftment. This may actually be the undoing of the aborigines as it robs them of their capacity to be self-reliant. With only an oral history and no script, aboriginal culture is fast fading in the face of modernization, and these unfortunate people are trapped in an identity warp.

It was warm as we heaved our two anchors and sailed out of Kennedy Harbour. The sharp outline of compact Booby Island, the last of the Torres Straits Islands, with its prominent radio mast and lighthouse, was abaft the port beam by dusk. Its three-in-fifteen seconds flash stayed with us for a while before receding, and we began our passage across the Gulf of Carpentaria which is so huge that its two ends were, at one time, thought to be part of different land masses.

In following gentle winds, we boomed out our biggest sails in a flat sea. Currents were favourable too, as was the forecast for the week. Things couldn't be better. Soon, it was to get hot and sticky below decks, and rather uncomfortable in direct sunlight. The protective awning was again required on the cockpit. The gentle sailing continued for the first four to five days, with winds dropping at times. However, the currents ensured that we made over a hundred miles each day. Energies once more began to be diverted to reading, star-gazing and cooking.

Bhatta revealed that he had brought a fishing line and spoon from the local fishermen in Thursday Island, and the first day out we caught a 3-kilogram tuna. Bhatta ripped off the crepe bandage from around his wrist (twisted earlier while weighing anchor), and set aside the pain along with the bandage, to transform the slippery tuna into delicious fried fish and curry in less than thirty minutes! Even before this was served, the line tugged again, and in came a mackerel, which Mathur began cleaning under Bhatta's guidance. We caught a barracuda and two more tuna—one over 10 kilograms in weight—on the sail to Darwin.

Also crossing the Gulf with us was the US yacht *Magic*, with Carl and Jolene Burton and two Australians. We picked them up on the radio as Carl was trying repeatedly without success to raise a ship bearing down on them from astern. We had a brief conversation. Carl sounded hassled after a sleepless night, negotiating the Torres Straits from Port Moresby.

Now he blurted, 'This ship is climbing up my bum, and not responding on the radio'.

The master of the ship responded a little later and *Magic* was much relieved. Carl told us, over the VHF radio of course, that they were headed the same way as us, all the way to Sri Lanka. We promised to call again later, and hopefully meet at Darwin.

Spirits on board zoomed as Bharti regained radio contact with home, still over 4,500 miles away. Two days later, Mathur had a HAM breakthrough when he contacted HAM operators in Visakhapatnam and Nagpur. The next day, he spoke to amateur radio operators in Hyderabad and Bangalore, and soon was on the Indian HAM network. By now, communication with our home stations had become the main daily occurrence everyone on board looked forward to.

Darwin

Darwin is on the mouth of a fairly long bay. The approach to the port from the east is an intricate affair. After entering the Dundas Straits going south, one must pass the Abbot Shoal buoy, thence rounding Cape Hotham, leaving it at least 10–15 miles to port, and on to the Vernon Islands, which straddle the extremely narrow and treacherous Howard Channel and Clearance Straits.

Fresh following winds built up as we charged down Dundas Straits on the evening of 5 October 1986. Abbot buoy passed by rapidly to our starboard, indicating a strong flooding current taking us along way too fast. Soon, Cape Hotham was passed. By now, it was dusk and flashing beacons came up, making it easier to identify points on land even as the dark night increased the dangers inherent in the close and intricate navigation through reefs. The passage past an infamous wreck marked prominently on the chart and written about in the *Coastal Pilot*, and the Vernon Islands was swift and electric. With currents pulling us through, it was important to stay in the middle of the narrow and unlit channel, or suffer a disastrous wrecking.

While moving extremely fast, I was constantly taking bearings of the beacons using a handheld compass as KS plotted these in rapid succession. It was past midnight as we entered the bay and made for the mouth of the river. But the strong and confused current pattern was playing havoc with us so that although we steered for the now visible light marking the mouth, we were constantly pushed

David Howell fitting the new limb at Sydney.

off course and had to be ever vigilant and correct ourselves lest we sail over a shoal or a sand bank. The weather chose this moment to compound the misery and send us a squally thundershower with extremely erratic winds.

By daybreak, we were sailing up-river to the naval base at Larrakeyah where we were granted berthing facilities, making life so much easier in the 20-feet tidal variation. These small courtesies from one service to another, from country to country and, finally, from man to man, are really what make life so much warmer. As we worked on board next day, two young school children came by. I gave them a souvenir postcard with *Trishna*'s photo on it. They gave me their addresses:

'Please write to us from India,' they said.

The military garrison commander, Colonel BM Kemp, called us over for drinks at the officer's mess, after which Captain Grant, a friendly officer, drove us back.

'Are you a Sikh?' he asked. 'We have been keeping a close watch over you for the impending visit of Mr Rajiv Gandhi to Australia.'

We had heard that the Prime Minister's plane was to refuel at Darwin the next day on its way to Sydney. So this was why Colonel Kemp had steered the conversation to Rajiv Gandhi twice during the evening! What with my beard and the name Singh, anyone would be fooled.

We celebrated our one year out at sea with the good Sri Lankan couple, Nissi and Amara Mendis, who fed us wholesome home food, and opened two bottles of Australian white sparkling wine for the occasion.

Dussehra is the Indian festival when the tools of the trade are cleaned, decorated, and worshipped. It fell on 12 October. We scrubbed *Trishna* clean, and festively decorated her before offering a silent prayer to the Gods: thankfulness for the voyage so far, and fortitude for the future.

CHAPTER 14

RETURN TO ORIENTAL WATERS
THE SAIL FROM DARWIN
TO SINGAPORE
13 October 1986–19 November 1986

Darwin to Singapore

Our long Australian romance, stretching over 2,000 miles and forty days, was coming to a close. It is a continent, but it has a total population of only 16 million—roughly equal to that of Kolkata! The next day, we were on our way to Indonesia.

As we sailed northwest into the Timor Sea on the morning of 13 October 1986, we noticed we were not leaving the harbour by ourselves. There was another sail, bent to wind, about 2 miles astern on our port quarter, heading the same way.

Over twenty-four hours later, the sail was exactly at the same bearing and distance from us. We immediately began keeping it under observation, from one watch to another. When an Australian Custom's aeroplane flew above us, and called out to our shadow-boat several times without drawing any response, we decided to come up on the air.

'Custom plane, this is yacht *Trishna*, anything for me?'

'No *Trishna*, nothing for you, we are calling the sloop two miles to your south east'.

Upon this, the yacht, silent so far for reasons best known to itself, came up loud and clear:

'Yes, this is New Zealand yacht *Wanderer*. What's your problem?'

It certainly was odd to begin a conversation in that tone, and we strained our eyes to see him. It is rather unlikely for two yachts, even when sailing in company of one another, on the same course, to maintain stations so accurately. So he certainly seemed to be shadowing us. After taking details of her crew, their nationality, etc., the plane flew off, and we felt better. The crew included a Swede and two New Zealanders

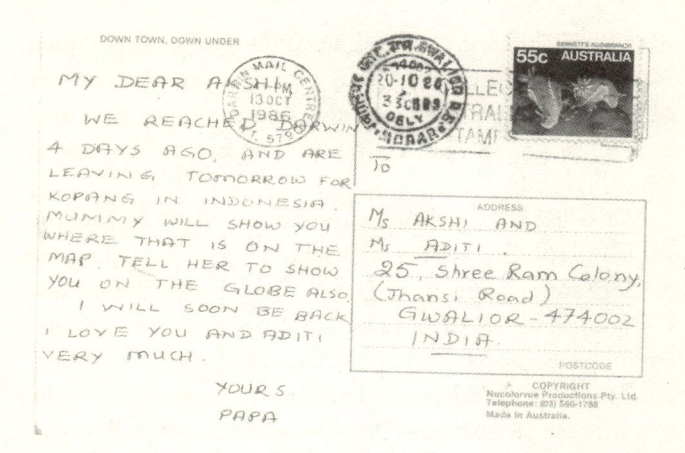

> DOWN TOWN, DOWN UNDER
>
> MY DEAR AKSHI,
> WE REACHED DARWIN 4 DAYS AGO, AND ARE LEAVING TOMORROW FOR KOPANG IN INDONESIA. MUMMY WILL SHOW YOU WHERE THAT IS ON THE MAP. TELL HER TO SHOW YOU ON THE GLOBE ALSO.
> I WILL SOON BE BACK. I LOVE YOU AND ADITI VERY MUCH.
>
> YOURS,
> PAPA
>
> To
> Ms AKSHI AND
> Ms ADITI
> 25, Shree Ram Colony,
> (Jhansi Road)
> GWALIOR - 474002
> INDIA

calling themselves Ryan, Pebbles and Burton, supposedly bound for Sri Lanka on their way to the Mediterranean. All along, conversation with *Wanderer* was not spontaneous. Even mundane queries received studied and delayed replies, and our suspicions grew.

One of them said: 'I was into Sai Baba and all that'.

We knew that drug trafficking and illegal migrants from the South China Sea and other areas had combined to make these waters rife with piracy. Any hazard the sea may pose is small compared to these ruthless modern operators.

Probably warned off by the customs plane, our shady companion withdrew that night, and was not sighted again.

ʚ ɞ

By now, Mathur had acquired various nicknames on board. One was 'Hook', a reminder of his barely audible chats with some Australian HAM operators, who would ask him to say a sharp 'hook' in reply, if he could hear them. Various HAM radio terms like 'QSL' were also used to refer to Mathur. Thanks to him and the amateur radio network, most of us got news directly from our families in various cities all over India.

We sailed for Bali with a short stop for fresh water at Kupang. The Indonesian Army kindly gave us a jeep for driving around the tiny Timor Sea island. The driver, Corporal Riwu ('I was a captain in the Portugese Army, but am only a corporal in the Indonesian Army now'), was an instantly likeable roly-poly chap, forever laughing. We'd all pile into the Toyota, and Riwu would take off, rally style, through the dust tracks of various villages. Chickens and dogs would scatter as Riwu drove, and we'd shut our eyes, suffering quietly, with hearts pounding and palms sweating, as he narrowly missed pedestrians, vehicles, poles, trees and even a bus stand! Riding out a 60-knot storm at sea had felt safer! Imagine sailing all the way around the world only to die in a car crash there!

The mere thought was unnerving.

Driving through a village, we passed the house of a local Raja. When we asked if we could take a picture of his widowed Rani, with their hut-like house in the backdrop, a local go-between told us that the Rani was willing, provided we paid her 15,000 rupyah!

We sent her a lapel badge souvenir of *Trishna* along with the reply: 'No thanks!'

We did, however, manage to photograph the dead Raja's grave for no charge.

At those latitudes, days are hot, with frequent precipitation and an occasional thundershower. There were a lot of fishing craft about. A few dhows, some with colourful sails, passed us. Favourable winds and currents pushed us westwards. Once in a while, the winds would die down to nothing, making it hot and sticky below decks.

On the morning of the 26th, *Trishna* emerged, after a dark and squally night, into waters merging with the Indian Ocean. We sailed at an exhilarating pace the whole day and night towards Benoa Harbour, Bali. But the winds died off on the 27th, and we could enter the harbour only the next morning.

Benoa, Bali

The entrance passage to Benoa was extremely narrow—barely 100 metres wide at places—and turns at sharp angles every few hundred metres. There were several underlying reefs and shoals on both sides, and the eddy currents were strong. Also, old, disused channel-marking posts of steel, twisted and rusted, abounded. Nothing would have saved us from certain disaster had we entered at night. We could well understand the anxiety of the master of the small merchant ship probably under 500 tons, which took more than three hours to laboriously negotiate the treacherous 1.5-mile passage.

Early morning, fishermen in their dug-out canoes, much like sampans fitted with outriggers, and tiny v-shaped sails fixed to vertical bamboo masts and a bamboo yard arm, were fanning out to sea from Benoa as *Trishna* sailed in with the early morning sun. There were dozens of them around, bobbing up and down in the gentle swell, as we sailed to the small-boat anchorage. Close by were moored some thirty or more mechanized fishing trawlers, in an apparent state of disuse and decay. They were all named *Samodara*—from *Samodara 1* to *Samodara 40*.

The hot and spicy Indonesian food was very welcome. By now, we were in a relatively carefree and light-hearted mood, and with good reason—having sailed over 30,000 sea miles, we were poised once more to sail home across the Indian Ocean. Boat handling and various crew drills had become second nature to us, and all our hard work had paid off. Even in fierce storms, we knew we could keep all the systems of our seventeen-year-old *Trishna* working. Barely a couple of ports away lay the Indian port of Car Nicobar in the Andaman group of islands.

The passage to Jakarta was covered in eight days. A gentle current appeared to be helping us along as we sailed north.

Diary entry:

7 November 1986

> Voyage so far from Bali (we had left on the 2nd) has been good. Free winds most of the time (meaning sailing with the winds, not against them), overcast skies, showers now and again. On the last two nights, winds would switch off as if by an electric switch, exactly at 11 p.m., followed by rain, with lightning and thunder. The celestial wind switch would be put on again at 7 a.m.

This was to carry on for another two days and, in the pre-dawn darkness of the 9th, we sailed up the Sunda Strait towards Tanjung Priok in the midst of a post-thunder squall, charging past the fishing stakes and oil rigs, and anchored in the inner basin. Around us were tiny tankers, LPG carriers, and general cargo ships, with familiar names like *Bhima* and *Shakti*. The murky waters appeared only a shade less polluted than Mumbai's. By 10.30 a.m., we were secured alongside the jetty, at berth number 301.

Our Military Advisor, Colonel BR Naik, Vir Chakra, and his gentle wife Nalini, as well as Captain Gopalachari of the Indian Navy and his gracious wife Hema, took us straight to their homes—three to each home. The two wonderful ladies mothered us weary sailors, cheerfully taking away even our washing from us, and ordering us: 'You are now to rest and relax'.

So polluted was the air here that *Trishna's* decks were soon covered with a thick layer of dark muck! Some enthusiastic visitors even brought black soot-like dust mixed with oil on their shoe soles from the tanker jetty nearby, and trampled the whole deck with it. The white fenders lapping the waters as well as the once-sky-blue sides of the graceful boat had become an ugly black oily mess, as we prepared to sail at midday on 14 November 1986. We cast off to a flurry of waves and cheers from ashore.

Spirited following winds enabled us to make rapid progress virtually all the way through the Banka Strait. The passage was lively, with plenty of shipping, fishing trawlers and barges, both towed and propelled. Radio calls to passing ships often went unanswered, enhancing the feeling that you needed to 'fend for yourself' in the busy shipping lanes. Those who answered spoke only Indonesian. Our searchlight was our main protection against being run down by those ships on dark nights.

Singapore

On 18 November 1986, we crossed the Equator for the fourth and final time. Just past midnight, we were hit by a squall and visibility came down to zero. It lifted with the break of day, and the beautiful island of Singapore was suddenly in full view. We sailed round to the north, going anti-clockwise, past Keppel Harbour, and entered the Johor Straits, going west with favourable currents, past lots of small yellow buoys laid out as if they were boundary-markers around the island. With Malaysia to our north and Singapore to our south, we sailed past fishing huts on stilts of bamboo, jutting a long way out into the channel from the land.

They were like tottering jetties, each with a fluorescent tube light below the bamboo huts, a little above the water, illuminating the stilted bamboo jetty as also the thatched hut, and the dark flowing water in an eerie, ghostly cold light. Not a soul stirred on any of the contraptions, adding to the eeriness. The light was probably meant both for warning plying boats from colliding with the intruding jetties as well as to attract fish into the nets cast below them. Soon *Trishna* was berthed at Sembawang Naval Harbour, Singapore.

Several of us had family visiting us here, since it was not so far from home. Vani Rao, Bina Mathur,

Mrs Bhattacharya, Manju Bharti and Asha were there. So were Shekhar's mother and Nisha Bassi, Rakesh's sister. It was good to see Asha after having sailed more than halfway around the world.

The headmaster of the United World College of South Asia wanted me to talk to the students on the travails of sailing around the world on one leg.

I spoke instead of the pleasures and the satisfaction of doing so.

At the steering wheel while on watch.

CHAPTER 15

THE SAIL HOME
SINGAPORE TO MUMBAI
27 November 1986–10 January 1987

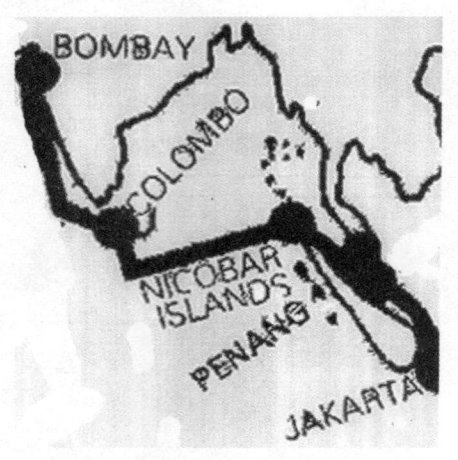

Singapore to Mumbai

On the morning of 27 November 1986, we retraced our route from Sembawang Wharf to the Malacca Straits, going clockwise half around the island. By the evening, we were well on our way up the narrow and busy straits.

Cloudy skies with bad visibility during the days and worse at night, alternating calm and squalls, a favourable 1-knot current were the general sailing conditions. It was a troublesome passage, and we stuck to the eastern shores. It was mostly wet and clammy outside, and hot and stuffy below decks. Scores of fishing boats were all around. Often during the day, one of these was sighted sitting right in the middle of the shipping lane, hastily starting engines and motoring off as an oncoming ship threatened to run her down. As we sailed in the dark, moonless, squally nights, a blinding light—white or green or red, no matter— would suddenly come on dangerously close to us, shaking and startling us completely into our immediate collision-avoidance drill. Clearly, in those waters, there were no sailing norms, no order. These fishermen were the masters of the dark waters. We sure were glad to be out of those harrowing, narrow straits.

Georgetown

In 20 knots of wind, we raced past the island of Penang on our starboard side before turning right to head for Bandar Raya at Georgetown, which we reached at noon on 1 December. Georgetown obviously is the most common name for a port—this was our third!

Pulau Pinang means 'island of betel nuts'. We will remember it for its deep green tropical forests with a multitude of palm varieties in all sizes, and the idyllic road to nowhere running all along the waterfront. There were dozens of hotels and beach resorts, some yet unfinished, with exquisite names like Batu Ferringi, Rasa Sayang (which means 'feeling of love'), and Tolok Bahang (which means 'bay of the reflected heart').

Most memorable, indeed, was the hour-long meeting with the legendary Tunku Abdul Rehman[1]. It took place in his house which was really more of a museum, with thousands of artefacts and curios, each presented by a visiting dignitary—usually a Head of State. Gifts from at least five Indian Presidents or Prime Ministers were on display.

We sailed from Georgetown on 5 December 1986.

Diary entry:

> 5 December 1986
>
> Sailed out of Penang. From the Pacific, entering the Indian Ocean through the Malacca Straits. Although on the threshold of success, we still have the run up to Mumbai to complete successfully. Care and vigilance is key.

---

[1] Tunku Abdul Rahman(February 8, 1903 – December 6, 1990) was Chief Minister of the Federation of Malaya from 1955, and the country's first Prime Minister from independence in 1957. He remained as the Prime Minister after Sabah, Sarawak, and Singapore joined the federation in 1963 to form Malaysia. He is widely known simply as "Tunku" or "The Tunku" (a princely title in Malaysia).

After an early thundershower, the first night passed under fair winds.

Our biggest problem was the indiscriminate and heavy coastal fishing fleet. Not only would they be buzzing around like bees during the day, criss-crossing our path both close ahead and astern, in total disregard of rules of the road and safe sailing, they would also startle us by near collisions on dark overcast nights. That piracy has been an endemic problem here, did not help our nerves and we had to be ever vigilant.

Campbell Bay

With favourable currents, we sighted the Great Nicobar Island in the afternoon of 8 December, but the winds were still to die down. We sailed into Campbell Bay only the next morning, escorted by the vessels *INS Nideshak* and the Coast Guard Ship *(CGS) Vikram*. Campbell Bay looked pretty as a picture that morning—perhaps more so because it was our first home port. After all, the eyes only see; it is the mind that 'feels' the sight.

AP, Tipsy, Navin and Bassi were there to meet us, and it was a pleasing reunion for us all.

The simple and kind islanders wanted to be with all of us at once. They hosted us to simple and frugal social gatherings and meals, offering all they had. Two young lads even composed songs in Hindi and Punjabi in our honour. We were deeply touched and moved beyond words. I would not trade those moments for all the gold on earth.

A thousand miles to the southwest lay Colombo, the capital port of Sri Lanka or the 'pearl of the Indian Ocean'. It was to be our last port before Mumbai. By now, the Australian limb had begun to fit well, and I was thankful to Mr Howell for having made it ready in record time. Having started my voyage with two Indian legs I was destined to return home with an Australian one to boot!

Just as a funny aside, apart from the initial discomfort, I had had only one problem with the import. In the short time he had been given, Mr Howell had not been able to find a stocking of my skin colour to cosmetically cover the limb. I had been forced to go to the women's section of a store in Brisbane, embarrassing enough by itself, only to be told that they had no stockings in stock, and that I should try the exclusive women's lingerie shop next door. Trying hard to beat down my feeling of helpless embarrassment, I casually strolled into the well-stocked, shop. Fortunately there was no other customer visible. What had to be done, had to be done. But the question was, how?

'Guess what I could be doing in a women's lingerie shop?' I said to the petite sales girl. It was an awkward attempt to start off the conversation in a light vein. She looked bewildered at being confronted with such a query in an empty shop by a tall, weather beaten, bearded and limping sailor. 'Er yes, er yes sir, I guess you are looking for something for your wife,' she stammered.

'Not at all,' I said, by now unable to hide the twinkle in my eyes. 'What I buy here, I will wear myself!'

Without further dilly dallying I explained what I was looking for and her face was awash with joyful relief. I was glad to have saved the situation as the last thing I needed was for her to explode into emergency action and make an urgent call to the police! Happily, the stocking colour was quickly matched, and soon the till rung home with my payment.

All these felt like events from some distant past as *Trishna* and her crew, limb stocking and all, were readied for the sail from Campbell Bay to Colombo.

The accompanying motor launch with our four teammates who had sailed the earlier legs with us and had come here to be with us in Campbell Bay, dropped off astern as we sailed out of the bay, and the Coast Guard Ship *Vikram* escorted us out to open seas—home to good sailing boats.

Only a few days earlier, *Vikram* had captured a poaching Taiwanese fishing trawler whose crew had beached the vessel, and hidden on the island. We sailed past *Vikram* as she hailed and cheered us on, and then set a course around Indira Point, with its red-and-white lighthouse at the southernmost tip of the archipelago, as also the southernmost tip of India, before settling down on a course of 260 degrees magnetic for Sri Lanka. *Trishna* charged towards Colombo with strong following winds of over 20 knots at times. Clear hot days and cool nights, and we averaged over 160 miles a day, all the way into port!

This, in fact, was the fastest passage of our voyage.

There were plenty of flying fish to be picked each morning from the deck for breakfast. Once every few days we also caught a large tuna or two, and my diary entry on one such day reads: 'Two days of fish food'.

Sighting Sri Lanka

At 8 a.m. on 20 December 1986, we sighted Sri Lanka. We passed the Dondra Head Lighthouse a couple of hours later, just as we saw three huge sperm whales lounging in the tropical waters, spurting plumes of water and nudging each other playfully. We circled and filmed them, a lot of our earlier fears having faded with so many whale sightings. We also had the feeling that this may be our last opportunity to film them on the voyage. Turning north along the western coast of the island, we passed Galle and then Barberyn lights that day and Colombo was abeam by daybreak on the 21st. Three hours later, we entered the protective breakwaters of the harbour, past the imposing lighthouses of the eastern entrance.

As a naval and a customs launch escorted us in, half a dozen vessels in the harbour opened up with blaring horns in a crescendo of welcome! Surprise mingled with emotions of humility and thankfulness for the large-hearted acknowledgement of our near-complete circumnavigation. Thank you, good people of Colombo. You stole our hearts away!

In Colombo, we met President Junius Richard Jayewardene, and also the Chief of the Armed Forces. KS spoke on the phone with Tipsy in Mumbai, who wanted to know the exact date of our arrival. 10 January 1987 seemed like a good date. It would, of course, all depend on the winds. We still had more than 800 miles to go.

A Sri Lankan naval patrol boat escorted us out of the harbour at 1400 hours on 29 December. As we pulled away from the enchanted land, we radioed our farewell to the grand old man of Colombo harbour, Mr Henricus, who had been its strong-willed and dedicated Harbour Master since 1969.

And finally, we set course for Mumbai, and home. *Trishna*'s home run was on at last!

Second New Year Celebration

Diary entry:

> 7 January 1987
> About 80 NM short of Mumbai
>
> Had an eventful stay at Colombo. Sailed out on 29 December with our High Commissioner, Mr JN Dixit, Military Advisor Captain Gupta (IN) and others accompanying us in Sri Lanka Navy patrol boat, which sailed with us till the harbour mouth. Other harbour craft blowing their horns wished us Godspeed! Warmth in our hearts, and a yearning for the home-bound departure. Captain Kanal and 2nd Officer D'Silva of the Indian LPG carrier ship *Harvester* bade us farewell on VHF radio.
>
> We ushered in our second New Year of the voyage with all hands being woken up by a loud blaring foghorn, hooted close to the ear by the crew on watch, at midnight. We hugged each other emotionally, wishing each other a Happy New Year, since our journey was drawing to a close. We had spent a long time together—too close and in too small a boat—and soon the rest of the world would re-enter our lives.

Those were sweet moments. The journey's end was in sight.

We crossed the Palk Strait separating the two countries as the orange orb that governs our world sank slowly below the western horizon on the 30th. The rocks of Kanyakumari were now in plain view, barely 15 miles away. The New Year was rung in at sea, and it was 1987. A wind pattern of northeast land breeze during the day and a westerly sea breeze at night began to settle down as we coasted northwards. To avoid this, and the intervening patches of calm, we sailed 50 miles further off shore in more steady breeze.

The atmosphere on board was charged with eagerness for Mumbai. All talk was of home and what we would do after the voyage. A near collision with a whale, sighted by Surendra Mathur barely metres away, reminded us that our voyage was not yet over, and any more than 6 feet of water depth needs to be treated with respect even when the journey's end is in sight.

Diary entry (undated):

The last step in the uphill climb which has spanned eight years of my life is at hand. In many ways, these moments hold richness far greater than the aftermath of success. The task seems over, only loose ends remain. The green shaded oasis at the end of our near-endless journey, the summit at the very top of the blue skies, the peak, is now visible. The driving human ego which, in its seemingly insatiable urge, drives body and soul mercilessly to unimaginable heights seems quenched with the seeming certainty of success. It is simply this feeling of well-being, of delirious contentment, of an indefinable sweet intoxication that spurs man to ever greater achievement.

Even before we sailed from Colombo, Bharti was displaying signs of a fever. It wouldn't come down, and by the New Year Day, his fever had risen to 105 degrees Fahrenheit, and held. Crocin didn't help. Skipper ordered antibiotics and even chloroquin, anticipating malaria; but nothing helped. Wet towels were applied, which helped keep the temperature from shooting to dangerous levels. Since the fever would not go down, it soon became imperative to evacuate him. Skipper spoke to Dr. Das of the Navy's Hospital Ship, the *INHS Aswini* at Mumbai, and the navy swung into action. We altered course for nearby Mangalore. The naval warship *INS Ganga* conducted a textbook rescue operation for the benefit of us sea-faring army 'pongos' and, within six hours of the radio call, she was within 200 metres of us. Her executive officer, Commander KV Subramaniyam, came alongside in an inflatable to evacuate Bharti to the ship. Bharti had been my watch-mate all the way around the world, as well as on our earlier voyage from the UK to Mumbai, and it was sad to see him go so close to the finish line. But we all agreed it was for the best. He was later reinstated on board after treatment for malaria, enabling him to complete his circumnavigation.

CHAPTER 16

MUMBAI

Goa was passed on 5th evening, and Ratnagiri went by the next night.

On 6 January 1987, between 2 and 4 p.m., our present course intersected with our outbound passage from Bombay. At that moment, we technically completed our circumnavigation of the world.

Diary entry:

> 7 January 1987
> Just outside Bombay
>
> A deep feeling of gratitude, of exultation, of profound peace and silent happiness, of very personal emotions of thankfulness to the Gods of the Seas and Winds for our success, as much as for the deep etched lasting lessons we have learnt from them, fills me. To express it adequately, one needs to be better at words. The feelings defy

Beyond Horizons

articulation; yet I am overwhelmed—thankful for life itself. Some shipping and an odd dhow around—Bombay only 75 nautical miles ahead! Oh what a dream it has been—full enough to flood a lifetime for ever!

Asha Speaks—'They are Back!'

They were coming back! They had made it! They had completed their fantastic voyage—their dream—and sailed the *Trishna* all the way around the world and back to Mumbai! They were alive, well and back home!

Thank you, God! Thank you. The feelings of apprehension, the fear of bad news, of hope, of waiting for their next news—all these had receded into the background as the months had piled on, and my daily routine with the two baby girls in and out of their growing-up tribulations, had taken centre stage.

However, while the fire of hope and prayer had receded, its power had not dimmed. In fact, with each passing day, the thread of hope had been gaining strength. And now, our prayers were being answered—they were sailing into Mumbai tomorrow!

Fifteen months of gut-wrenching anxiety were finally over on 10 January 1987, at Mumbai. Our two daughters were waiting for their dear 'Papa', scarcely aware of what that word stood for, on the steps of the Gateway of India, with flying placards reading 'WELCOME PAPA, WELCOME TRISHNA', as *Trishna* sailed home, bringing in lots of excitement and joy.

As the anniversary of Trishna's arrival to Mumbai, 10 January will always be a special day for me. The Gateway of India had been decorated, and all the people we could think of were there to welcome them. As naval ships blew their horns in salutation, helicopters showered petals, and fire-tender ships jetted out water spouts. All kinds of sailing boats in Mumbai were there to welcome them. And among those world-weary sailors was my lanky, one-legged hero!

I had the girls dressed in their best, and I myself was as presentable as could be—for him to set his eyes upon us, the quietly waiting party. Happy thoughts of gratitude and anticipation kept bubbling in our hearts, sending waves of happiness.

And then, there they were!

He was wearing my hand-knitted cap, with 'AK' emblazoned on it. There was a huge grin on his face accompanied by unending, inspired waving.

And we were together again! What had begun in uncertainty was over. After the excitement, the tiredness of the long wait came on. And all we could do was let the moments grow on us—too rich to break up by banter or small talk.

Someone pointed out AK to his young daughter, saying, 'See baby, that is called Courage.'

My heart heaved—could it take any more pride? Or would it just burst? Each moment brought wave upon wave of pride, joy and relief. Was it all really over?! So much seemed to be happening! I wanted to soak in each moment. I actually did not want the moments to end. I wanted them to last for ever and ever—after all I had waited a long time. Now, I felt proud of him, as always, and of being his wife.

Smile on my face, lump in throat, emotional tides roaring in and out, breathing anything but normally, and swelling with pride, the minutes swirled past as the reception ceremony with the Minister KPS Deo, General Krishnaswamy Sundarji, the then Chief of the Army, and a host of very senior dignitaries from the Army, Navy and other departments progressed. The welcome ceremonies were concluded with the release of a commemorative postal stamp on their voyage by the Department of Post.

The Grand Plan, the unending wait—it all seemed worth it now, as I took in as much of my man with my eyes as possible. Yes, God had heard our prayers, and we were together again.

Some days later, I spied on our elder daughter Akshi, all of six years old, in the secrecy and solitude of her room, imitating AK's walk, complete with his signature limp. 'Pa' was no longer an ephemeral phenomenon who lived in a photo frame. He was a real person who lived, breathed, laughed and loved her—a life-transforming discovery for a young person.

Yes, we were finally together again.

AK Speaks—The Morning After

Trishna sailed into the Mumbai harbour to a resounding welcome on 10 January 1987. Everything afloat in Mumbai harbour escorted us in, from the Captain's launches of all the naval ships in port, to port trust boats, private launches, sail boats, dinghies, and even surfboards. Several naval helicopters hovered overhead as we made our way to the Gateway of India, where numerous dignitaries, including the then Army Chief, General K Sundarji and Mr KP Singh Deo, MP our Chief Patron, welcomed us ashore. A commemorative stamp and first day cover on the voyage were released.

Trishna then made an overland passage by rail to New Delhi, and on 26 January, it 'sailed' down Rajpath on a specially fabricated trailer as part of the nation's proud display in the Republic Day Parade.

Felicitations by the President, the Prime Minister and various other important people followed. Honours and awards were bestowed on us, and soon we were back at our Army jobs.

Was it all over? Not really. Each of us now had enough wonderful memories to last us the rest of our lives.

For me, there never will be a better boat, nor a better crew to sail with—ever.

CHAPTER 17

QUIET THOUGHTS

The voyage was over. All of us were picking up the threads of our personal and professional lives in the normal material world. The human mind is very adaptable. Soon things returned to as near normal as is possible after such a voyage, and only when some talk or thoughts would open the mind's window back into the days on board *Trishna* would we be transported back in time, the salt air and the blue sea would seem once more to be all around us in the mind's eye in all its enormity.

I asked for, and was sent to my field engineer regiment in the hilly and jungle areas of our north eastern borders and I tried to get on with what I had been trained to deliver for eight years through RIMC, the NDA as well as the IMA—soldiering. Being an above-knee amputee and not having the knee joint to articulate my lower limb, unable to run or jog with troops in field or to climb over the undulating country as soldiers are required to, I was in a way relieved when I was boarded out of the Army on medical grounds in 1990. Much as Asha and I loved the uniform, I could not dream of being carry-on baggage for my Regiment or my men. And if I was to push papers from a desk for the rest of my life, I would not do so in uniform—for I had not worn it to push papers in.

We moved with our daughters, one six and the other nine years old, to Lucknow, to rebuild life on the 'civvy street'.

ॐ ॐ

Republic Day celebrated on 26 January each year is the day of the big parade at Delhi, where the nation showcases its cultural diversity and richness. Cultural floats with energetic, colourful participants acting out a representative theme from their part of the world, keep time to loud regional music. These are followed by the show-of-might floats, with the Army, Navy and the Air Force displaying some of their impressive hardware, as a huge audience looks on, awestruck. The flawless military marching of the various contingents are a treat to see. Then comes the time when the grateful nation confers its highest military honours on those men and women who have shown exceptional courage in facing impossible odds, at times paying with their lives for the particular act of duty they upheld, invariably blazing a trail of glory and sacrifice for the nation. Unfortunately, due to cross border insurgents and terrorists, these days, we are witnessing an increasing number of these distinctions being conferred posthumously.

It was 26 January 1994. Watching the Republic Day Parade on TV in Lucknow, the mention of one name sent the mind racing. He had laid down his life, they said, while carrying out a frontal assault, leading his men as Commanding Officer of the Maratha Regiment, to break a deadly ambush set up by over a hundred anti-national militants somewhere in the North Eastern sector. He is survived by his wife, serene, in a white sari as she walks with resolve and dignity towards the podium to receive the Ashok Chakra from the President of India. Tears of anguish may flow, because she hasn't control over them right now. But helplessness? Never! The face does not flinch—the inevitability, the pride, the sorrow, the determination, the sheer loneliness—make the mask on her face difficult to describe, deeply marked as it is with as much grace as grief. Her only child is a son whom they had together named Shivaji after the great Maratha warrior as a tribute to the Maratha soldiers he had led.

Hey! But I know his name backwards. It is not a Maratha name. I spelt it out in a manner I can never ever forget—one letter for each ground push-up. Neelakantan Jayachandran Nair. He was no Maratha—or was he? One with his men for always?

ॐ ॐ

Days and years were passing, as we settled into the humdrum life of an ex-army family, bringing up our children the best we could.

Life's mornings began with the newspaper over a cuppa—a luxury ill-afforded during service life. One such day, as I sipped tea and read the paper, a small news item jolted me. I read it again in disbelief. Something about it did not seem right.

It was Him. The mind went racing back to our NDA days. He had, quite unobtrusively, requested and been assigned to the toughest of the tough branches of the Indian Army—the Indian Para-Commandos on getting commissioned from the IMA. I had secretly marvelled at and admired the steely determination that had clearly shone through his firm eyes then. This funny boy who had joined the NDA aged sixteen, and was in grave danger of permanently damaging his tendons since he had never ever run in his life up until then! What a lean and handsome soldier he had grown into. And Miss Pretty Face too flashed before my eyes. They had gotten married after so many years of waiting. And now this, so soon...too soon!

The news report stared me in the face, as I read: his JCO[1] had been captured by terrorists who had then holed up in a hut 'somewhere in the forward areas' in north India. He led an assault to get his man back. He was shot several times. They could not save him.

Oh God in Heaven, this is not right!

Get a hold of yourself. Wasn't this what you were trained for?

Why do you think all was taken away from you at the Academy—all but the wry jokes?

The grateful nation conferred on him one of its highest gallantry awards.

---

[1] Junior Commissioned Officer

Over two hundred and fifty cadets pass out of the hallowed portals of the National Defence Academy at Pune every six months. If you see them during the passing out parade, they are virtually clones of each other. Is one a Maratha, a Tamil, a Brahmin, a certain caste? These narrow identities are obliterated forever at the NDA when we are all transformed in to the nation's soldiers.

We heard that DK Paul, my RIMC mate and later, my batchmate at NDA, had died when he single-handedly took on looters and thugs who began looting passengers at gun point in the train he was travelling in; they had thrown him off the running train.

'Grow up, buddy,' I told myself.

But it does hurt.

Maybe something was left unattended during the training. Or was it?

It happens. It happens in this world, to others—and sometimes to ourselves too!

What is the difference—between us and others? Is it supposed to be worse if it happens to us? Or, when it happens to others?

Yes, it had been a long journey in life starting from the day we joined NDA, black steel trunks and bed-holdalls and all, to almost the other end of life's rainbow. Each having traversed his own path as life unfolded for him differently.

Each of the clones had delivered, in his individual way.

NDA had done its job well.

ஒ ஒ

Asha speaks:

AK has always said that we don't show this much concern to so many others to whom similar misfortunes happen every day. Isn't it a bit selfish to try to sort out people, or the system, only if something happened to us?

He has always held the belief that life is worth living and enjoying for its pleasant moments, of which he firmly believes there have been, and will always be plenty. One only has to look out for them!

And so we moved on.

EPILOGUE
IN RETROSPECT—A DISCLAIMER

Trishna was the best boat one could hope for to embark on a voyage around the world. It was just the right design, and built to the best possible specifications.

Also, in retrospect, the *Trishna* crew was, and has been, the best bunch of buddies one could hope for. As is understandable under the conditions, each of us had our own equations, as also our differences. That is only normal, considering the size of the boat—a mere 36 feet, floating in the middle of the oceans, day and night, for months on end. That we stuck it out and never once faltered under even extremely trying conditions, that we joined as one at sea to see that boat and crew were as safe as we could make them, each and every time, that we put boat and crew before our prejudices, has joined us together, over the years, into as strong a team as we always were. Yes, we were the best crew one could hope to be with. It is a lifelong honour to have had such buddies.

My perceptions and interpretations of the events during our voyage, both on land and at sea, are personal; it is possible that other crew members have a different take on the same episodes. I shall always be quick in correcting any factual data, or even interpretation, once brought to my notice. I shall always wish to stand by my crew members.

The Academy (NDA) at Pune has, at any given time, over fifteen hundred cadets. There were scores of mates at the RIMC at Dehradun as were Gentlemen Cadets at the IMA, Dehradun too with whom I grew up, trained and lived. While the situations I have narrated are true, some have been woven into my story without the mention of actual names. Some situations have also been attributed to, and spun around, fictitious characters with the intention of capturing the essence of what happened and how, without exposing or hurting feelings. All the events interwoven into the story have actually happened, though not always to the same person, and not in the same sequence, or the connecting build-up that has been portrayed. If I have failed in my attempt to bring out the essence of what, I feel, were the best years of our lives in the best places and circumstances that could have moulded us, please forgive me, and attribute it to my various shortcomings. My intent is to bring forth and make those facts, emotions and events shine in their true light, which occupy a place deep inside all of us who had 'been there, and done that', feelings and events that refuse to go away, and instead appear to become more precious as the years pile on.

Many of us who were then together are now Lieutenant Generals or Major Generals, and their equivalents in the other two services: the Indian Navy and the Indian Air Force. They are commanding Corps, Fleets and Air Bases, and some will soon move up and command armies. A select few may even have the privilege of higher office. We are their honoured course-mates, and will be always proud of them. When I look back, I am more than convinced that Ronnie and Phyllis achieved what they set out to do—to turn out some of the finest human beings on God's Earth, and the finest soldiers at that.

Ours has been a great bunch. Again, I wish to state categorically, that I would like to correct any difference in facts or in perception or interpretation as soon as they are brought to my notice. My intention has been to make as best an attempt as possible to bring out, in my own limited way, the greatness of these institutions, and how much we owe to them for what we are today, individually, and as the collective Defence Forces of this great nation of ours. Yes, Ronnie certainly achieved what he set out to do when he took over as the Dep-Com of the NDA, and as the foster-parent, along with Phyllis, to fifteen hundred of us; he created good robust men, in body and soul, for our Armed Forces.

One day in 1993, I received a letter from Phyllis, telling me of his demise.

'And He one day shall make it plain/That earthly loss is Heavenly gain!'

Farewell and Godspeed, Ronnie!

Phyllis too has passed away since to enrich the heavens... since that is exactly what Ronnie and Phyllis have always striven to do, make the very space they occupy richer with their simplicity, goodness and sheer strength of moral character. They have influenced and inspired each of us who has had the privilege of their association in a manner that few can.

RIP Ronnie and Phyllis.

Ronnie and Phyllis, we all owe you one, and will always love you, wherever you are—since bodies may go, but what you stood for will never go away.

ANNEXE 1

PERSPECTIVE ON SAILING IN INDIA

Sailing—the art and sport of moving a boat using wind power on sails—is probably amongst the least understood sports in India. Although we have an extensive coastline, sailing for conquest has never been the nation's forte. Probably the fine living conditions Mother Nature blessed this land with, and the consequent reluctance to embark upon off-shore conquests as a nation or a race, have contributed, over the centuries, to the idea of using the oceans merely for livelihood—local fishing, and occasional trade forays to neighbouring lands in the vicinity.

Even this has never really been a survival activity in the land of plentiful vegetation. Neither has this trade shown the aggressive dynamism visible in the conquistador races who were constantly in search of better pastures. In any event, sailing escaped being a national activity of necessity in India in the way it was destined to become for the countries of Northern and Western Europe. Indeed, the history of their dominance over oceans and thereby colonization of the world is closely linked to the art of sailing—in fact, it is a consequence of it.

ॐ ॐ

Thus, in India, sailing has not the stature or the popularity, of most contemporary sports that come to mind.

When the *Trishna* set sail, no attempt had been made from India to sail around the world, much less to sail single handed, or to sail around Cape Horn.

Like all ultimate adventures, a sailing voyage around the world is more often the result of a lure —an urge for the wide blue yonder rather than a calculated personal achievement or career mission. Most people I know initially thought that such a plan was akin to cavorting on Goa beaches in summer—with the added bonus of doing it across countries across the globe. I have heard well-educated people say 'They are planning to sail around the world', and gesticulating with a rowing-like movement of the hands!

Others have said, 'Sailing the oceans will be fine and easy I guess. It's the entering and leaving ports that will be the adventure, na?' Or, 'How far from the coast will you be? Not much na?' I suppose all these people wanted to confirm that the boat was actually going to go coasting around the world! I wonder which route would permit that to happen! Yet another wanted to know if we were going to have a ship accompanying us, till I told him there are storm situations at sea during which I may be happier on a well-found sailing boat than on a ship—lying quietly, riding up and down the huge wave-lift in sync with the large wave lengths. A large ship would take a pounding on its plates as it powers its way like a drunken wild horse, out of sync with the high waves, at times lying within crest and crest, unable to ride the wave slopes the way a small yacht could, taking the drubbing of its life. And the best one came from one of the officers directly in charge of promoting adventure activities: 'So many people have sailed around the world from the western world without so much planning as you are doing—and by the way, why have you asked for a helicopter to accompany the boat?' Our bewilderment was complete.

At one stage of our planning, someone up the line thought sailing the seas was a cake-walk and, in his opinion, the project didn't deserve any merit. I am presuming he hadn't spared the oceans much thought. He was probably thinking about seas since these are closer to the nose than oceans—and seeing beyond the nose wasn't the 'done' thing!

☙ ❧

A total lack of any information at hand during conceptualization and the initial planning of our trip resulted in our setting modest goals instead of attempting the highest bar at the first go. Those were days well before computers, internet, or mobile phones. Probably the only medium of gaining any knowledge about any subject were books. These were eagerly devoured, despite being out-of-date technically, and describing voyages sailed decades earlier. But they gave us a strong foundation, since oceans, winds and waves do not change over decades whereas technology does. So, a basic understanding of these, and approaches to boat handling and survival at sea are bound to outlast the frequency with which technology changes. Bluntly said, while technology can make things far easier, it is so only as long as gadgets do not start failing at sea. Being prepared for that eventuality, really, is the cornerstone of a sound around-the-world sailing plan.

Under those conditions, it seemed prudent to route our voyage westwards rather than go east-about, via Cape Horn.

Around fifty yachts under 38 feet had sailed around the world until the time *Trishna* set sail. A lot of water has since flowed up and down the Agulhaus and the Benguilla currents, and the number is bound to be larger now, although boats sailing across oceans have generally been larger than 40 feet. This is purely as far as statistics are concerned. Technological advancements have completely changed the scene, making a lot more possible, which was not earlier so.

Even so, at that time, there was much romance attached to the voyage drawing several TV shows, front page headlines, and even a comic book for children. If anything we have done is a beacon of light to help draw more people out to sail the majestic and mighty oceans, the voyage of *Trishna* will have served its purpose.

ANNEXE 2

'ABANDON SHIP' SURVIVAL AT SEA

Following are some of my notes on the very pertinent subject of survival in case we were ever forced to abandon *Trishna* at sea. I had made these after reading various accounts of yachtsmen and seafarers who lived to tell their tales; many did not. In one particular case of shipwreck in the south eastern Indian ocean, two lifeboats were cast adrift with survivors. One was under command of the Captain, and the other under the First Officer of the ship. The detailed accounts maintained by them have doubtless done great service to seafarers, in understanding the harsh realities of such situations, which every seafarer must be prepared to face in case of an eventuality. Desirable actions are suggested point-wise, those backed up by the accounts of the crew of the unfortunate shipwreck are given alongside each point.

I salute these noble men, who gave to the seafaring world whatever they could by way of their own case studies, even in their hour of gravest misfortune.

- High energy foods like chocolates, condensed milk and biscuits are the best form of survival rations from the point of view of storage, long life, and calories per unit weight. Biscuits must not get wet in sea water. In the case studied, extremely limited supplies of condensed milk, some biscuits and water was all they had.
- In the absence of fresh water, thirst can be mitigated by drawing sea water into the nostrils and blowing it out again and keeping the face and head wet. One must guard against trench foot and frost bite, if one is in cold areas.
- In this particular documented case, the first survival water ration was issued on the third day. For the first twenty-four hours, no food ration was given.
- Rations given per day were as follows. 8 a.m.: one cigarette-tin lid full of condensed milk and one biscuit per man. At 2 p.m.: a one-third full cigarette tin of condensed milk per man. And, at 4 pm: milk ration as at 2 p.m.
- One man drank paraffin oil from the lamp, and another drank spirit from the compass; both were terribly sick and delirious. Sea water drunk by some in desperation had the same effect.
- Watches were maintained and, at times, some rowing done to keep the mind occupied, and to gauge the limit of exhaustion. Some became semi-comatose

after six to seven days. Dousing oneself completely in sea water, and wetting the head, neck and body with sea water was done daily.
- Sucking on buttons seemed to help; some rowing was done to stretch the body and for exercise.
- Feet were rubbed with stove oil, and sun dried as much as possible to prevent trench foot. A good rub now and again was also considered a must.
- Mouths grew white, lips and tongues swollen after sixteen to eighteen days, when sea bath was discontinued, since weakened men could not stand the cold.
- First death occurred on the eleventh day in the First Officer's boat, and on the sixteenth day in the Captain's boat, another on the seventeenth. Boats were at sea for a total of twenty-two days, in high southerly latitudes of 19 degrees south and more, hence it was cold southern winters in June–July. The latitudes were between 28 degrees 50 minutes and 19 degrees south, in southern winters.
- On the eighteenth and nineteenth days, one boat reduced rations to half in preparation for a longer survival period, in case they missed Mauritius and would then have to drift and partially sail/row on to Madagascar; however, Mauritius was reached.
- From the eighteenth day onwards, there was almost a death a day on the First Officer's boat, the final tally being nine deaths in his boat, and two in the Captain's, indicating the role that leadership enforced discipline can play under such trying conditions.

- Captain's boat sailed 1,513 miles to Rodriguez Islands in twenty-two days and nineteen hours; and the First Officer's boat sailed 1,747 miles to Mauritius in twenty-four days and twenty hours, once more highlighting the importance of the quality of navigation and leadership which finally translated into lives saved.
- Catch, store and drink as much rain water as possible. This lesson cannot be overemphasised however obvious it may appear. Each drop collected and saved translated into lives saved in this case study.

ANNEXE 3

A NOTE ON THE BEAUFORT WIND AND SEA SCALE

Sir Francis Beaufort, British admiral and hydrographer to the Royal Navy, was the first in 1805 to introduce and describe a scale of wind for estimating wind strengths without the use of instruments, a system based on subjective observations of the sea. The scale is still widely used to describe the wind's speed and strength. The Beaufort scale of wind velocity relates wind speed to the physical appearance of the sea surface by considering such factors as apparent wave height and the prominence of breakers, whitecaps, foam and spray. It is the oldest method of judging wind force. It has since been repeatedly modified to make it more relevant to modern navigation. Wind speed measured at 11 m (36 feet) above sea surface is usually applied to use the scale. The wave heights are approximate. He developed the scale by measuring the effect the wind had on the flags and sails. In 1838, his 'Wind Force Scale' was introduced by the British Navy for use in log entries. The original Beaufort scale stayed in use until 1905, when Sir George Simpson adapted the scale to modern steamships. In 1921, the International Meteorological Committee (now defunct) approached Sir George to develop a new wind scale, acceptable by all nations. He included indications which were easier to understand for the shore-based part of mankind, such as ascending smoke, leaves rustling and the swishing of trees. He also added instrument measured wind speeds to the scale.

Force	Wind (Knots)	WMO Classification	Appearance of Wind Effects	
			On the Water	On Land
0	Less than 1	Calm	Sea surface smooth and mirror-like	Calm, smoke rises vertically
1	1–3	Light Air	Scaly ripples, no foam crests	Smoke drift indicates wind direction, still wind vanes
2	4–6	Light Breeze	Small wavelets, crests glassy, no breaking	Wind felt on face, leaves rustle, vanes begin to move
3	7–10	Gentle Breeze	Large wavelets, crests begin to break, scattered whitecaps	Leaves and small twigs constantly moving, light flags extended

(*Contd.*)

(*Contd.*)

Force	Wind (Knots)	WMO Classification	Appearance of Wind Effects On the Water	Appearance of Wind Effects On Land
4	11–16	Moderate Breeze	Small waves (1–4 ft). becoming longer, numerous whitecaps	Dust, leaves, and loose paper lifted, small tree branches move
5	17–21	Fresh Breeze	Moderate waves (4–8 ft) taking longer form, many whitecaps, some spray	Small trees in leaf begin to sway
6	22–27	Strong Breeze	Larger waves (8–13 ft), whitecaps common, more spray	Larger tree branches moving, whistling in wires
7	28–33	Near Gale	Sea heaps up, waves (13–19 ft), white foam streaks off breakers	Whole trees moving, resistance felt while walking against wind
8	34–40	Gale	Moderately high (18–25 ft) waves of greater length, edges of crests begin to break into spindrift, foam blown in streaks	Twigs breaking off trees, generally impedes progress

(*Contd.*)

(*Contd.*)

Force	Wind (Knots)	WMO Classification	Appearance of Wind Effects	
			On the Water	On Land
9	41–47	Strong Gale	High waves (23–32 ft), sea begins to roll, dense streaks of foam, spray may reduce visibility	Slight structural damage occurs, slate blows off roofs
10	48–55	Storm	Very high waves (29–41 ft) with overhanging crests, sea white with densely blown foam, heavy rolling, lowered visibility	Seldom experienced on land, trees broken or uprooted, 'considerable structural damage'
11	56–63	Violent Storm	Exceptionally high (37–52 ft) waves, foam patches cover sea, visibility more reduced	Widespread damage
12	64+	Hurricane	Air filled with foam, waves over 45 ft, sea completely white with driving spray, visibility greatly reduced	Excessive damage and much destruction

ANNEXE 4

GETTING TO KNOW NOBBY

Ex Squadron Leader DH Clarke DFC, AFC (Royal Air Force):

> Since I joined the RAF in 1937, I have been nicknamed 'Nobby'; everyone calls me that, so please feel free to do so...I have been their (Guiness Book of World Records) consultant since 1970.

I received Nobby's first letter dated 21 May 1986 somewhere in the Pacific Islands. We were to exchange about half a dozen letters on matters relating to everything under the sun. With his wealth of wisdom, his letters were always inspiring, informative and philosophical, and helped in seeing life more clearly. He wrote on sailing—*The Blue Water Games (Ocean Sailing)*—of which he was the global authority. He also wrote about why one should not write a book—but then again, he reasoned why one must! On his days during the World War II, he describes how he flew alongside the legendary Douglas Bader (an ace fighter pilot despite being a double amputee), the number of aircraft he shot down, life aboard a sailing barge on the Thames which was all he could afford as home after leaving the RAF, advice on having to leave a steady job in the Army, and the important points to remember while settling down on 'civvy street'.

> I see that your retirement was effective at 0900 hours 3.9.90. At this time, on 3.9.39, I was Orderly Officer at Gosport aerodrome—near Portsmouth—when the adjutant sent for me and relieved me of the duty. War was not declared officially until 1100 hours, but the Adj sent me by train to the Isle of Sheppey where he told me, 'The Germans are going to invade, set up big guns, and shell London.' My job was to fly out a xxx (illegible text) aircraft from Eastwich aerodrome on the island, before the Jerries captured it.
>
> The only Indian I know who skippered his own yacht from England to Australia was VIK Radhakrishnan, who sailed one of my trimarans over this route in 1964. (He was an astronomer). His 35 footer trimaran was named *Cygnus* A...When TRISHNA ties the knot, your voyage will (to the best of my knowledge) be a 'first' for India...
>
> On 28 March 1990, I corrected the proofs for the 1991 Guinness Book of Records for the last time, having given them six month's notice that I intended to retire from supplying them with BWG (Blue Water Games) records. At 71, I feel I have done enough!

And on my expressing the desire to set up a sail training school for children after I left the Army, he says:

> As to a sail training centre for children, I am in two minds about this... As an entirely self-taught sailing man, I believe that it is a mistake to over-encourage youngsters into believing adventure consists of merely sitting in a boat, or on a ship (supplied by someone else) and doing what he is told. When I was 13, I had saved enough pocket money to buy a 14-foot sailing dinghy, and I taught myself how to sail her without any outside help. At the same time, inevitably, I learnt how to maintain her and had to pay for her upkeep—and to pay for my mistakes! ... Fifteen years later, when I bought my Thames sailing barge *John & Mary* (81' x 18' x 3'6"; 115 tons, no engine) to convert into a floating house, again I was entirely responsible for everything...and I did it all on very little money. ...Certainly give youngsters the benefit of all your sailing experience, but never let them forget that adventure is a harsh and expensive mistress who totally lacks compassion.

About writing a book:

> The simple reply is DON'T! Sailing round the world and soldiering are child's play compared with the discipline of writing a book. ...On the other hand, with the above horrible warnings in mind, I say GO AHEAD AND WRITE YOUR BOOK. For the personal satisfaction it will give you—even if it is never published—for what you will rediscover about yourself, which long ago you dissipated on the fair winds as you battled from infancy towards the mighty gales of maturity; and above all, for

> the self-discipline which you will be forced to re-discover despite your belief that you are a well-disciplined soldier (I make this remark because I found out for myself, after 9½ years' service in the RAF, that service discipline is nothing when compared with the absolute essential self-control which is required to order one self to sit before a blank piece of paper, pick up a pen, and WRITE!)
>
> You will never enjoy it, but by the time you complete it, you will undoubtedly have much greater respect for yourself.
>
> It costs at least 1095 pints of beer and 1095 hours of writing time a year, plus 2920 miles of driving. The beer costs 898 Pounds, my car petrol costs 135 Pounds; total 1033 Pounds. So it costs me about one pound per hour to write (plus pens, paper, typist, etc., but that is a different addition). As the seaman said in days of yore—'Different ships, different long splices.' I repeat—there's no money in writing.

And again, on my querying about other physically handicapped circumnavigators with whom I may be able to bond:

> I don't think you would find many members if you tried to form a club of physically handicapped circumnavigators. The following list of the approximate number of yachts which have sailed round the world will explain why.
>
> Solo (all sizes of craft)
>   120   1st 1895–98   (USA)
> Small Crewed (under 15.5 mtr LOA)
>   110   1st 1923–5   (Eire)
> Large Crewed (over 15.5 mtr LOA)
>   90   1st 1847–8   (Great Britain)

The first one-legged sailor (to make it) almost across the Atlantic was the Italian Teresio Fava in 1928; he sailed his 19' 6" (15.94 mtr) gaff cutter from Italy, and was last reported by the French steamship *Providence* crossing the Newfoundland Banks. (Presumed lost at sea thereafter).

Possibly the most outstanding was the single-handed crossing of the Pacific, from San Francisco to Honolulu, by the totally blind Hank Dekker. He sailed his 25' (7.62 metre) Bermudian sloop *Dark Star* 2376 miles in twenty-three days; his charts and compass were in Braille and he had a speaking Loran for position.

Unfortunately, apart from listing PH 'firsts', I have not collected every handicapped person's voyages...in my experience, the majority of ocean cruising yachtsmen are very poor correspondents! ...I have a strong suspicion that genuine record breakers are embarrassed at the thought of being publicized as 'record breakers'.

...famous transoceanic voyages of the past are often quoted inaccurately by historians—probably the most ridiculous being one which eventually I solved after a prolonged search: a 15 footer, said to have been sailed from Cape Town to Alaska in 1800–1801, turned out to have been a 15 metre trader (sailed by an American, Richard Cleveland), the vessel had been purchased in France, and so was measured in metric; but the Americans probably thought it meant 'feet', or maybe they thought 'm' or even 'metre' meant feet! Who knows? Anyway, for some 180 years it was presumed that a brave American had sailed single-handed across the Indian and Pacific oceans...!

Concerning introducing your wife to sailing: DON'T! I mean blue water sailing, not afternoon and weekend cruising. After living afloat for 20 years, and receiving many, many letters from disgruntled wives (seeking a divorce from their ocean-cruising husbands) I KNOW that the vast majority of wives seldom take happily to sailing the ocean blue. Oh, they might loyally follow their husband's desires, but at least 90 per cent soon begin to hate it. Psychologically, a woman prefers a secure nest in which to raise her chicks; she does not consider a floating home to be a secure nest. She may tolerate it at first, but eventually...

I had a marvellous time throughout WW II; which I attribute to the fact that I never stayed long enough in any place to get shot down (although I had many close-to-death miraculous survivals). I used to volunteer for suicide jobs on the premise that inevitably you were looked after better than merely as a cog in the squadron—when all you could do was what you were told until eventually you were shot down.

In his letter dated 4 May 1987:

I had a letter from Mr Gulshan Rai in March, asking if you were the first handicapped yachtsman to circumnavigate. I...suggest the word BELIEVED be used with the claim. I am perfectly happy for you to use my name as the authority, provided you prefix the claim with BELIEVED the first...etc.

And finally:

For myself, a peaceful life in Suffolk is all I ask. I have had more than a fair share of adventure, and now: 'Sleep after toil, port after stormy seas, ease after war, death after life doth greatly please' (Spencer). But you never know...

ANNEXE 5

GOOD WILL
THE REAL MANTRA
Letters During and After

I had a plan, a dream as well as a career in the Army that had certain terms and conditions of service. Could the plan fit in? The answer was for the Generals to find out—not puny Captains who could afford to dream. There was certainly no money!

My letter to the Engineer-in-Chief's branch, May 1980, in an effort to 'pitch in my bit':

> I offer to contribute Rs 10,000 which is my six month's gross pay, for this venture. I am willing to pay this amount in monthly installments of Rs 300 each, with effect from 1 July 1980.

Reply dated 29 May 1980, from the then Engineer-in-Chief General SN Sharma, the famous skydiver and the

Corps of Engineers' living face of adventure:

> At this moment, we are unable to acquire a boat. ...We will certainly take this money from you (once we have the finances for the boat).

In all fairness, in those days, money was in very short supply in the country for anything at all, leave alone adventure or sailing. India was emerging from the list of countries termed 'Have Nots', and had not yet joined the list of Developing countries. Years later, in 1986, the project was kickstarted again with the help of the erstwhile Commandant of the College of Military Engineering and the then E-in-C, General PR Puri, and Brigadier (later General) HK Kapoor.

Letter dated 28 November 1986 from General SN Sharma, ex-E-in-C, now retired on my writing to thank him after our voyage was successfully concluded, for having been a pillar of strength right from the inception of the project:

> To think of me is perhaps undeserved; by far the greatest credit goes to you, as the very first person sent to UK to find a yacht, after which other things followed. ...I especially admire the way you have got over the hang gliding accident, where you lost your leg, and thereafter continued with this adventure around the world, for which you were the first person ever selected.

Second Letter General SN Sharma (Retd.), 29 March 1987:

> Your personal contribution to this was the culmination of a task you had taken on at the very beginning when the expedition was just a dream. Few indeed are fortunate to

put their hand on something and go through it right to
the end with success. You have earned yours the hard way
and in spite of the hang gliding accident in which you lost
your leg.

My correspondence with other yachtsmen from different parts of the world drew positive responses. It was the encouragement received from all quarters that kept the push going. All the advice I received on all aspects of the venture, the boat to start with, was worthwhile, useful and highly motivating. Much of it was also heady stuff, and very gratifying!

Letter from Major PGF Martin, MBE of the Joint Services Sailing Centre (JSSC), Gosport, UK, 20 August 1980:

> I must say that I admire your enthusiasm which is reflected
> in every sentence of your letter. ....A good 34 or 35 ft yacht
> should suit your purpose. For a round the world trip the
> bigger the better. We can discuss this later.

Letter dated 12 January 1981, from Colonel LGS Thomas, OBE, ex Royal Indian Gurkhas Batallion, then with the JSSC:

> ...wondered what had happened to your imaginative
> project as...after writing and signalling to Brigadier
> Kapoor, we heard nothing in reply. I hope that your
> project is not dead.

Letter from the intrepid Tristan Jones, written from Galle, Sri Lanka, on board his yacht *Outward Leg* (ironic, since he himself was a one-legged yachtsman):

As my old friend (now deceased) Bill Tilman of Nanda Devi fame, used to say when people asked him how to get started: 'Put on your boots and Go!' I suppose in our case it is 'boot'.

Letter from David East, David East Yachting, UK (who helped us find a suitable boat for our voyage):

> Certainly—with the funds available for the project—it would have been hard to find a more generally suitable yacht, and I hope she will give you much pleasure in the years to come.

Letter from Colonel TPS Chowdhury (later Brigadier), Team Manager, and one of the change-over crew on *Trishna*, 26 June 1987:

> You have been the architect of the Sailing Cruise and I personally know the hard work and personal devotion you have put in the project.

Letter dated 27 April 1987 from Vice Admiral MP Awati, erstwhile Commander of India's Western Fleet, Mumbai (he had earlier flagged us off from Mumbai on our voyage):

> [The voyage around the world] was a milestone in Indian Adventure. A national renaissance is composed of such feats. Let us hope that there will be many more both on land and sea and hopefully in the air.

Letter from Lieutenant General Sami Khan, Commandant of the National Defence Academy, Kharakvasala, Pune, 31 January 1986:

You and other members of the *Trishna* team have done all of us proud. We wish you success and glory in this rare and adventurous endeavour. It is indeed a great source of inspiration for all cadets and will motivate them for times to come. Well done and keep the NDA Flag 'Sailing' High.

Letter from Brigadier Ashok Joshi, Military and Naval Attache at the Indian Embassy, Washington DC, USA, 6 January 1987:

What a tremendous achievement, and what an adventure! You have done something remarkable of which everyone is proud. ...Your feat will be remembered for many years and will be a source of inspiration. You have shown great courage and perseverance. Only, your wife, I think, has shown greater courage and fortitude. Bravo!

Letter from Mr Bhu Dev Sharma, President of the Bhartiya Association of the Caribbean, 3 February 1986:

You and your colleagues' decent, cordial and highly cultured disposition have won the hearts of the people of Trinidad and Tobago. Many people whom you have met have spoken very highly about you and your colleagues. They have wished their great appreciation to be conveyed to you...This very enterprising feat of sailing round the world is also an act of goodwill of India towards the citizens of the countries you are visiting, and we Indians settled or working abroad are really very proud of it.

Letter from Major General JJN Taimni, India's Security Advisor to the Prime Minister of Mauritius, Port Louis, 19 May 1987:

> You and your team mates have indeed done us proud. I, for one, am all admiration for your guts and courage. You have blazed a trail which, I hope, other Indian young men will follow to bring honour and glory to the country in the same way as you have done.

Letter from Mr JN Dixit, Indian High Commissioner, Colombo, Sri Lanka, 11 May 1987:

> All of us in this mission were thrilled to receive you and your colleagues in December 1986. We are all very proud about both your success, and your adventurous spirit.

Letter from Lieutenant Colonel SK Jain (later Major General), limb surgeon at the Artificial Limb Centre, Pune, to the illustrious amputee, General YN Sharma:

> I recollect only the few names (sic), like Douglas Bader, Norman, and A.K. Singh in the history of the modern world who have reached such heights. It is an example to others and that is why on many occasions I say 'what you think is the end, actually is a new beginning'. It is not possible for me to express my feelings in words.

Letter from Ian Morrison, Public Relations Manager and Fund Raising Officer, Auckland Crippled Children Society (under which the Takapuna Grammar School runs) 11 August 1986:

> Knowing how little time you had to spare with us, makes us all the more grateful for the way in which you made it

a point of meeting and encouraging our disabled young people. On their behalf and ours, may I send you our most sincere thanks.

Second Letter from Ian Morrison, Public Relations Manager and Fund Raising Officer, Auckland Crippled Children Society (under which the Takapuna Grammar School runs) 11 May 1987:

> All of us at the Auckland Crippled Children Society were delighted to hear of Trishna's safe and timely return home. Many of our young disabled people will be particularly inspired by your own personal example.

Letter from AJ Joglekar, Honorary General Secretary, Fellowship of the Physically Handicapped, FPH Building, Haji Ali, Mumbai, 23 January 1987:

> On behalf of our fellow handicaps and on behalf of our entire institution, we extend to you our heartiest congratulations on your remarkable achievement of sailing round the globe. We at the Fellowship of the Physically Handicapped are especially proud of you and treat it as a personal glory. You have indeed proved what we have always believed in, that there is nothing that a handicapped person cannot achieve in this life, if he so wills and endeavours to pursue, and as such you will stand out as a beacon of light for the disabled of our country and of the world at large.

Letter from Major PHJ Wilcox (Retd.), Training Officer (and earlier Skipper) of the fifty-five-footer Sail Training Yacht *Khukri*, Joint Services Sailing Centre, Gosport, Hants, UK, 8 May 1987:

A great personal achievement with two legs, but even more so in overcoming such a handicap as a lost leg. Will you ever be able to settle back to routine army duty...?

Letter from Major General RK Singh, VSM, ex Centre Commandant and Colonel Commandant of the Bengal Sappers, Roorkee, 22 September 1986:

> *Trishna's* one year on the sea is over—one year of tremendous achievement—unparalleled! My regards to all members of the crew and to the skipper, especially to the four of you who have dared it all the way—the vagaries of nature, the ills of confinement and the mental conflict because of proximity of living and surviving. Cheers to all of you on the Anniversary. ...Four more months! We look forward to your return.

Letter from Mr TP Sreenivasan, India's High Commissioner, Fiji, 1st January 1987:

> [I would have written earlier]...but we had a coup on our hands. I cannot imagine how perfectly human soldiers suddenly change when they assume power! ...We were following your odyssey back to India with great interest. The pride with which India welcomed you back must have sufficient compensation for all your travails! Congratulations once again. More than your heroism and courage, what remain in our minds are your personal warmth, humility and cheerfulness.

Letter from Major (Retd.) PS Pammi (leader, Corps of Engineers' earlier sailing voyage in an 18-footer, open day-sailor boat, the *Albatross,* from Mumbai to Bandar Abbas in the Persian Gulf, and back), 11 February 1987:

> ...I wanted to hug you and say: 'AK, you are the pride of this country today, and this soil has not produced many like you.' I am aware that the presence of a loyal, dedicated, brave and noble soul like you on board must have given a great deal of confidence to Rao, especially when the going was rough. The comradeship of a man like you will always inspire an outfit to perform near miracles.

Foreword to Dom Moraes' book, *Trishna* by the Engineer in Chief of the Army, Lieutenant General PS Roy:

> They...at one point thought that they had reached the end...since one of the most brilliant and innovative of the crew, Major A.K. Singh, lost his artificial leg. Singh bravely carried on, and became the first handicapped person ever to sail round the world.

Letter from ex-Chief of the Indian Navy, Admiral (Retd.) (Ronnie) RL Pereira, 26 January 1987:

> Your voyage has entirely been a most memorable one, and I do hope someone will sit down and write a book. I think it is absolutely necessary for the younger generation.